LEARNING, ADAPTABILITY AND CHANGE

LEARNING, ADAPTABILITY AND CHANGE

THE CHALLENGE FOR EDUCATION AND INDUSTRY

JOHN HEYWOOD

P·C·P

Paul Chapman
Publishing Ltd

T
14.5
.H48
1989

/

This edition first published 1989
Paul Chapman Publishing Ltd
144 Liverpool Road
London
N1 1LA

British Library Cataloguing in Publication Data
Heywood, John
   Learning adaptability and change: the challenge for
   education and industry.
   1. Technological change.   Social aspects
   I.   Title
   306'.46

   ISBN   1-85396-067-5

Typeset by Inforum Typesetting, Portsmouth
Printed in Great Britain by
St Edmundsbury Press Ltd, Bury St Edmunds, Suffolk

for
Anthony, David, Caroline, Sarah and Christopher

CONTENTS

PREFACE

Technology is so much part of our everyday living and expectation that we seldom, if ever, stop to consider its impact on our lives. Because our everyday contact with technology is with the video, washing-machine, car and like devices it is very difficult to appreciate the extent of social change bred by technology unless it directly affects our life-style. Nevertheless, events such as the Big-Bang in New York and London, changes in office organization, mechanization in industry and persisting unemployment have made us more aware that we, and in particular our children, will have to be more adaptable than in the past.

We might think that it is easy to adapt, but a little reflection will remind us that our values and dispositions are deeply held and difficult to change. We want security, and the thought of change can make us feel very insecure; some of us may, for a time, become emotionally unstable. Yet technology will force on us changes in the way we work and live more quickly than was the case in the past. If the peoples of nations are to compete in the world economy, they will have to be much more adaptable than previously. No wonder the Chairman of Rank-Xerox titled a lecture, 'Can we teach ourselves to change?'

Unfortunately, the answer to this question is by no means simple. It depends not only on our dispositions but also on the way we interact with others in the family, at work and within the culture generally. In certain cultures it may be necessary to support changes in attitudes with educational programmes. The goals may be so well understood by the people in other cultures that no educational support is necessary because everyone works toward the achievement of those goals. Nevertheless, change is a characteristic of all cultures, albeit slow in time and soft in impact. The experience of the Japanese railways has been no different from that of the British. Both organizations have experienced a great deal of resistance to change. We are all called on to adapt, some more so than others, and some more frequently than others.

If we are to accommodate the demands for change that will be made on us, and, at the same time, retain our commitment to the goals of the organization in which we work, we need to understand the factors that contribute to or impede the organization achieving its goals.

This book is about the factors that enhance or impede change. It is an examination of the factors that cause some societies to be more successful, some organizations to be more adaptable, and some individuals to be more responsive to change than others. It is a study of the factors that influence the interactions between individuals, industrial organizations and governments in the pursuit of economic and social goals.

The text is founded upon three principles. The first is that the factors that impede innovation in an organization, or prevent a society from adapting to new circumstances, are the same factors that inhibit individuals learning. From the perspective of change, individuals and institutions may be regarded as learners, or learning systems. Neither individuals nor organizations can adapt if they cannot learn. Thus a key function of those who govern or manage is to create an environment conducive to learning. Since intelligence is the ability to select and to shape the real world in which we live, we, too, have a responsibility to help those whom we allow to lead and to manage to create that environment.

It follows from this that, if this is to come about, a much greater participation in the management of enterprises by all the workforce will be required if there is to be a creative response to the continuing effects of technological development and social change. This will require a communality of understanding and education among management and workers, in which the principles to be understood relate to adaptability, and thus to learning how to learn in a changing environment.

In this sense we all have to exercise direction and control – that is, manage ourselves and sometimes other people. We are all managers and we are all managed. In a democratic society and in participatory management, it is an act of management or leadership to let someone else manage or lead. We all have something to contribute to the task of management, and this is the third principle.

If learning and decision-making are held to be the same thing, that is, goal-seeking behaviours, then the activity of learning is an adaptive response. Since the transfer of learning cannot be accomplished without knowledge, adaptation to change in life, whether at work, in the community or family, cannot be accommodated without an understanding of the factors that contribute to economic and social behaviour. It is the aim of this book to foster such an understanding. Because it is concerned with the effects of the interaction between individuals, organizations and society, it is interdisciplinary and thematic.

With these issues in mind, the following general questions are considered throughout the text:

1. Why are some individuals more able to adapt to changing circumstances in the home and at work than others, and what are the circumstances that encourage or inhibit adaptation?

2. Why do some individuals work well in some systems of organization and not in others, and what are the characteristics of organizations that make for effective work?

3. Why are some individuals better able to provide leadership than others?
4. Why, in the industrialized nations, is the creation of wealth important, and how is wealth created in an industrial society?
5. Why are some countries more successful at creating wealth than others, and is this a transient phenomenon?

The problems discussed are those considered traditionally to be the province of individual and organizational behaviour placed within the broader perspective of the culture in which we live. I have given courses based on this approach to experienced and senior personnel in industry, teachers in need of retraining, undergraduate engineers and scientists, and sixth-formers. It is intended, therefore, for

- teachers who want a fundamental rationale for the new courses in the school curriculum on the human aspects of technology and economic well-being;
- undergraduates taking courses on the engineer and society;
- decision-makers in the political sphere;
- persons preparing for a career in management who have not had any previous management training, to provide them with a framework for a greater understanding of industrial, economic and social behaviour;
- and experienced managers and workers, with ideas for their reflection that arise from the perspectives of learning and culture within which the traditional approaches to the study of behaviour in organizations are set.

John Heywood
Dublin, 1989

ACKNOWLEDGEMENTS

I am indebted to Dr N. Carpenter who encouraged me to develop the inter-disciplinary courses in the Department of Industrial Studies of the University of Liverpool from which this thinking has emerged.

Continuing encouragement has come from Professor G. Carter of the University of Salford to whom I am most grateful. I am similarly indebted to many industrialists and in particular to the late W. Bill Humble and Barry T. Turner.

The continuation of this work in Dublin was greatly encouraged by Michael Murray of the Christian Brothers to whom I am most grateful. Finally to Paul Chapman for his many suggestions and great patience during the editing of the manuscript.

1

ADAPTATION, INTELLIGENCE AND LEARNING

Introduction

Few, if any of us, have escaped the need to change. For some, such changes are small and the stress induced is negligible. For others, large changes may induce debilitating stress or apathy. Yet some cope, if passively, with whatever it is they are caused to do. And some not only cope but also control both cause and effect. The more unexpected the change, the greater the demands on the coping skills that help us accommodate the new circumstances.

Today we sometimes call the behavioural response that is made to a need for change 'adaptive behaviour'. A new cliché, coined by educationalists, calls for programmes in 'education for adaptability'. They argue that one of the reasons why some young people join the ranks of the long-term unemployed is that they are not able to adapt to the continuing restructuring of employment and skills caused by the incessant flow of technological and social innovation. These educationalists recognize that everyone is affected by technological development, for it is happening not only at the workplace but also in the way we live.

Just as individuals have to adapt, so, too, do organizations, be they bureaucracies, agencies of service or manufacturers. They, too, have to respond to the demands of both social and technological change. So it is important that we should understand how we cope with change, and whether or not we can learn skills that will help us both to evaluate the merits of 'change' and to accommodate those changes imposed on us independently of their merit.

We learn to adapt from the moment we are born. The same is true of organizations, and throughout this book one of the underlying themes is that of the organization as a learning system. Thus, if we understand how people learn and what enhances and impedes learning, we can also understand what factors enhance and impede the collective learning of organizations. The first three chapters of this book are concerned with these factors.

1

This chapter begins with a brief description of the early development of children, more especially as it relates to perceptual learning. We observe that when we talk about other people, we rate them along many dimensions. These have to be understood if we are to understand the contribution learning can make to adaptability. Among these dimensions are intelligence and personality. The two sections that follow look at intelligence from two different perspectives. In the first we consider the nature of intelligence. In the second we discuss the significance of spatial aptitude in learning and intelligence. The use of imagery learning in the development of spatial aptitude is considered, as is its more general role in learning. It is clear that inventiveness, which is one of the aptitudes that society needs, is encouraged precisely when students are allowed to be unconventional in their approaches to learning. Such approaches are often those used to develop creativity or divergent thinking. The inability of companies to diversify successfully is sometimes a cause of failure.

This chapter ends with a discussion of two recent theories of intelligence. Gardner's theory of multiple intelligences is considered first. In this theory, intelligence is defined as the ability to solve problems in a particular cultural setting. Gardner's theory approximates in many ways to the views that the person in the street is likely to hold about intelligence. Intelligent and academic behaviour are not the same. Intelligence is exhibited in many activities and, moreover, it is often demonstrated in personal and intra-personal behaviour. Some support for Gardner's theory is to be found in the work of Sternberg, who defined intelligence as a mental activity directed toward purposive adaptation to, and selection and shaping of, real-world environments relevant to one's life. To be intelligent is to be adaptive, and to acquire the skills of intelligence is to acquire a positive disposition to adaptation. Skills of adaptation may, therefore, be learnt. If intelligence can be developed, then – given the parameters of Sternberg's theory – the answer to the question, 'Can we teach ourselves to change?' must be 'Yes'. Such learning begins with an understanding of how we learn.

Aspects of our Early Development[1]

It is now a cliché that the first five years of a child's life are of immense importance to his or her subsequent development. The pathological theory of human development described by Freud and modified and developed by his successors in the psychiatric field is within the very broadest interpretations accepted by most of us. Because of the very high rates of divorce in Western countries, there is much interest in the structure of the family, and whether, for example, (and under what conditions) surrogate parents have an equal and positive effect on the child. Because many women go out to work, there is an equal interest in the effects of the working women on child development. Research indicates that parenthood – real or surrogate – is of tremendous significance in the development of the child. The purposes of this chapter are to look at some of the actions parents can take to support the intellectual needs of their children and to prepare them for the changes they will inevitably meet in life.

Learning for life begins at birth as the child perceives the environment and relates it through sight and touch to his or her movements. This process is called perceptual motor-skill development. Early[2] and others have suggested that this development takes place in seven stages.[3] During this process, the infant acquires a knowledge of his or her position in its environment, and so learns to distinguish between left and right, top and bottom, and so on. Early argues that if the sequence of the stages that lead to these discoveries becomes disordered, the child is likely to experience learning difficulties as he or she grows older.

Of course, other factors influence learning. Erikson has pointed out that while much experience of learning is frustrating, too much frustration or indulgence can be harmful. In such a world, infants have to decide whether they can trust their environment and the individuals within it. If the infants continuously perceive a hostile environment, this is likely to influence their subsequent development. Mistrust, which, as experience tells us, is a common impediment to learning as well as a common experience in employment, must influence the drive to adapt negatively.

To return to the problem of perceptual motor development, the movements of the infant who is functioning at stage 1 (motor level) produce internal information that becomes the frame of reference for future activity, in the sense that new actions are checked against this frame of reference – which is called the motor base. This system becomes fully organized when the infant is able to use both visual and aural information.

Both teachers and parents can impede the sequence of development. For example, if a young child is made to draw with a crayon before he or she can differentiate the hand, wrist, elbow and arm, he or she will force their fingers to draw, but the drawing will be characterized by rigidity because the child has acquired a skill in isolation, which is not related to the motor base. Early describes a 9-year-old who, when writing at a chalkboard, kept his whole arm rigid. He made the writing movements from the shoulder because he could not differentiate the components of his arm. Children need to, and normal children do, develop generalized movement patterns. This provides them with an awareness of their potential for movement at any given time.

Children have to build an internal structure for position, and this is difficult because all positions in the universe are relative. So children have to use their body as a reference point to define right and left and up and down. Part of the function of this internal structure is the co-ordination of hand and eye. The developmental sequence for this is hand–eye, eye–hand. Observe how the child's eye is attracted to the hand. It is only later that the child learns there are two sources of information.

When the child's perception has fully developed, the motor aspect drops and the information is organized directly. To illustrate the significance of perception in learning, close your eyes and see if you can locate in your mind all the objects that surround you. The final stage of development is when previously learned concepts condition the perceptual activity (more of this in Chapter 2).

It is claimed that children with learning difficulties resulting from the perceptual motor sequence being disturbed, can be helped to overcome them if they can be taken through the correct sequence of development with content and materials more appropriate to their age. Early has described several syllabuses that are intended to achieve this goal. One of them requires the child to construct a large globe, and the sequence of construction is related to its construction and use.[4]

There is also a positive side, as recent interest in holistic learning in the classroom has shown. Exercises related to perceptual motor skills can, it seems, help to develop important intellectual skills. For example,

> students are directed to work with their non-dominant hand; right handers work with their left hand, and vice-versa. They are then led through a series of exercises such as finger, hand, arm, shoulder, head, hip, leg and foot movements on the non-dominant side. These movements are orchestrated with classical music selections. Once everyone is comfortably engaged in these 'non-dominant side waltzes', the entire procedure is rehearsed mentally. Following this covert rehearsal, physical rehearsal is again repeated for the dominant side followed by another period of mental rehearsal, and ending with physical rehearsal. Once a balance between the two sides is achieved, students are directed to draw and write first with the non-dominant hand, then with the dominant hand.[5]

It is claimed that such exercises not only improve handwriting and drawing skills but also creative thinking, which is to suggest that such thinking is related to spatial awareness.[6]

As perceptual learning takes place, often on a trial-and-error basis, so the child learns to adapt. The acquisition of knowledge through experience and the learning of the skills of adaptation go hand in hand. As we see in Chapter 2, they can come into conflict in later life, for too much experience can impede adaptation.

We learn from the study of infants that the way we perceive the environment is of tremendous importance to our development. It is our perception of the environment through the senses that enables us to accommodate that environment. We also learn that we do more than merely accommodate what is found, for it is evident that we also try to adapt and control the environment. It is not a wholly passive operation of trial and error that leaves us where we are: all our actions take us forward in little steps. So we learn that accommodation and adaptation arise from exchanges with the environment. Neither is it merely a matter of receiving information from the environment, for to adapt we must also provide the environment with information. But there is more to it than that, for we observe that those who look after children can encourage or impede their learning. Finally, we see that the behaviour of the child in the cot is not something that is random, but an activity that we can with confidence call intelligent.

It is self-evident that children go through different stages of physical development until they reach adulthood. I do not use the term 'maturity' as physical maturity is too readily associated with mental maturity, yet everyday wisdom tells us that this is not so. I also hesitate to use the term 'mental maturity', for it is equally a matter of everyday observation that mental maturity, or intellectual development, does not necessarily mean that a person is wise in the ways of the world. In this sense, a person will have high levels of moral and emotional development coupled with the skill of reflection.

Adaptation is not always accomplished with ease, and sometimes not at all. Moreover, anxiety can lead individuals and groups to resist change totally. Such behaviour is often observed in industrial relations – a recent example of which is the opposition of the British Transport and General Workers Union to the development by the Ford Motor Co. of a single-union plant at Dundee in Scotland.[7]

The American psychiatrist, H. S. Sullivan, argues that anxiety is interpersonal in origin and as such can be used to threaten our feelings of self-esteem. Thus, when technology threatens work, many individuals (afraid that they cannot cope with the new technology) resist its introduction, and this has been characteristic of the history of innovation. The ability to adapt is thus a function of the total environment of the objects in it and the people who inhabit it.

However we define security, there is no doubt that part of the problem of adaptation is the fear of insecurity. Thus there is a lifelong tension between the demands of the new, and the safe haven where we are. Young adolescents, as they seek their own identity, find – as do their families – the break away from their parents perplexing. The drive to develop new and independent forms of behaviour is counteracted by the security of the structure from which we have to depart. It is my opinion that this search for identity, with its attendant conflicts, continues throughout life. What is clear from the psycho-analytic view of development is that if the innovators create an environment that appears hostile to those whom they wish to adapt, adaptation will be all the more difficult.

So we observe that when we talk about other people we rate them on many dimensions. The trouble is that, not only do we simplify and rationalize our observations, but we also tend to give black-and-white evaluations about those whom we judge. Yet, if we were invited to defend similar judgements about ourselves, we would probably argue that such judgements cannot be made because we are complex, and that part of that complexity arises from the way the combined force of intellect and personality reacts with the environment.

Intelligence and Intelligence Testing

It is this very complexity of the human being that makes psychological research so difficult, because the psychologist's tools provide us with very limited information.[8] Today, psychological investigations are based on sophisticated forms of questionnaire, interview, observation and test, each of which yields relatively little about individuals that is generalizable, unless the investigator is prepared to go beyond the evidence presented. Because of this, we have no general theory of human behaviour. However, there are many theories that, taken together, give us important insights into human behaviour and that help us understand how children develop. In this chapter we consider some of these theories to the extent that they throw light on the development of children in their first ten years. Because of the peculiar relationship they have with work and learning, intelligence is considered first.

There is now much scepticism about intelligence tests and what they measure. Nevertheless, their study has much to offer both parent and teacher, so it is particularly important to understand the nature of such criticism.[9]

In Britain, intelligence testing is often associated in the public mind with an examination that was taken at the age of 11 for the purpose of selecting pupils into grammar, technical and secondary-modern schools. It was held that this created an élitist society, and that children in particular from secondary-modern schools were disadvantaged. Since it was not possible to predict the performance of children with great accuracy at the age of 11, this examination was unfair. To offset the effects of this examination – the results of which were found to correlate closely with social class – politicians from all parties in the 1960s supported the development of a comprehensive system of education.

An important feature of the debate between the psychometricians (as those concerned with mental measurement are called) and sociologists, was the influence of heredity on intelligence. If, say, 80 per cent of the attribute called intelligence was due to heredity, then the environment could make little contribution to its development. The early work of psychologists led to this conclusion, but some of the pioneering studies were recently found to be fakes.[10] However, this is not to deny that there were no hereditary components in intelligence: it is to say that the way in which intelligence reacts with the environment is complex.

In America, the interpretations of Jensen's studies caused a furore, since it seemed from his arguments that black people were necessarily of inferior intelligence because of the hereditary factors.[11] And these arguments continue. The year 1982 saw an almost surfeit of books on this topic. Despite this debate, testing in America and Britain (which followed different paths) has yielded considerable information of use to parents and teachers.

Binet was the first to devise tests to measure intelligence: modified at Stanford, these tests have withstood the test of time. Binet does not, however, give a straightforward definition of intelligence but writes that

> in intelligence there is a fundamental faculty, the impairment or lack of which, is of the utmost importance for practical life. This faculty is called judgement, otherwise called good sense, initiative, the faculty of adapting one's self to circumstances. To judge well, to comprehend well, to reason well, these are the essential activities of intelligence.[12]

Binet's criterion of intelligence was based on chronological age. He established the norm of performance of his tests by the given age of the group to be tested. Thus, the intelligence quotient for the average person in a given age group is 100. Persons who perform at a lower or higher level may then also be described as having an intelligence equal to this or that age.[13]

Since intelligence has been thought to be a fundamental capacity, the tests designed to measure it have, in theory, to be both culture and knowledge free. That is, they should not be influenced by the environment in which a person has lived, or by the knowledge attained in that environment. Neither should it be possible to train pupils for an intelligence test. Such parameters are almost impossible to achieve, and more recent theories of intelligence by Gardner[14] and Sternberg[15] take the effects of culture into account.

Tests that require some knowledge for satisfactory performance are called achievement tests when they are used as examinations, or aptitude tests when they are designed to measure potential. An important issue is the extent to which aptitudes depend on general intelligence. Indeed, a range of aptitude measures is likely to produce a better measure of general intelligence than a single test, but the British approach, as it emerged in the 1950s, to the analysis of aptitudes (using factorial analysis) gave rise to the view that human abilities are hierarchically ordered (see Figure 1.1).[16]

The family tree shows a general factor commonly called intelligence (indicated by the letter *g*) and *g* makes a contribution to any test. When allowance is made for the general factor, the tests fall into two main groups, one of which is characterized by verbal and numerical aptitudes, and the other by spatial, mechanical and practical aptitudes. Each of these divides into specific factors associated with the minor factors.

Spatial Ability, Imagery and Play

MacFarlane Smith evaluated the significance of the spatial factor.[17] Apart from his own work, MacFarlane Smith analysed all previous studies of spatial ability. With regard to Britain, he concluded that in the general population spatial ability was underdeveloped and that this accounted for what was believed at the time (1964) to be a shortage of scientists and technologists. Students who had highly developed numerical and verbal skills but who lacked in spatial aptitude would be unlikely to enter high-level careers in technology that demanded high levels of spatial skill. At that time, the system of secondary education in England was still organized along tripartite lines. He argued that the academically oriented grammar schools developed the verbal and numerical skills at the expense of the spatial because of the type of curriculum they offered. Such subjects as metalwork, technical drawing and woodwork, which would help pupils develop spatial ability, were undervalued and held in low esteem, and were only studied in depth in technical and secondary-modern schools. This argument has been maintained by McCallum, who followed up MacFarlane Smith's work.[18] Independently of any

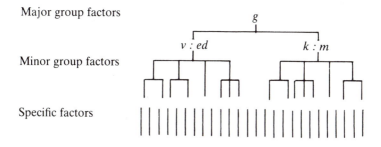

Figure 1.1　Hierarchical ordering of human abilities

debate about the supply and demand for qualified scientists and technologists, persons who lack spatial perception are unlikely to want to pursue careers where such perception is likely to be of some importance, such as in engineering and science.[19]

But quite apart from the argument about technologists, there is the more general point that a poor spatial facility may inhibit learning in many other subjects, especially in mathematics. Often in primary schools, children with learning difficulties are found to lack spatial aptitude and some improvement is obtained if deliberate attempts are made to foster spatial skills. Parents can aid the development of spatial skills by giving children puzzles, encouraging drawing and providing them with the wherewithal to make things. They can also insist that their children pursue practical activities throughout their school career.

In the hierarchical view of intelligence, the spatial, mechanical and practical abilities are related to the right-hand side of the brain, whereas the verbal and numerical abilities are related to the left-hand side.[20] The call for a holistic approach to education is a call for an approach that pays equal attention to the needs of each side of the brain. In MacFarlane Smith's view, the evidence tends to support the view that mathematical ability is different from numerical ability and depends on spatial ability. Numerical tests would not, therefore, necessarily predict mathematical ability.

MacFarlane Smith argued that such creative geniuses as Einstein solved their problems through the perception of inner images. In America, educators have taken Einstein's and other autobiographical and psychological studies of creative thinkers[21] as an argument for the provision of imagery exercises in the curriculum. Philosophically these ideas have a foundation in the Kantian notion that thinking in pictures precedes thinking in words. Guided-imagery exercises go well beyond the provision of technical drawing or woodwork, as the following example quoted by Galyean shows:

> In a tenth grade geometry class, students are memorizing definitions for trapezoid, rhombus, parallelogram and quadrilateral. After reading the definitions and looking at the shapes, the students close their eyes, breathe deeply and visualize a shape in their minds. When they open their eyes, they check to see if this internalized shape agrees with the definition. With eyes closed again, they change the shape in any way they wish as long as it fits the general definition. When they open their eyes, they check to see if their recreated shape fits the original definition. They then draw the internalized shape, and the teacher checks the drawing for accuracy.[22]

It is claimed that in this way the students learn the definition more quickly and for longer periods of time than when geometry is presented in a traditional, instructional mode.

Apart from guided cognitive imagery of this kind, Galyean reports on guided imagery exercises that focus on the affective domain, and beyond that to the structural (transpersonal) dimension. She describes an experiment with remedial English students in their tenth grade, who were asked to view a slide of a rose:

> They were given one minute to draw the rose and two minutes to write about it. Then they were told to put these papers away and prepare for guided imagery activity. They

closed their eyes and created a garden where they could see, smell, touch, and feel the vibrancy of many flowers. Suddenly they were to see a rose bush with one special rose on it. They became the rose and felt what it was like to sway in the breeze, warm their petals in a friendly sun, wash their leaves in a gentle rain, and watch people admire their beauty.

Following this ten-minute imagery, the students opened their eyes, viewed the slide once more, and were given one minute to draw the rose and two minutes to write about it. Analyses of their compositions revealed a significant increase in vocabulary and complexity scores.[23]

The evaluator of this exercise concluded that the drawings completed after the exercise had more balance, richness and depth than those done before the exercise. There is nothing new in this technique. It has been widely used in radio for the presentation of programmes to young children. What is new is its application in the later years of schooling.

It is in imaginative activities of this kind that the practitioner can find time for reflective thinking. Imaginative activity is, according to Arendt,[24] the foundation of all thinking for, to quote Barell,[25] 'Imagination is the ability to transcend conventional and accepted ways to thinking and acting to transform facts, ideas, and concepts into novel combinations. It is the ability to form, manipulate freely and react emotionally to images in the mind'. Such thinking requires the thinker 'to enter into the subject . . . to imagine what it is like to be . . . and in this way the thinker is able to develop a new perceptual framework. It is this activity which some authorities call insight and explains how some people find it easy to see a face in diagrams which most of us would think of as inkblots.'[26]

What can we learn from all this? First, I think we underestimate the importance of play. When children are playing they imagine themselves into all sorts of situations and some of them become real as they grow up. Despite all the efforts of household names in education, such as Froebel and Montessori, parents and teachers often miss the point of play.[27] As has been pointed out by others, many childcare centres in the USA deprive children of what they need most to grow,[28] that is, opportunities to play, interact freely, experiment and discover who they are. As Bruner says, 'A game is like a mathematical model, an artificial but powerful representation of reality. Games go a long way to getting children involved in understanding language, social organization, and the rest; they also introduce the idea of theory to these phenomena'.[29]

In play we notice that the child also learns to adapt and that adaptation and new learning are often synonymous. It is when learning fails that we fail to adapt or, to put it in another way, adaptation is an action consequent on learning. The consequences of not adapting will depend on the particular circumstance, for in some situations, particularly those involving moral dilemmas, it may be essential for the person not to adapt if he or she wants to avoid severe distress.

Nevertheless, we should remember the dictum that 'Every time one teaches a child, one prevents him or her from inventing or discovering'. In the discovery method the teacher becomes, to use Suransky's phrase, a 'Child-watcher instead of a child teacher',[30] or the teacher becomes a manager of learning.

I don't suppose the many primary-school teachers who practise these methods recognize that they are involved in the management of learning. Their work might be improved if they did, because it would remind them that part of their managerial role is to relate theory and practice continually in the understanding of how children learn. It is only with such understanding that curriculum programmes can be designed. That this applies equally to managers in industry should be easy to see. This theme pervades the chapters of this book. It is essential that managers in industry and business should 'see' themselves in these pictures of the teacher and ask themselves whether they are people watchers or people-minders. The analogy is penetrating, for managers should be vitally concerned with the 'learning' that people undertake in groups as it affects the output of their particular organization.

All the same kind of pressures we find at work are to be found in the play of young children, and these processes of socialization continue throughout life. They provide the basic skills for adaptability. If it is a social complaint that adults are not readily adaptable, then we must look first at the process of socialization and the way it is handled in schools, and only then at the content of knowledge as it relates to socialization. Thus everyone is concerned with an understanding of learning. The more we understand about the factors that enhance and inhibit learning, the more adaptable we are likely to be.

We were led to this point from a discussion of the role of imagery in education. This in turn led us to the value of play, but it also leads us to consider the value of day-dreaming and, more positively, reflective thinking. I call this 'the Martha-Mary dimension of education', and take my analogy from the gospel.

All too often we take 'doing' as the measure of effectiveness. A child must be seen to be doing something that is productive: A worker, even a research worker, must be seen to be at work. Day-dreaming is not allowed. Yet it is clear inventiveness, which is one of the aptitudes we are told society wants, is encouraged precisely when students are allowed to be unconventional in their approaches to learning.

In the hierarchical view of human abilities, intelligence influences performance in every specific ability. Using another technique of factorial analysis, an American psychologist, L.L. Thurstone,[31] argued that there were seven primary mental abilities that were largely independent of each other. These were verbal comprehension, word fluency, numerical fluency, spatial visualization, associative memory, and perceptual speed and reasoning. They were not hierarchically ordered.

Creativity and Intelligence

Following in this tradition, J.P. Guilford suggested that there were 120 factors of the intellect.[32] His model is usually shown in the form of a cube that shows the interrelations between the three main categories, called (1) operations, (2) content and (3) products.

The operations are cognitive, memory, divergent production, convergent production and evaluation. The contents are figural/visual, figural/auditory, symbolic, semantic and behavioural. Size, form and colour etc., make up the figural aspects, letters and digits etc., the symbolic, and verbal meanings and ideas the semantic. Behavioural relates to the way in which we deal with social situations. When a mental process acts on the 'content', a product is produced. The products are units, classes, relations, systems, transformations and implications. The model includes the activity of memory.[33]

In Guilford's model, creativity is the process of divergent thinking. This is a 'searching activity'. In contrast, convergent thinking is an information-processing activity. In a pencil-and-paper test, convergent problems would produce a single-solution answer that would be correct. In divergent thinking, problems are set that require several realistic answers: the more divergent the thinker, the more unusual the answer. To illustrate this point, you can ask a group of children or adults to write down as many uses of brick as possible in, say, two minutes. Some will produce traditional answers, others will present unusual ones. It is the latter group of children who are said to be creative.

In Britain, Hudson used pencil-and-paper tests to test sixth-formers (16–18 years) and concluded that high-IQ, low-creativity students tended to enter science and technology.[34] But his tests were pencil and paper, and it is by no means clear that creativity in these fields depends on verbal ability and, in consequence, on verbal expression.[35] Nevertheless, Hudson, unlike MacFarlane Smith, had a profound influence on those concerned with engineering education in Britain, for the Council of Engineering Institutions established a working party on creativity that subsequently organized a symposium on the matter.[36] A significant feature of that symposium was the lack of attention and disinterest in defining creativity. This seemed to be due to a widespread and unconsciously accepted assumption that everyone knew what everyone else meant by creativity.

Whatever we might think about creativity as a separate and equally important factor in mind (the intellect) to intelligence, there is little doubt that the ideas generated by Guilford, and those who have tried to develop his work, such as Getzels and Jackson, and Hudson, have been very influential in education.[37]

First has been the recognition that, in contrast with primary-school teaching, the techniques of play and small-group activities allow scope for original work, even when divergent thinking is not actively encouraged. In contrast, the teaching methods used in post-primary education at all levels tend to encourage convergent thinking, and this is often reinforced by the examination system. Happily, examinations are becoming more flexible and allow the development of more flexible learning. There have also been attempts to design questions that will force creative responses. These do not seem to have been successful because, once a question is set, the very preparation of an essay answer involves the student in a substantial analysis of the problem. It is by no means clear that it is the solution of the problem that is tested rather than the analysis.

Second, creativity research has focused on the fact that in certain circumstances teachers may prefer children who are convergent thinkers, since the divergent thinker may be difficult to handle. At the same time, many teachers rate the possession of high intelligence and high creativity as the most desirable characteristic in a pupil.[38]

Inability to diversify has caused many companies to fail.[39] Using the Guilford model as an analogy, it might be argued that those firms that succeed are more likely to exhibit 'divergent behaviour' than those that don't. But not all divergent thinking in pencil-and-paper tests is sound and creative. So too with companies: while an organization may want to diverge it can diversify into markets for which it is not fitted. Adaptation requires intelligent as well as creative behaviour. But intelligence does not necessarily mean high IQ as measured by paper-and-pencil tests. Many successful business people did not demonstrate high IQs at school. For this and other reasons, traditional IQ tests have been criticized as they do not assess many activities that we regard as intelligent behaviour. The limitations of pencil-and-paper intelligence tests are fairly obvious. There is no sound reason why they should pick out a musician or an artist or, for that matter, an entrepreneur.

Frames of Mind, Gardner's Theory of Multiple Intelligences

Criticisms of pencil-and-paper intelligence tests have led to important developments in the theory of intelligence. In contrast to Guilford, one of these theorists, Gardner, suggests that we possess a number of 'intelligences'.[40] He lists the following human potentials: musical intelligence, bodily-kinesthetic intelligence, logical–mathematical intelligence, linguistic intelligence, spatial intelligence, interpersonal intelligence and intrapersonal intelligence. That he is open to the use of other terms to describe 'intelligences' (e.g. intellectual competences, thought processes, cognitive skills), illustrates one of the differences between his approach and those that went before. He argues that, because of the interaction between heredity and training, we each develop these 'intelligences' – some to a greater extent than others. From the beginning of life these intelligences build upon and interact with each other. At the core of each intelligence is some kind of device for information processing that is unique to that particular intelligence.

Gardner suggests that the presentation of information to the nervous system causes it to carry out specific operations, which, by repeated use and processing, are eventually generated as intelligent knowledge. These 'raw' intelligences are developed through their involvement with symbol systems. Children demonstrate their various intelligences through their grasp of these symbol systems. Then, with further development, each intelligence and its associated symbol system come to be represented in a notational system. For example, at the symbol-system level there is a response to the sound of a musical instrument: at the second-order level there is a response to music. Finally, these intelligences are expressed in interest and vocational pursuits. Gardner defines intelligence as the ability 'to solve problems in a particular cultural setting'.[41] His theory is in contrast to traditional theories that are culture dependent.

Most of us, it is suspected, will probably feel that Gardner's intelligences are reasonably representative of reality. We do know people who are highly successful, for example, in sport and business, who are not highly intelligent as measured by intelligence tests. Whether Gardner's human potentials are the only 'intelligences' is, for Gardner, an open question. He would agree that perception, memory and judgement are active in each intelligence. If I have a doubt it is that perception might be an intelligence. We will be in a better position to make a judgement on this issue after reading Chapter 2, which considers the significance of perception in learning.

Gardner does not detail how the higher-level cognitive operations come into his framework, although he makes suggestions on how common sense (at least, his definition of that capacity), originality and metaphoric capacity may possibly be embraced within his framework. In contrast to Guilford, he does not believe that originality is a general capacity since it only occurs in single domains. Rarely, if ever, does one come across a person who is creative across the board. Gardner is careful to describe originality and draws attention to the fact that superb musical performers do not demonstrate a skill in experimentation that is a characteristic of originality. However, the person who becomes a gifted composer does demonstrate this characteristic. Because there may be a relationship between this kind of giftedness and personality, there is no necessary reason why creativity scores should correlate strongly with IQ scores.

Gardner's view that the ability to discriminate among one's own feelings and label (describe) them as an intelligence (personal) will have considerable appeal, as will the idea of intrapersonal intelligence (the ability to notice and to make distinctions among other temperaments, motivations and intentions). Industrialists are as much concerned with intrapersonal relations as they are with basic skills in mathematics and language.

We may conclude that Gardner's theory is one that approximates in many ways to the views the person in the street is likely to hold about intelligence. It is a theory that embraces the many talents owned by men and women. There is some support for this view in a study by Sternberg.[42]

Intelligence and Purposive Adaptation

Sternberg and his colleagues asked a representative group of lay persons in the USA, and a substantial number of experts in research on intelligence, for their descriptions of intelligence, academic intelligence, everyday intelligence and unintelligence. They found that the research workers considered motivation to be an important function of academic intelligence, whereas the lay persons stressed interpersonal competence in a social context.

When they put the significant ratings together, they came up with the following description of intelligence:

1. Practical problem-solving ability: reasons logically and well, identifies connections among ideas, sees all aspects of a problem, keeps an open mind, responds thoughtfully to others' ideas, sizes up situations well, gets to the heart of problems, interprets information accurately, makes good decisions, goes to original sources of basic information, poses problems in an optimal way, is a good source of ideas, perceives implied

assumptions and conclusions, listens to all sides of an argument, and deals with problems resourcefully.

2. Verbal ability: speaks clearly and articulately, is verbally fluent, converses well, is knowledgeable about a particular field, studies hard, reads with high comprehension, reads widely, deals effectively with people, writes without difficulty, sets time aside for reading, displays a good vocabulary, accepts social norms, and tries new things.

3. Social competence: accepts others for what they are, admits mistakes, displays interest in the world at large, is on time for appointments, has social conscience, thinks before speaking and doing, displays curiosity, does not make snap judgements, assesses well the relevance of information to a problem at hand, is sensitive to other people's needs and desires, is frank and honest with self and others, and displays interest in the immediate environment.[43]

Like Gardner, Sternberg recognizes the influence of culture and, from the analysis above, argues that motivation is one of four factors in the common core of intelligence. The others are a problem-solving factor, a verbal-ability factor and a social-competence factor. Of more importance to the context of this chapter is Sternberg's definition of intelligence. He defined it as a mental activity directed toward purposive adaptation to, and selection and shaping of, real-world environments relevant to one's life. Thus, to be intelligent is to be adaptive, and to acquire the skills of intelligence is to acquire a positive disposition to adaptation. His definition is, it seems to me, both attitudinal as well as cognitional. This is because, in this theory, intelligence is defined in terms of real-world environments that are related to, or potentially related to, one's life. It cannot, therefore, be completely understood outside of our socio-cultural context. Technology, for example, is likely to change our ideas about what we regard as intelligent behaviour. Numerical skill as a function of intelligence is likely to decline as a result of the introduction of calculators. Thus Sternberg argues that we see changes over time in what constitutes adaptive intelligence and, in consequence, intelligence is not only purposive but involves adaptation to the environment. Intelligent behaviour in these circumstances is not passive because we are able to choose, to a certain extent, the environments in which we are prepared to adapt. Moreover, intelligent behaviour will be demonstrated by the way we shape the environment. As Sternberg says, the most successful individuals in a particular sphere of endeavour are likely to be those who shaped this field.

If intelligence can be developed, then, given the parameters of Sternberg's theory, the answer to the question, 'Can we teach ourselves to change?' must be 'Yes'. It is with the outcomes of business and technical activities in the personal, social and economic spheres that this book is concerned, and, more especially, with the knowledge, skills and behaviours that constitute adaptive performance. It is with the problem of perception in our learning of the environment that we begin.

Notes and References

1. The developmental aspects referred to in this section relate in particular to perceptual learning, with some attention to the personality theories of E. Erikson and H.S. Sullivan. See, for example, Engler, B. (1979) *Personality Theories: An Introduction*, Houghton Milfflin, Boston,

Mass. Neither is this section concerned with the well-known cognitive development theories of Bruner and Piaget. See also Murray Thomas, R. (1985) *Comparing Theories of Child Development*, Wadsworth, Belmont, Ca (2nd edn).

2. Early, G.H. (1969) *Perceptual Training in the Curriculum*, Charles Merrill, Columbus, OH.

3. A slightly longer summary of this work, with details of this curriculum project, is to be found in Heywood, J. 1982) *Pitfalls and Planning in Student Teaching*, Kogan Page, London.

4. Early, *Perceptual Training* (note 2).

5. Jean Huston quoted by Galyean, B.C. (1983) Guided imagery in the curriculum, *Educational Leadership*, Vol. 40, no. 6, pp. 54–8.

6. For example, see Chapter 8. Visual-spatial intelligence, in H. Gardner (1983) *Frames of Mind. The Theory of Multiple Intelligences*, Basic Books, New York, NY.

7. In 1988 the Transport and General Workers Union, which is one of the large unions represented in the Ford Motor Co., GB, successfully prevented the Amalgamated Union of Engineering Workers from making a single-union plant deal with Ford US for an electronics plant to be built at Dundee. Because Ford US could not obtain total support from the Trade Union Council, it withdrew its plans to build the plant. This event is likely to be recorded as an important one in the annals of British trade union history.

8. In regard to the work of psychologists, see Colman, A.M. (1981) *What is Psychology?*, Kogan Page, London.

9. There has been a spate of books in recent years, of which Heim, A. (1970) *Intelligence and Personality: Their Assessment and Relationship*, Penguin Books, Harmondsworth, is among the best. Among the outstanding but substantial introductions to the subject is Butcher, H.J. (1968) *Human Intelligence: Its Nature and Assessment*, Methuen, London.

10. Burt's studies of twins have been found to have been based on constructed evidence, although this is not to negate the major contribution he made to the development of educational psychology and, in particular, factorial analysis.

11. Several books that have been stimulated by this controversy are Jensen, A.R. (1969) How much can we boost IQ and scholastic achievement?, *Harvard Educational Review*, Vol. 39, no. 1, pp. 1–123. The original article and commentaries by seven critics are contained in *Environment, Heredity and Intelligence* (1970) Reprint Series no. 2, *Harvard Educational Review*.

12. Binet, A., Simon, T. H. (1915) *Method of Measuring the Development of Intelligence of Young Children*, Chicago Medical Book Company, Chicago, Ill.

13. Intelligence quotient = (Mental (test) age − Real age × 100). For a simple introduction to the measurement of intelligence, see Valentine, C.W. (1978 reprint) *The Normal Child and some of his Abnormalities*, Penguin Books, Harmondsworth.

14. Gardner, *Frames of Mind* (note 6).

15. Sternberg, R.J. (1985) *Beyond I.Q.: A Triarchic Theory of Intelligence*, Cambridge University Press.

16. Both for an explanation of the British approach and factorial analysis, see Vernon, P.E. (1950) *The Structure of Human Abilities*, Methuen, London; and Vernon, P.E. (1963) Creativity and intelligence, *Educational Research*, Vol. 6, p. 163.

17. MacFarlane Smith, I. (1964) *Spatial Ability*, University of London Press, London.

18. McCallum, I. (1983) New training initiatives – another name for the Emperor's Clothes, *Educational Management and Administration*, Vol. 11, no. 2, pp. 153–6.

19. For a study of the role of spatial thinking in science, see Walkup, L.E. (1965) Creativity in science through visualization, *Perceptual and Motor Skills*, Vol. 21, p. 35.

20. Bogen, J.E. (1982) Split brains and the human duality, lecture at Tarrytown Conference Centre, New York, NY. See also Bogen, J.E. (1969) The other side of the brain, *Bulletin of the Los Angeles Neurological Societies*, Vol. 34, no. 2, p. 105.

21. See MacFarlane Smith, *Spatial Ability* (note 17), for many examples. For studies of creativity among scientists, see Taylor, C.W, and Barron, F. (eds.) *Scientific Creativity: Its Recognition and Development*, Wiley, New York, NY.

22. Galyean, Guided imagery (note 5).

23. *Ibid.*

24. Arendt, H. (1976) Reflections – thinking (part II), *The New Yorker*, 28 November, p. 26.

25. Barrell, J. (1983) Reflections on critical thinking in secondary schools, *Educational Leadership*, Vol. 40, no. 6, pp. 45–9.

26. Abercrombie, M.L.J. (1961) *The Anatomy of Judgement*, Penguin Books, Harmondsworth.

27. Maxwell, W. (1983) Games children play, and Mills, B.S. (1983) Imagination: the connection between writing and play, both articles are in Vol. 4, no. 6, of *Educational Leadership* and provide a useful introduction to this topic.

28. Suransky, V.P. (1983) The preschooling of childhood, *Educational Leadership*, Vol. 40, no. 6, pp. 27–9.

29. Bruner, J.S. (1966) *Towards a Theory of Instruction,* Harvard University Press, Cambridge, Mass.

30. Suransky, Preschooling (note 28).

31. Thurstone, L.L. (1947) *Multiple Factor Analysis,* Chicago University Press, Chicago, Ill.

32. Guilford, J.P. (1967) *The Nature of Human Intelligence*, McGraw-Hill, New York, NY.

33. See Baddeley, A.D. (1976) *The Psychology of Memory*, Harper & Row, New York, NY, for recent research on memory see Cohen, G. (1989) *Memory in the Real World*, Lawrence Erlgaum, Sussex.

34. Hudson, L. (1966) *Contrary Imaginations,* Methuen, London.

35. A point made by Christine Heward and this writer, and discussed with Hudson in a BBC Radio Broadcast, 'The Tongue Tied Scientist'. Heim *Intelligence and Personality* (note 9) also criticizes this work in Chapter 3 of her book.

36. Gregory, S.A. (1972) *Creativity in Engineering,* Butterworth, London.

37. Getzels, J.W. and Jackson, P.W. (1962) *Creativity and Intelligence,* Wiley, New York, NY. See also Heim, *Intelligence and Personality* (note 9), for an introduction to their work. Note the methodological difficulties, and Cattell, R.B. and Butcher, H.J. (1968) *The Prediction of Achievement and Creativity*, Bots-Merrill, Indianapolis. For a review of work on creativity up to 1971, see Freeman, J. *et al.* (1971) *Creativity: A Selectivity Review of Research*, Society for Research into Higher Education, Guildford. For a study that discusses these issues in relation to engineering education, see Jordan, T. (1981) An evaluation of the effectiveness of the 1st-year Electronic Engineering Laboratory Studies at the University of Salford, PhD thesis, University of Salford.

38. See Heim, *Intelligence and Personality* (note 9), Chapter 3; and Guilford, *The Nature* (note 32).

39. Jay, A. (1967) *Management and Machiavelli,* Penguin Books, Harmondsworth. Insight from the writer of the award-winning British TV series, 'Yes, Minister', unfortunately now out of print.

40. See Gardner, *Frames of Mind* (note 6), for a short version of the theory applied to education. See also Walters, J.M. and Gardner, H. (1985) The development and education of intelligences, in F.R. Link (ed.) *Essays on the Intellect*, Association for Supervision and Curriculum Development, Alexandria, Virginia, U.S.

41. Gardner, *Frames of Mind* (note 6).

42. Sternberg, *Beyond I.Q.* (note 15).

43. *Ibid.*

2

PERCEPTION AND LEARNING

Introduction

Our starting point is Sternberg's view of intelligence, with which the last chapter ended. That is, intelligence is a mental activity directed toward purposive adaptation to, and selection and shaping of, real-world environments relevant to one's life. It would seem self-evident that intelligence can be trained in such a way that the intellectual and emotional traits that result from heredity are well-disposed to do that to which they are intelligently directed. Such training requires us to learn about ourselves and our environment, which in its turn requires an understanding of how we learn and what impedes our learning. It is with learning and the factors that impede learning that this chapter is concerned, because it follows from the definition of intelligence at the end of the last chapter that the factors that impede learning must also be those that impede adaptability.

We saw in the last chapter that the infant learnt by interacting with his or her environment. After the infant has acquired information, he or she can manipulate data in the mind without reference to the environment. Eventually the infant sets him or herself a new task that causes the infant to experiment again with his or her environment.

The activity of sending a signal to objects in the environment and receiving a pulse back – to use the analogy of radar – is what we call the activity of perceptual learning. Thus impediments to perception, seeing, touching and feeling, are impediments to learning. If we misunderstand a 'situation', how can we be expected to adapt to the 'situation'? Unfortunately, we are all too easily deceived, and one of the greatest deceptions we undergo is the fact that most of us do not believe we can be easily deceived. If we are to understand the environment, we have to accept it as axiomatic, that it is easy to be deceived. By accepting this, we begin to develop a sensitivity toward the environment. Even so, we continually lose this sensitivity and this makes adaptability more difficult, particularly as we age. This chapter is based on the view that if we are aware of the factors that influence learning, we will be better able to adapt because the new learning required for adaptation will not then come as a strange activity.

The Significance of Perception in Learning

To begin at the beginning, look at the two lines in the diagram in Figure 2.1.

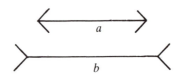

Figure 2.1   Which one of the following is a correct statment about the diagram: (a) Arrow-head 'a' is longer than arrow-head 'b'; (b) Arrow-head 'b' is longer than arrow-head 'a'?

Which one is the longest, *a* or *b*? If you have not seen this illusion before, you may be tempted to say that *b* is longer than *a*. If you put a rule along the lines you will find that they are of the same length. If you thought one was longer than the other, you were deceived. There are many such examples.[1]

The problem is that we see these illusions as a one-off activity, like watching a conjurer on the television. We find it difficult to believe that such deceptions happen to us all the time, or that the first perceptions we gain of 'others' are a powerful influence in the attitudes we adopt to those individuals. At the most elemental level, consider the well-known picture of the lady in Figure 2.2. Is she an old lady or a young lady? Is she a blonde or a brunette? Those who have seen this picture before will know that the angle of vision influences the result. Some people take a very long time to see the alternative to their own first image.

The perceptions we have of people are important. Many adults take against youngsters because they relate the perceptions they have of dress and demeanour to particular behaviour patterns for which there is more often than not little justification. In their turn, children make unwarranted assumptions about their parents. The combination of parental and youthful misperception can cause conflict in the family. An interesting test for you and your friends is to go for a pre-ordained walk in the town where you live or work. When you have completed the journey, write down all the things you saw on that journey.[2] The chances are that your friends will produce a different list from your own. Ask yourselves how this comes about and you will soon find that it is to do with your past experiences, interests and worries. A major influence on our perceptions are the many 'problems' we have to solve – where to go tonight, what to buy for dinner, the row with the girl or boy friend. These divert our focus away from the environment, and it is the objects in the environment related to our thinking that we observe.

One doesn't have to send people out for a walk to demonstrate this point: many games on television show that people differ in their perceptions of the same activity or object. Once I was in a classroom watching a student teacher when midway through the class he asked the pupils, aged 12 to 13, to write down what they thought they had learnt. Among the answers they wrote were the following:

- I have learnt how a contra entry works.
- I have learnt to keep my work tidy.
- I have learnt how to balance a cash book properly.
- I have learnt to look more closely at the question.
- I have learnt to be neat and tidy.
- I have learnt that if you take your time everything will be correct.
- I have learnt that the teacher gets nervous in the class when an inspector is present: and I have learnt a bit more about balancing accounts.

Some of these answers relate to and converge on what was done in the previous 20 minutes, but the last one shows an imaginative leap, or a broader perspective. Sometimes we apply the word 'insight' to this perception. Jane Abercrombie illustrates this point with two pictures.[3] On one side of the page in her book is a large sketch that looks as if a pen has splattered black ink over the page. Asked to explain the picture, few see the face of a prophet or Christ, which is shown on the following page. After a few flips backwards and forwards most people see the face

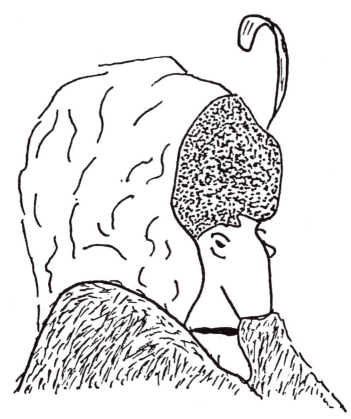

Figure 2.2 Is she an old lady or a young lady? You should be able to see both. Many different versions of this drawing have been published.

of 'Christ'. This 'insight' requires a substantial focusing of the observer's perceptual capacity.

The Problem of Ambiguity

The different perceptions teachers and pupils have of each other can inhibit learning. Quite simple phrases and actions on the part of the teacher can give rise to misunderstanding among the pupils. Such misunderstandings could lead to conflict in the classroom or personal conflict in learning, particularly when children are on their own wrestling with homework. The same is true of students and teachers in higher education, or, for that matter, trainers and trainees in industry. A competent teacher will help children to develop their perceptual skills by encouraging them to ask questions about the matters they find difficult. But at some stage, young students need to have their attention drawn to the fact that they have perceptual skills that need to be exercised. In that way they may cope better with the situations they will find in later life in the community, in the family and at work. Some analyses may come as a shock. Imagine what the student in the example that follows would feel if he had correctly understood the situation that surrounded him:

> A student had to make a work sampling study of chargehands in a fairly confined factory, *without a complete introduction*. He started on a Monday morning. A new product was assembled and production was under time stress. Because he often spoke to chargehands and was continually making notes, he appeared to most of the young assembly workers as controllers of their bosses. His appearance near their assembly lines was welcomed with some satisfaction: they became bolder towards the chargehands. They made jokes and nudged each other when he was approaching. To the chargehands he became a menace: they became uncertain and nervous and they concerned themselves more with the production process itself than with their group of workers. To the departmental manager he became a scapegoat: he blamed several production faults on this work sampling study and he walked about the factory more than usual.[4]

In this situation there is a great deal of ambiguity. It is fairly easy to see how it has arisen. The person responsible for the student had failed to explain to *all* those involved what was expected of the student and to what use it would be put.

Ambiguities of this kind are a powerful influence on behaviour. They occur all the time in all kinds of human relationships. They are particularly prevalent in the perceptions we have of the way individuals exercise power and control. Ambiguity is seen in the fact that even when power is used 'for a good end or purpose, such as to be generous, it often has the ambiguity of giving a feeling of goodness and of being patronizing both to the person who gives and the person who receives'.[5]

It is important to clear up ambiguities because they affect communication, information, interpretation and subsequent action. As Woodhouse says, 'A consideration of the reality of ambiguity of tension and conflict throughout all aspects of human life can be not just a theoretical exercise but can illuminate the human scene and nerve us to worthwhile efforts in many areas and affairs of daily life'.[6]

Ambiguities are not merely inherent in the data presented to our senses but in the way that data is reconstructed by our perceptual learning processes. Thus it is that any understanding of human behaviour must begin with an understanding of the factors that influence perception. The five dimensions with which we are concerned are as follows:

1. Data, and its acquisition.
2. The sampling of this data.
3. The language through which we communicate our experience.
4. The collective of that experience.
5. The internal dynamics within us that contribute to our behaviour.

Data and its Acquisition

In this section we are concerned with the nature of data and its acquisition, not with how we process the data in problem-solving activities. It is a matter of experience that we collect data all the time. It is also a matter of experience that we are sometimes aware that we are acquiring new knowledge and that sometimes the images of new knowledge are rather vague. We at times call the development of a vague image into a picture of clarity 'insight', and the pursuit of that insight 'understanding'. To be able to understand the influence of both ourselves and the environment on the acquisition of data, we have to define that data even though we do not know exactly how data presents itself to us. Thus, from the 1930s, psychologists interested in learning, such as Bartlett,[7] have postulated that we acquire very small items of data, rather like the computer's 'bytes', which we store and arrange in the memory, and in that part of the brain called memory. These have been variously called schema, schemata, categories and, in my own work, frames of reference,[8] since it is only associations of schema that have meaning. Without a concept of this kind it is difficult to analyse how we learn, for by learning we mean that process by which experience acquires new concepts and reorganizes old ones.

The problem of perception is confounded by the sheer quantity of knowledge available to our senses. We have, of necessity, to 'sample' that information if we are to give meaning(s) to that data. This is what happened when students walked round the town in the test suggested earlier. The sampling was conditioned by the interests and dispositions of the participants. So it is with almost everything we do. A wife may see quite different facets in a dress from her husband. Nevertheless, there are fundamentals about the dress on which both will agree. Fortunately it is a fact of experience that we are able to assent to universals or common propositions because without them there could be no communication. It is for this reason that formal education has to be concerned with the provision of first principles on which further generalizable knowledge can be built. What those principles might be is another, most contentious issue. My own view, for example, is that the aims of this book should be met in senior-cycle, second-level education.

It will be appreciated that frames of reference are acquired, as it were, 'unconsciously' as well as deliberately. The more attention we give to them, the greater our understanding. Level of interest and motivation relate to the depth of attention we apply to frames of reference currently attracting our attention. It is also evident that the more we attend to schema, the more complex the frame of reference that can be handled. If we are called on to respond to frames of reference in which our attention is low, our response is likely to be naïve.[9] Such responses may well be dogmatic, for it is only when the frames of reference are well developed, and more than elemental 'bytes' of information, that the higher-order thinking skills of analysis, synthesis and judgement are brought into play.[10]

The Influence of the Environment

We can see at once that we are very dependent on our environment for the acquisition of knowledge. Since no two environments are entirely similar, and since our previous knowledge acts on the data it samples, and even though universal understanding is possible, communication between different groups of people can be difficult. This is because the knowledge frames of reference (categories, schema) they have derived from their previous experience may be very different.

It is in this sense that we can say that knowledge is socially constructed. The environment and, more especially, the other people within it, create the knowledge patterns that are open to us. If we move to other frames of reference outside our realm of knowledge, we cannot expect to grasp the new information except with difficulty. The problem is that while these frames of reference help us to see, evaluate and respond, we often distort the information we see in order to make it fit our own frames of reference. We see what we want to see. This is especially true of arguments in the moral and political spheres.

This is no better illustrated than by the report on 'The Belgrano Affair' by the House of Commons Foreign Affairs Committee. In 1982, Argentina had annexed the Falkland Islands from Britain. The British government, led by Mrs Thatcher, went to war and in a short time wrested the Falklands back from the Argentine. In the process an Argentine cruiser, *The Belgrano*, was sunk in circumstances that led some Labour Members of Parliament to suppose that the sinking had broken the rules of war. Writing the day after the publication of the report on 24 July 1985, *The Times* leader-writer said the following:

> Two groups of individuals sit together for months reading and listening to the same evidence. At the end of this process no individual breaks with his group's identity but the two groups reach fundamentally different conclusions about the evidence. Moreover, the differences between them provide subtle pointers to the different political philosophies espoused by each group.
> The majority of the Committee examined the evidence and were satisfied that the sinking of the Belgrano was, in the circumstances, a reasonable decision of war, that the Peruvian peace plan was not intentionally or in fact scuppered by that sinking and that though there were deceptions at the House of Commons which were regrettably prolonged by ministers, they were more the product of caution than of deliberate mendacity.

and in a later paragraph:

> The minority group of Labour members clearly approached the affair with a fundamental belief that the war as a whole was wrong and the Belgrano affair, as a particularly striking episode, was one of the most scandalous. Consequently wherever the evidence provided to the Committee left some element of doubt, their tendency was to suspect the worst and to seek further evidence of a conspiracy to withhold facts, or else to substantiate their own suspicions that the whole war was a put-up job to help Mrs Thatcher win the subsequent election. No pragmatism there but rather the time-worn tendency of the left to see patterns and conspiracies in other people's behaviour because that is so familiar a part of political life on the left.[11]

We may confidently predict that there is sufficient ambiguity in the selections I have made for Conservatives to accuse me of prejudice in favour of Labour, and for Labour supporters to view their choice from an opposite perspective.

We see the same in Irish-American congressmen who visit Northern Ireland and who, regardless of what they hear or see, are expected by the British to blame the British for the situation, and do so. For example: 'Mr Kennedy's use of the language of Irish republicanism was seen as confirming the suspicions of Ulster Unionists that his four-day fact-finding visit was loaded in favour of the nationalist cause for a united Ireland.'[12]

The term 'prejudice' is often applied to such dispositions. Perceptual learning theory tells us that we cannot help being prejudiced. This is a necessary consequence of the need to sample data and the environmental conditions to which we are subject. The more sophisticated our frames of reference, the more objective we can be. I say 'we can', because often we choose not to, especially when an ideology dictates that we take an action with which we do not necessarily agree. This is particularly true of politicians when they are obliged to vote with their party. They need to be prejudiced in favour of their ideology, just as the salesperson has to be in favour of the goods he or she is selling. There is nothing wrong with this, because society requires that some individuals should pursue their beliefs in this way. Nevertheless, it does prevent politicians from a more objective assessment of reality.

In subjects that are value-laden, students often switch off a lecturer whose views are contrary to their own. We call this 'cognitive dissonance'.[13] The distortions we make inevitably limit our flexibility in situations where adaptation is required, such as arguments with our friends or colleagues at work where compromise, concern or tolerance may be required. Limitations in our frames of reference may well limit our understanding of a particular situation for we impose reality on the objects of knowledge, that is, the situations we perceive. If individuals are to adapt with relative ease to a new situation, it is necessary that they should understand that they have to find new ways of perceiving the environment in order to make it work for them. Education can help them do this by providing them with the widest possible frames of reference. It is easy to see how, in theory, the comprehensive organization of schools and a common curriculum should achieve these goals. But the environment, both present and historical, can defeat the best-laid plans, for language usage derives from the environment and persons whose contextual experiences differ widely from one another may not necessarily be able to communicate among themselves. Just as language can be a source of ambiguity, so it can be an impediment to effective communication.

Language as a Source of Ambiguity

We continually come across examples where the words and phrases we use can cause ambiguity. Other people not only listen to our words but also observe our gestures. They understand that language is closely related to behaviour and that the truth of a matter demands an understanding of both. Language has a regulative function for it co-ordinates, stabilizes and facilitates other forms of behaviour. We use words to instruct ourselves and through continuing interaction with words we achieve our goal.[14] Reflection on our mental processes soon confirms that this is the case. So we observe as well as listen, and further reflection will show that we often misinterpret what we hear and see.

The language forms used by different groups of people may lead to conflict between them because they simply do not understand each other. The methods of communication used in Britain by the tabloids, on the one hand, and the serious press, on the other, illustrate this point. The tabloid gives over many columns to photographs and cartoons. Its headlines are 5 to 8 cm high. The amount of text is relatively small and no subject demands too much attention. The sentences are short and sometimes badly constructed. In contrast, the serious newspapers devote much attention to comment. There can be many paragraphs in an article that use complicated words, phrases and subclauses.

More observation shows that everyday language usage among different groups of people follows similar patterns. Bernstein, when analysing his earliest observations of language usage by individuals, distinguished between public and formal language. Later on, as he refined the concept, he called them restricted and elaborated codes.[15] The children of unskilled workers tended to use short, simple sentences with simple words. Sometimes the sentences would not be completed. Such children would not be able to concentrate on a specific topic for very long, and, in argument or aggression, they would use a language of implicit rather than explicit meaning. In contrast, the higher socio-economic groups use a language of explicit meaning. They reason, they conclude and can hold a topic of conversation for substantial periods of time. These children are fortunate because they are able to use the restricted and elaborate codes. One problem that arises from these differences in language codes is that the disadvantaged child may well perceive a different reality in the words and actions of a teacher from the one the teacher wants to display. Teachers often use a language children cannot understand.

Not everyone would agree with Bernstein's analysis or the sociology of knowledge to which it has led. Nevertheless, simple observations in public places suggests that the grammatical usage of the lower socio-economic group is limited, and its argument categorical without logic, although in some spheres it may have considerable understanding that it finds difficult to express.

This has been particularly well illustrated in a recent study of religious belief in white working-class London. The level of abstract thought required, to discuss questions about religion systematically was inhibited by the lack of an appropriate language. Thought, it seemed, could not be shaped without a suitable vocabulary and this caused many respondents to express anxiety.[16] Nevertheless, on a 1 (not at all) to 10 (very important) scale, God was given 6.3 importance in their lives.

We should not make too hard and fast a dividing line because anyone faced with abstract concepts with which he or she cannot cope will avoid the issue. The middle classes have the ability to bluster and waffle and may overawe other people with verbosity that lacks logic. You see this at work in the examination answers of undergraduates. I have called this elsewhere the 'fudge factor'.[17]

The anxiety that was felt among these working-class respondents to questions about religion may well explain their not being able to participate in middle-class religion. Individuals who are unable to express themselves and fear that they will not know what to do and say will not want to venture in. This is true of many social situations. But more important than this is Longley's point that there is something fundamentally incompatible between working-class culture and cerebral middle-class protestantism.[18]

The closeness of religion to morality suggests that such persons may have difficulty in explaining and/or justifying their moral position. They may operate from what the middle classes sometimes call a high-moral position.

Kohlberg, who suggested a stage theory of moral development,[19] wrote

> While social environments directly produce different specific beliefs (e.g. smoking is wrong, eating pork is wrong) they do not engender different basic moral principles (e.g. consider the welfare of others, treat other people equally etc.). In so far as basic values are different, then it is largely because we are at different levels of maturity in thinking about basic moral and social issues and concepts. Exposure to others more mature than ourselves helps stimulate maturity in our own value processes. We are, however, selective in our responses to others and do not automatically incorporate the value of elders or authorities important to us.

Kohlberg's idea is that we develop through stages in the moral sphere just as we do in the cognitive domain.[20] We do not all develop at the same rate. This means that those at a lower stage of development would have difficulty in understanding those at a higher stage. These difficulties would be compounded if those at the higher stage had difficulty in articulating their positions.

At a time when there is much interest in the relative qualities of male and female managers, it is of more than passing interest to note the challenge to Kohlberg's theory by Gilligan and Lyons.[21] They argue that women have a different view of social morality from men. The primary concern of women is a systematic, lifelong concern for individuals. Thus in judging, an individual whose morality is based on justice will make judgements based on 'how decisions are thought about and justified; or whether values, principles or standards are (were) maintained, especially fairness', whereas an individual whose morality is based on response and care will consider 'what happened/will happen, or how things worked out; or, whether relationships were/are maintained or restored'.

The value of Kohlberg's work lies not so much in its developmental nature as in the fact that it highlights the conflicts that can emerge when the moral positions of individuals differ. Moreover, experience suggests that these standpoints relate to the stages in the theory. At the very least it is possible to argue that many problems in industrial relations arise from different moral perspectives, and that this is a major problem in negotiation. We can see at once the relationship between this theory and perceptual learning, on the one hand (especially in the way we acquire values), and industrial relations on the other.

Having observed and analysed shop steward/management relations on a number of occasions, I came to the conclusion that many industrial-relations problems arise because individuals among the negotiators are at different levels of moral development. Thus, a shop steward might be at a higher level of development than a manager. Since their schema as expressed through language (to restore the argument to language and perceptual learning) would be different, there could be no communication or 'real' understanding between them.

Given such differences, it is easy, therefore, to see why so many industrial-relations problems arise. It is conceivable that neither side understands each other. Each side comes out of its cocoon for the occasional or regular meeting and then goes back to its group. There is no incentive to learn the language of the other group. As Bernstein says, once they identify with the group who have the same language code, there is no further attempt to grapple with the broader and more complex aims of the wider society or organization.

If such groups are to get together, they either have to appreciate each other's language codes or there has to be a much more substantial attempt to find methods through which propositional thinking can be developed among those whose language competency is limited.[22] It is for this reason that there is much interest in the potential of Latin to achieve this goal.[23]

Specialist languages are not confined to the socio-economic classes. Every grouping of tasks, such as medicine or engineering, acquires its own specialist language, and this is as much part of its desire for status as it is of a need determined by the nature of the problem to be solved (i.e. the language of method). Ultimately, specialization and the language of specialization can impede adaptation. This is the problem of experience within specialist tasks and it is a major problem for those who wish to induce change in organizations.

Experience and Learning

Hesseling, among others, drew attention to the effects of specialization on communication between employees in different sections of a manufacturing organization. He wrote that

> In the general sense a production manager can be as much a specialist as a mathematician or a commercial manager. A commercial manager may develop, by virtue of his working circumstances and experience, a gambling orientation whereby he interprets the incoming information as probabilistic. Or the mathematician may develop a style of categorisation to interpret events as relational structures. A production manager may

categorise information in terms of technical process and work performance. When a sociologist, for example, points out interpersonal rivalries in his department it can surprise him. These interpersonal relations did not yet fit into his system of categories and had mainly to be seen as differences in performance.[24]

It is evident that the specialist languages impede the performance of the specialists to the detriment of the organization. Hesseling called the effects of specialism on the task 'deformation professionelle'. In order to function within their specialisms, engineers have to make their frames of reference highly efficient: this is the deformation. Unfortunately, the information related to their specialist tasks and the modes of thinking that are forced on them by those tasks are often transferred to the solution of problems in other fields to which the mode of thinking is not really relevant.

In Britain, the problem of specialist languages is especially complicated because of the educational origins of the different specialists. It is still a fact that production engineering is a low-status occupation. Many production engineers come from the shopfloor via an apprenticeship. Manufacturing engineering has only just begun to acquire some status in engineering departments of universities in the UK. Semantic differences, not as sharp as those described by Bernstein, will inevitably intervene. These will be compounded by the fact that the modes of learning among persons in these two groups are likely to differ and this will cloud the perceptions they have of what each other ought to be doing. Burns has said in a much-quoted article that 'production management cannot bring itself to believe that a development engineer is doing the job he is paid for unless he is at the bench doing something with his hands; a draughtsman is not doing his job unless he is at the drawing board and so on.'[25] As we have seen, the engineeer who has been trained by a university is much more likely to think in the abstract than the person on the shopfloor who has been trained to deal with matters in the concrete.[26] Inevitably that engineer will have to rely more on past experience than on principles. An organization that values experience will ensure that this value is acquired by every group.

My colleagues and I found in a study of an industrial enterprise that at around the age of 40 engineers in that firm came to value experience more than training, although training was highly regarded by up-and-coming young engineers. At the same time, we were able to demonstrate that this reliance on experience could prevent engineers from finding successful solutions to new problems.[27] Development and design involve relatively small changes in design. As Peters has pointed out, most improvement in quality in products and organizations comes from simplification of design, manufacturing, layout, processes and procedures.[28] Design and development are ongoing processes that depend on the collective experience of the organization with its products.

Knowledge about why some components or ideas succeeded and why others failed is readily built up and stored, and these are the schema that form the bases for future development. Too often design changes are forced on technologists. They are not trained to anticipate change but to respond to problems. Often in these circumstances they look backwards to see how these problems were solved in the past. For example, when the engineers in our study came face to face with a problem that was radically different from the ones related to their experience, they were sometimes unable to relate this experience to the solution of the new problem. Knowledge of the principles of engineering science learnt in their college courses did not seem to come to their aid.

They were not trained to look at problems from a fresh point of view and a different perspective. Experience had cushioned them against adaptability. They have, as Peters says, or at least their leaders have, to create a structure in which teams seek to create new worlds, destroy them and create again. In these circumstances we might ask the question, 'What is the paradox that provides security, on the one hand, and the drive for change on the other?' Peters' answer to this problem is to suggest that security – he calls it *stability* – has to be focused on the maintenance (my term) of superior quality and service that can only be achieved by the *dynamic* constant improvement, not merely in products, but in individual skill-building.[29]

Such skill-building demands an understanding of how perception influences our learning for the dynamic of constant improvement is a dynamic of learning that utilizes both convergent and divergent styles. Since our perceptual frames of reference are greatly influenced by our experience, it is clear that those managers and management teams that succeed are likely to be those who have had, and which bring together, a wide variety of personal and professional experience.

Support for this view is to be found in recent research by Norburn, who has said that

> the more experience of a subjective judgemental nature an executive has, be this in childhood, in lateral education, in several differing functions within the organization or in broad-based international exposure, the more likely that he or she will form part of a management team in a growing industry, or be a candidate for a chief executive position.[30]

Once again the findings of research that go back to the 1960s are confirmed. Education should provide individuals with the widest possible range of frames of references. But perceptual-learning theory suggests that it is not sufficient to define it in terms of a range of subjects as is the case with the Education Reform Act in England, or with the classical education that it is often argued generalist managers should have. There is evidence enough to suggest that this has failed.[31] The breadth of vision with a meticulous eye for detail, which Mant describes as the characteristic of the competent manager,[32] cannot be achieved without a thorough understanding of the task in hand or without the development of convergent and divergent thinking skills in a variety of learning situations.

If experience is not to inhibit learning, then everyone ought to be exposed to training or renewal at regular periods throughout their life. They need, as Hesseling says, to be exposed to a *choc des opinions* at regular intervals.[33] That this is the approach of the large companies in Japan should not come as a surprise. The quality-circle approach for which they are renowned amounts to almost continuous training.[34]

The Development of Perceptual Skills

Our internal and perceptual development go hand in hand. Learning depends on an exchange with the environment. It is equally dependent on our abilities, aptitudes, dispositions – interests and values – and personality, more especially motivations. The learning system is complex. The cognitive style a person brings to the solution of problems is the result of a complex interaction between motivational, interpretive, evaluative and memory systems, as Figure 2.3 shows. When performance is considered, be it that of a learner or a worker, it is easy to see that it is influenced by seveal significant factors. It is also easy to see that some relate to the performer – e.g. abilities, aptitudes, attitudes and disposition, education and training, health and personality – while others are a function of the working environment – e.g. environment for work (equipment methods), climate, goals of the organization, incentives, leadership and organizational structure.

It is argued in Chapter 4 that all workers are learners, and the implications of this for the organization of work is also discussed.

Because we are unable to look at the brain, we can only draw conclusions about how we think from the behaviour of children and adults in learning situations. Generally speaking, we go along with the view that in the solution of problems individuals move from the concrete to the abstract.[35] Some investigations support the work of Piaget, who believed that children had to go through fixed stages of development until they reached a stage when they could think in the abstract.[36] Others feel that children are capable of abstract thought appropriate to their age, and one at least has argued that children ask all the essential philosophical questions but in their own language. It seems to me that there is some truth in both perspectives. Teachers observe that children find it difficult to undertake propositional thinking in their subjects. Their reasoning is not seen to be very powerful except among those deemed 'bright'. But this is not to say that within certain topics on their own, students cannot achieve a high level of competence. The learning system is complex.

Nevertheless, within particular spheres of competence it is a matter of observation that individuals differ considerably in their capability to handle propositional thought. It is a function of their cognitive development and intellectual ability. Undoubtedly these differences can be a source of conflict. In debate, the contestants must be limited by their particular levels of cognitive development in the sphere of argument.

Perceptual-learning theory suggests that if there is a conflict situation arising from a different perception of concepts, it will only be resolved if the two sides undergo some joint learning exercise that will enable them to resolve the misunderstanding. At the general level of education, it is clear that much more attention ought to be given to the economic and human factors that influence our behaviour. For example, the conflict of interests between those who do and those who do not 'own' is heightened by the differing perceptions that owners and workers have of the concept of profits. Yet pupils are not required to have a basic

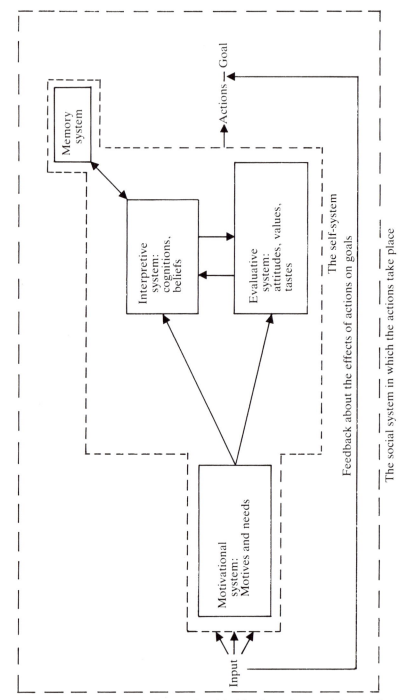

Figure 2.3   A systems model of the learner (modified by the inclusion of the social system from an idea by MacDonald, F.J. (1969) Educational Psychology, Wadsworth, Cal.

understanding of how business works or how wealth is created. Neither are they given the opportunity to discuss the uses to which wealth should be put. At the level of the company, such misunderstandings will only be resolved by greater participation in the running of the organization and shares in the profits. Even at the operational level it is possible to provide for learning experiences that will assist the better understanding of the value judgements being made in conflict situations. Such experiences aim to broaden the frames of reference the mind acquires as it develops, as the next section shows. At the same time, it has to be appreciated that the complexity of economic issues often leads to 'cognitive dissonance'. That is, that individuals, and especially politicians, often seek certainty in their own beliefs when faced with alternative value positions to their own.

Changes in industrial behaviour that are substantial and will continue, can only be in response to substantial changes of attitude at all levels in society. This in turn will influence the structure and organization of industrial and commercial concerns. Thus, individuals need to see themselves as lifelong learners if they are to remain adaptable and at equanimity with themselves in a world in which technological and social change continues apace. It is not sufficient for this purpose that they should obtain skills in autonomous learning, for that learning will have to be seen to have purpose within that technological and social structure. Thus a fundamental change in orientation in the purpose of learning is required, and it is with this that the final section is concerned.

Society and Learning

We owe to two American sociologists, Berger and Luckmann, the notion that 'Society not only controls our movements, but shapes our identity, our thought and our emotions. The structures of society become the structures of our own consciousness. Society does not stop at the surface of our skins. Society penetrates as much as it envelops us'.[37]

Society assists us with our sampling and helps us develop bias. But despite the fact that society provides the values and the information that constitute our knowledge, it is necessary to argue that it does not prevent the development of ideas or independence of thought. Indeed, without them there would be no change. However, I do not wish to suggest that all knowledge is relative. In my view it is not. The perennial issues of epistemology and metaphysics remain independent of the prevailing plausibility structure and, in effect, of what we come to believe is meaningful knowledge.[38]

Nevertheless, as Berger says, very few people feel the need for reappraisal

because the world view into which they have been socialised appears self-evident to them. Since it is also so regarded by almost everyone they are likely to deal with in their own society, the world view is self-validating. Its 'proof' lies in the reiterated experience of other men who take it for granted also. To put this perspective of the sociology of knowledge into one succinct proposition: Reality is socially constructed.[39]

To put it another way, our particular environment provides a ready-made structure of knowledge that itself is limited. The environments in which middle- and working-class children grow up in England are quite different. Moreover, attitudes persist – apparently happily. It is difficult to believe that a revolution is nigh. The lesson in terms of industrial life has been well put by Mant:[40]

> It is here that the language reflects the awful split in British education between state and private schooling. Those who go into 'management' as it is perceived (not excluding management education, management consultancy, management research all the rest of it) probably attended an old-fashioned and rather strict school in which the prevailing model was one of team spirit, pulling together, self-sacrifice, not letting the side down and fair internal competition under rigid, but explicit rules; a world of order-mindless perhaps, and dependent, but above all, ordered.

He continues

> Those who go simply to 'work' in order to live are much more likely to have attended a school which 'teaches' anmongst other things, that the best you can do in this chaotic life is to survive, and you had better learn pretty soon to fight, either openly or, more likely covertly, by opting out altogether. Later on, such people tend to be deaf to exhortations from management to 'all pull together' to combat a common external enemy (Japanese importers now, instead of St. Custards). The only 'club' available to the workers is called a union and the enemy is plainly close at hand.[41]

As we have seen, the divide is great. It is a divide of language and a divide of perceptions. It is not surprising that some authorities argue that the cause of the British decline in the nineteenth century was its class structure. In so far as manufacturing industry is concerned, there is some truth in this view. The technical jobs in industry are low status. Worse, the acquired perceptions individuals have of their capabilities are limited and these limitations arise from beliefs about their potential that derive in no small measure from the limitations to opportunity such sub-systems as apprenticeship and the professions impose. In Britain it is very difficult to be mobile once one is in a slot. The slot defines the individual rather than the individual the person.

Experience is not only valued but used as the criterion to categorize individuals. Application forms seek career histories. To obtain these with ease a job title is given. From this title a personnel selector draws information about the potential of an applicant to fill a particular job. If this job falls outside the predicted range of potential, then the applicant will be screened out of the selection process immediately.

Individuals are prohibited from change because of the unwillingness of management to go beyond over-simplified job descriptions of the work actually done and the skills used. In consequence, the mobility of labour is considerably limited. Task analyses show that workers have the skills to undertake a variety of roles. The reason that persons are not adaptable lie as much in the perceptions of the managed and managers as they do in anything else. Thus, while experience is valuable, it can also confirm existing prejudices and acquire new ones associated with the situation in which we find ourselves.

To overcome this situation people, whether they are managers or workers, teachers or pupils, have to understand very much more about each other and realize that, in general, most of us have much more to offer than circumstances allow. We have to view learning as giving and management as service. We have to view ourselves as learning systems. In the interaction between worker and manager, and pupil and teacher, each brings something to the relationship. The pupil's mind is not simply a *tabula rasa* (blank slate) on which the data of knowledge can be written. His learning is influenced by home, society and, by no means least, by his or her peers. He or she is an active individual with attitudes, values and emotions that contribute to the pupil's being and to the moulding of the pupil's intellectual skills. The pupil contributes to his or her learning as much as the teacher does for, as well as being a response system, he or she is also goal seeking, as Figure 2.3 shows.

We can tabulate what students and individuals bring to their work as follows:

1. *Knowledge*

    (a) General.
    (b) About his or her specialism or subjects of study.
    (c) About business, school or college.

2. *Physical skills*

    (a) Health.
    (b) Related psychomotor skills.

3. *Cognitive and affective skills*

    (a) Abilities to recognize and to solve problems (creative skills).
    (b) Ability to make judgements.
    (c) Ability to communicate.
    (d) Ability in the development of satisfactory interpersonal relationships.

4. *Personality and drive*

    (a) A certain activity-level norm.
    (b) A certain level of risk-taking.
    (c) Aspirations and expectations.
    (d) Acceptability.

5. *Values*

    (a) Interests.
    (b) A moral disposition.

In their turn, the school, or college, or organization, helps people to be effective by the following:

1. *Job or lesson analysis*

    (a) Providing a definition of the key results the job is required to produce, or the aims and objectives of a curriculum programme.

    (b)   A definition of the knowledge and skills required for the performance of the task.

    (c)   Details of information and resources necessary for the completion of the job or, for homework, a project or a practical class.

2. *School, college or organization*

    (a)   Provides a structure in which people can work or learn.

    (b)   A management or teaching style that will motivate, whether in groups or individually.

3. *Recruitment, education and training*

    (a)   Matching what an individual brings to the job to the needs of the job, or matching student abilities to the requirements of the programme.

    (b)   Background knowledge and experience of similar work or instructional situations likely to be of use.

    (c)   Training or instruction in specific knowledge and skills for a defined function.

Most people would accept that this idea of the teaching/learning situation has direct relevance to the work situation. The traditional hierarchical model of work assumes that orders are transmitted in a downward direction to the levels below. In return, information is transmitted upwards to higher management. It is the traditional teaching model. This model assumes that workers have the same goal as management, just as teachers so often assume that pupils have the same goals as themselves. It neglects the fact that such individuals as pupils have goals of their own and that in consequence their actions are directed to the achievement of a multiplicity of goals that relate as much to their careers, family and personal needs as they do to their work orientation. They will take actions that best serve these interests. Management, like teachers, often fails to recognize what it is that workers have to bring to their work, and organize accordingly – sometimes with alarming consequences.

There is much to be gained by extending the notions inherent in this twofold tabulation to the idea of learning as giving and management as service. It is clear that the management function is to provide resources, and to facilitate work. Many strikes are caused by the failure to produce the resources at the right time and in the right place. The teaching function is no different from the managing function. Both are decision-makers and the teachers task is to manage learning, and that is what a lesson plan is about. That this is increasingly recognized is shown by the fact that the concept of a teacher as a facilitator is now frequently used. It seems to me that an important conceptual jump is made if we move beyond the idea of teachers as managers and facilitators to the concept of them as servants. If learning is regarded as giving on the part of the learner, then for those learners whose orientation is instrumental, the teaching service has as its first aim the determination of what it is that those students can give. Just as it ought to be possible to select personnel for effective work performance, so it ought to be possible to modify the work environment to match the 'gifts' they bring to their work.

It is only understood now that the frames of reference required to cope with an ever-changing world go well beyond the subjects of the traditional school curriculum. They require an understanding of ourselves, the world of work and the socio-economic framework in which we operate. In the chapters that follow, an introduction to these aspects of living is presented.

Notes and References

1. Abercrombie, M.L.J. (1961) *The Anatomy of Judgement,* Penguin Books, Harmondsworth. This topic is discussed in great detail, and several interesting examples are included.
2. Rollers, D.A., Giardino, R., Herman, G. and Woditzch, G. (1972) The first year of the first little college, *Journal of Higher Education,* Vol. 43, no. 5, p. 337.
3. Abercrombie, *Anatomy* (note 1).
4. Hesseling, P. (1966) *A Strategy for Evaluation Research,* Van Gorcum, Assen.
5. Woodhouse, H.F. (1979) Ambiguity: some implications and consequences, *Studies,* winter, pp. 265–76.
6. *Ibid.*
7. Bartlett, F.C. (1932) *Remembering,* Cambridge University Press, London.
8. Heywood, J. (1982) *Pitfalls and Planning in Student Teaching,* Kogan Page, London.
9. Sherman, T.M., Armistead, L.P., Fowler, F., Barksdale, M.A. and Rieff, G. (1987) The quest for excellence in university teaching, *Journal of Higher Education,* Vol. 58, no. 1, pp. 66–84.
10. Anderson, J.R. (1980) *Cognitive Psychology and Its Implications,* W.H. Freeman, San Francisco, Calif.
11. *The Times* (1985) Deep waters run dry (editorial), 25 July.
12. *The Times* (1980) 9 April.
13. Cognitive dissonance theory was proposed by Festinger. Put crudely, it says that when our intellectual and value systems are mutually consistent about a particular attitudinal disposition, the attitude is in a stable state. When they are inconsistent the attitude becomes unstable. Any unstable attitude has to be reorganized. Therefore we can reorganize it so that we obtain consistency, or make it so inconsistent that we do not think about it any more.
    A student or worker can like their teacher or manager and agree intellectually with the values presented in the message, in which case there is no problem. A problem may arise if a student or worker disagrees with the values in the message. In both cases this will cause learning, but in the latter this could be because the student or worker impose their own understanding on the communication so as to maintain 'apparent' consistency with the instructor. Sometimes *misunderstanding* is imposed to achieve this goal and it is that that is the dissonance. It is important in all situations involving the understanding of value positions. Dissonance may become severe if the inellectual proposition is not only difficult to comprehend but runs counter to the value dispositions of those to whom the argument is presented. See Rosenberg, M.J. (1960) An analysis of affective-cognitive consistency, in M.J. Rosenberg *et al. Attitude Organization and Change,* Yale University Press, New Haven, Conn.; and for a particular study, Marshall, S. (1980) Cognitive-affective dissonance in the classroom, *Teaching Political Science,* Vol. 8, no. 91, pp. 111–17.
14. Luria, A.R. and Yudovitch, I. (1971) *Speech: The Development of Mental Processes in the Child,* Penguin Books, Harmondsworth.
15. Bernstein, B. (1966) Elaborated and restricted codes: their social origins and consequences, in A.G. Smith (ed.) *Communication and Culture,* Holt, Rinehart & Winston, New York, NY; and Bernstein, B. (1971) *Class, Codes and Control,* Routledge & Kegan Paul, London. The remarks in this chapter do not explore in any detail the sociology of knowledge behind this theory and the substantial debate to which it led. It seems to me from analysis of student-teacher essays on the topic that they find it a useful theory for classroom action. See this author's (1984) *Considering the Curriculum in Student Teaching,* Kogan Page, London. Bernstein does not infer that children are linguistically deprived or that compensatory programmes should be developed from simple generalizations about working-class children. Linguistic difference is not the same as language

(in)competence (my brackets). Lawton would argue that there are sufficient things in common between the two groups for them to be offered a common-culture curriculum: Lawton, D. (1978) *Language and the curriculum*, in D. Lawton *et al. Theory and Practice of Curriculum Studies*, Routledge & Kegan Paul, London.

16. Ahern, G. and Davie, G. (1983) *Inner City God*, Hodder & Stoughton, Sevenoaks.

17. Heywood, J. (1989) *Assessment in Higher Education*, Wiley, Chichester. On this matter, see also Labov, W. (1973) The logic of non-standard English, in N. Keddie (ed.) *Tinker, Tailor, The Myth of Cultural Deprivation*, Academic Press, New York, NY, based on studies in New York. For Labov, the concept of verbal deprivation is dangerous because it diverts attention from real defects in the educational system to imaginary defects in the child. He makes a distinction between standard dialects used by the middle classes and non-standard dialects.

18. The quotation and remarks in the text are based on a commentary by Longley, G. (1987) Class gulf facing the church, *The Times*, 19 October, p. 18.

19. The four main levels in Kohlberg's theory are premoral, preconventional, conventional and principled. Within the preconventional level there are two stages. The first is simply obedience as a response to punishment. The second is instrumental. Right action is that which satisfies my needs. When good behaviour helps others and is approved by them the individual has reached the lower stage of the conventional level. The higher stage is when we do our duty and maintain the social order for its own sake. Up to this level, conscience has not played a great part in moral behaviour. At the principled level, and in its lower stage, right action relates to an understanding of individual rights that have been critically examined and agreed by society. At the highest stage, conscience informs decisions in accordance with self-chosen ethical principles. The stages are independent of age and not everyone will reach the highest.

The theory has been criticized because it is 'absolute' and not relativist. It has also been criticized because tests on female subjects suggest that female moral development is a morality of care. Although this view has been challenged, it seems to me to present a perspective that is observable. Kohlberg, L. and Turiel, L. (1971) Moral development and moral education, in G. Lesser (ed.) *Psychology and Educational Practice,* Scott Freeman, Chicago, Ill.

20. *Ibid.*

21. Lyons, N.P. (1983) Two perspectives: on self, relationships and morality, *Harvard Educational Review*, Vol. 53, no. 2, pp. 125–45; and Gilligan, C. (1977) In different voice: women's conceptions of self and morality, *Harvard Educational Review*, Vol. 47, pp. 481–517.

22. The development of skills in propositional thinking depends on the way in which we acquire and understand concepts, since without concepts there can be no transfer of learning. Concepts are built up from schema and influence perception, and their range (as has been indicated) is very much a function of our environment and its history. Concepts present themselves as easy and difficult. The more difficult they appear, the more likely they are to be abstract. Thus at one level we are concerned with concepts as a means of classifying experience while at another we are concerned with the process of conceptualization that enables us to handle more abstract thought, and in consequence handle generalizations. It may also help us become more objective in the value judgements we make. It is this kind of mental activity that is called propositional thinking.

23. Corson, D. (1982) The Graeco-Latin lexical bar, *Hesperiam*, no. 5, pp. 49–59. He also cites work by Masciantonio, R., in the USA – Tangible benefits of the study of Latin: a review of research, *Foreign Language Annals*, Vol. 10, no. 4.

24. Hesseling, *A Strategy* (note 4).

25. Burns, T. and Stalker, G. (1961) *The Management of Innovation,* Tavistock, London.

26. Youngman, M.B., Oxtoby, R., Monk, J.D. and Heywood, J. (1977) *Analysing Jobs,* Gower, Aldershot.

27. *Ibid.*

28. Peters, T. (1988) *Thriving on Chaos,* Macmillan, London.

29. *Ibid.* See also Peters, T. (1988) section E1, *The Sunday Times,* 14 February, and (1988) E1 *The Sunday Times,* 28 February.

30 Norburn, D. (1988) *Strategic Management Journal*, quoted in *The Sunday Times* (1988) E1, 13 March.

31. Heywood, J. (1978) Factors influencing attitudes to technology in schools, *British Journal of Educational Studies*, Vol. 26, no. 2, pp. 137–49.

32. Mant, A. (1979) *The Rise and Fall of the British Manager,* Pan, London.

33. (a) *'Choc des opinions'* – to be confronted with a frustrating experience, in this case, by specialists in other fields; (b) there is a growing awareness of the importance of retraining in Britain because of changing work practices brought about by changing technology. Retraining is required for the

introduction of new work practices, skill shortage and redundant workers. See *IDS Study 405 (1988)*, Income Data Services, London.

34. See, for example, Wickers, P. (1987) *The Road to Nissan – Flexibility, Quality and Teamwork,* MacMillan, London. For a description of quality circles, see Robson, M. (1982) *Quality Circles,* Gower, Aldershot; and also Fox, W.M. (1987) *Effective Group Problem Solving,* Jossey Bass, San Francisco, Calif., which goes beyond quality circles and relies on nominal-group technique.

35. Sivnicki, M.D. and Dixon, N.M. (1984) The Kolb model modified for classroom activities, *College Teaching,* Vol. 35, no. 1, pp. 141–6.

36. Piaget's own writings tend to be difficult. Piaget argues that a child goes through three main stages of cognitive (intellectual) development. He believes them to be invariant, that is, a child must go through each stage, and the child cannot pass from one stage to the other until they are 'ready' for that change. These changes are very broadly age related. They allow for a progressive construction by the child of his or her cognitive reality without entailing total preformation. Experience plays a major role in making probable the transition from one stage to another.

Briefly, the stages are from birth to around 1½ years (the sensorimotor stage), the period from around 1½ years to 11 or 12 (the stage of concrete operations), and the period from 11 to 12 to around 15 (the state of formal operations). Within the first stage there are six sub-stages. Beginning with the exercise of sensorimotor skills during the first month, a child becomes able to solve simple problems around 1½ years, as, for example, going round a barrier in his or her search for a goal. The elements of problem-solving and application are clearly visible to the observer.

In the second stage, the child begins to learn elementary concepts. He or she begins to classify objects and to try to make generalizations. It is a difficult stage. If B is like A in one respect, it must be like A in all respects, even though it is not. Adults, often in complex situations, analyse abstract concepts in this way.

After the age of about 7 the child is able to understand conservation of matter, weight and volume. This means, for example, that they can distinguish the quantity of water that is at the same level in two glasses of substantially different diameter. Objects are arranged in order and classified by some quality, such as colour. Eventually, structures can be represented in symbolic form (i.e. algebraically). But this stage depends on the handling of concrete objects. It is only when the child enters the stage of formal operations that he or she becomes capable of propositional thinking and the handling of abstract ideas.

While I would wish to argue that young children do grapple with philosophical problems, they use their own frames of reference, as Matthews (1980 – see below) shows, and while I would support the proposition that within limits – because the structures of knowledge are simple – they can be learnt in an intellectually honest form through any mode of representation (Bruner, 1960 – see below) I would also wish to maintain that in the handling of new concepts we often go through the Piagetian stages. We go from the concrete to the abstract. I would also wish to argue that not only does the ability to handle abstract issues mark the intelligent from the non-intelligent person, but also that our environment and experience can either limit or enhance these abilities.

For a review and criticism of Piaget's theory, see Brown, G. and Desforges, C. (1979) *Piaget's Theory: A Psychological Critique,* Routledge & Kegan Paul, London; Matthew, G.B. (1980) *Philosophy and the Young Child,* Harvard University Press, Cambridge, Mass.; and Bruner, J. (1960) *The Process of Education,* Harvard University Press, Cambridge, Mass.

37. Berger, P.L. (1963) *Invitation to Sociology,* Penguin Books, Harmondsworth and Berger, P.L. and Luckman, T. (1966) *The Social Construction of Reality,* Allen Lane, London.

38. The environment certainly dictates the ideas on which universals can be built, but no environment can avoid the fundamental issues. Children grapple with these problems as Matthews (note 36) shows. The problem is that the material of the environment tends to push thoughts of this kind out of the mind as we grow up. See Ward, K. (1982) *Holding Fast to God,* SPCK, London.

39. Berger, P.L. (1963) Invitation to Sociology, Penguin Books, Harmondsworth.

40. Mant, *Rise and Fall* (note 32).

41. *Ibid.*

3

SELECTING AND
SHAPING THE ENVIRONMENT

Introduction

When we adapt, we try to obtain as close a fit as possible between the environment and ourselves. We do not want to live in an environment in which we feel uncomfortable. So if our values or our temperaments don't fit, we look for an alternative environment, or we try to shape the environment better to meet our needs. We do not live in a single environment but in many – a plurality of social systems, as they have been described.[1] At times in the society in which we live, we are in the family group, at other times we are in our work group and sometimes we are in friendship groups. Depending on the particular circumstances, the goals of one group are likely to be more importnat to us than those of the other groups. The goals and their significance continually change, so throughout life we are required to adapt. None of us can escape the need to adapt: sometimes we will want to adapt and sometimes we will want to resist change. As we have seen, how successful we are will depend on the particular structure of the environment and our understanding (perception) of that structure.

But environments change and the pace of such change has accelerated in the last twenty years. The impact of technology on social structure is more apparent, although the rate of change has not been at anything like the speed that futurists have predicted. Neither has it been as worrying. This may be due in part to technology seeming to have had very beneficial effects in the home and at leisure. It is at work, and in the tragedies that result from mechanical failures, where its adverse effects and limitations have been noticed. Combined with unemployment – although by no means its main cause – technology has forced many workers to make radical changes in their roles. Because unemployment is highest among the least skilled, schools have been forced to provide vocational and life-skill training for this group, in the hope that they will be prepared to be more adaptable. Among its objectives, life-skills training is intended to help the participants understand their own behaviour in relation to others. Apart from the need to develop confidence, these courses are also intended to help individuals in this group to respond to the demands society is making on them for greater participation in the management of work, and more generally in the democratic process.[2] There are now many advocates for the inclusion of such programmes across the range of ability in schools, not least because the effects of unemployment among middle-aged managers have shown that they also have great difficulty in adapting to changed circumstances.

There is no better starting-point for the understanding of human behaviour than from reflection on roles, role behaviour and our responses to the particular situations in which we find ourselves. Effective change often depends on our ability to adapt our role. In this chapter we consider some of the situations that may cause stress and conflict, and how the general disposition of personality relates to our subsequent behaviour.

Roles and Role Definition

Whoever the individual, whatever his or her personality, they will adapt their behaviour to the situation in which they find themselves. Thus, just as human organizations can be conceived of as systems, so they may also be conceived of as conglomerates of role players, for in any social system the basic unit is the role.

A role is, therefore, a pattern of behaviour associated with a particular position. 'It' carries out activities that, if the system is to achieve its goals, have to be co-ordinated. One activity of management is, therefore, the co-ordination and integration of roles. 'It' (the role) does not have to be a human being; it could be a machine. However, the discussion that follows is confined to human beings.

The performance of students can be analysed in this way. For example, those students who have a *social orientation* and are concerned with the social life that the institution offers, are likely to do less well than those with either an academic (pursuit of examinations) or an intellectual orientation (concerned with knowledge as its own end).[3] The attitude of large numbers of students in secondary schools is clearly instrumental. They arrange their schoolwork so as to make their dislike of it tolerable. Such attitudes derive from the meaning that life and school has for these young adolescents. If school performance is related to work success, and they perceive that they will be unemployed, they will undoubtedly develop an instrumental attitude toward schoolwork, and why shouldn't they? The problem for the school is to provide a curriculum that has meaning for them, and this may mean a radical re-appraisal not only of what is taught but also how it is taught, with all the implications that this may have for the staffing of small groups.

Not surprisingly, problems arise for management because a variety of individuals, each with their own value system and idiosyncracies, occupy roles in the organization. Very often, personnel come into conflict with each other simply because of personality differences. Sometimes conflict is created because of the perceptions that individuals have of their role. Even in a bureaucracy it is not possible to define a role so exactly that there are no differences in perception about how it should be performed. A major problem for employers, indeed ourselves, is the fact that at one and the same time our goals create for us a plurality of social systems. There is not merely the role system that connects the job to other jobs in the organization for work purposes, but the career system, the peer-group system and, not least, the family system. All of these systems make demands on our energies and there is no way of escape. The ways we use to reduce these tensions and sometimes conflicts influence our performance at work for better or for worse.

The nature of the work undoubtedly influences our attitudes to work. A person in an assembly-line job may develop an *instrumental* disposition toward unpleasant work. Workers in this situation are likely to tolerate that type of work if the rewards are satisfactory, and they will look for satisfaction in life elsewhere, more especially in the family and with friends. Another person in these circumstances may be *solidaristically* inclined, in which case that individual may seek personal satisfaction through membership of a group, and this may well be a trade union. Work enables the individual to share in group activity from which he or she obtains the meaning. Other individuals, particularly those in management positions whose jobs give them satisfaction, are likely to have a *bureaucratic* orientation to work and to give service to the organization. Motivated by interest, this type of worker uses his or her work for steadily increasing income, social status and for long-term security.[4]

Such orientations undoubtedly have an influence on role behaviour, for they stem not only from personal(ity) disposition but *from the meaning that work, and therefore the type of work, has for the individual.* Thus one of the most powerful influences on role behaviour are role expectations.

Expectations, Role Adjustment and Role-Set

Whenever we anticipate a role, we generate expectations of what will be expected of us in that role. For example, when a student in his or her school-leaving year is looking for a job, ideas about what will be expected of them in different jobs will be generated. However vague their understanding, these expectations will have a strong conditioning effect on their subsequent choice. When they, and for that matter any worker taking on a new job, actually work in that job, they will in all probability have to make some role adjustments in order to perform their task. It will involve them in an adjustment of their expectations. Whether or not their performance meets the expectations of others is a different matter.

These new workers will also find that they are linked in a network with other people. Sometimes the bonds in the network will be 'tight', sometimes they will be 'loose'. Sometimes their dependence on another will be 'strong', sometimes 'weak'. They will not be able to avoid making contact with other people. This is as true of the teacher as it is of the assembly-line worker, refuse collector or postman. In this respect the example of relationship between shop stewards and trade-union officials in England in the 1960s is of considerable interest. It might be supposed that militant stewards would want to bypass union rules and so come into conflict with union officials. But this was not found to be the case.[5] Because the shop steward was the source of contact between members and full-time officers of the union, the stewards and the full-time officers needed to support each other. Stewards looked to the officers for advice and support and vice-versa. They shared important objectives and understandings about how those goals might be best attained.

We can only understand the behaviour of individuals within the social context in which they operate, and in this respect we have to take into account the perceptions that the individual has of his or her own behaviour and the expectations of others in his or her network. The social or organizational context may be complex. Sometimes it is possible to identify key persons who are at the focal point of a number of roles (individuals) that are necessary for the key person to perform his or her task. This grouping is called a role-set.[6] The individuals in the role-set will also belong to other role-sets and may be the focus of another role-set. Taking all the role-sets together, an organization may be viewed as a matrix of 'overlapping role-sets'. The role-sets of individuals will vary both in degree of bonding (dependence) and distance (closeness in organizational terms). Thus a shop steward, as a worker, may only be linked to his or her foreman and storekeepers from whom he or she gets their material if he or she is a specialist craftsman. But as a shop steward that person is likely to be linked with full-time union officials, foremen, other stewards, line management at all levels, personnel officers and union members. Sometimes the networks in which an individual is placed can cause role-conflict, and these may be harmful to effective performance. It is with this conflict that the next section is concerned.

Conflict

Conflict and tension are normal consequences of living in systems, be they as small as a family or as large as an industrial organization. It can be positive, negative or neutral in its effect. At its most simple, conflict may occur when there is a difference between expectation and reality. A teacher colleague of mine, writing to me about the problems of homework in his inner-city school, said:

> Homework is tied in to a certain extent with discipline. Students expect to get homework to do and the amounts to increase with the proximity of the exams. However, when students fail to provide even miniscule amounts of homework, teachers come to rely on the work done in the class. This subject is a very great source of worry for teachers and pupils because both wish for more homework but because of human failings, it cannot live up to expectations in reality. This causes what is known as 'conflict' – expectations and reality are in conflict, which gives rise to feelings of guilt for both parties.

Some individuals are particularly creative in conflict situations. Thus conflict may prevent stagnation, or it may cause a group of individuals to remain united and establish relationships that would not otherwise exist. At the same time, it is evident that the day-to-day running of organizations can be impaired by conflict. It is not so much the large official strike that is likely to do the damage but the little unofficial stoppages that last for one or two hours and that disrupt the flow of productivity.

The same teacher colleague also wrote:

> In the past year, the Principal has become much more involved in the Leaving Certificate students and he has taken a personal interest in them. He has stated his expectations of them plainly. They are punctuality, attendance, homework and effort during class. He also threatened to suspend the two lowest scorers in the Christmas tests. Even though they thought that he could not carry out his threat, they were still quite worried about it while at the same time they sought the easy way out by getting good marks in subjects such as physical education and religious knowledge. . .
>
> The students see obvious conflict between what the Principal expects by way of timekeeping and what teachers are giving. It is no wonder therefore that there is confusion in their minds because they do not see unity of purpose from the teachers. We have already spoken of homework and effort which is a 'two-way street' within the classroom itself. The Principal has never stressed to the teachers the need for homework or his feelings about it or indeed sanctions for not doing homework. Some of the teachers feel that it takes a lot more effort than they are willing to give, to try to drag homework out of students and they feel that this mothering of students is bad training in that the way to get the students to be responsible starts with the homework.

Conflict situations can also cause strain and tension between members of an organization, as, for example, when two unions represent the workers in a company and one does not support the industrial action of the other. For conflict to have positive outcomes, it has to be managed positively. Mant, for instance, has suggested that part of the problem in Britain is that fighting takes place within firms, whereas in Germany the fight is taken to the market-place.[7] He quotes A.K. Rice to the effect that 'Fight is not a problem in itself; the problem is to ensure the fights occur between the right people, at the right time and about the right issues.'[8]

One condition for role conflict arises when the actions of two individuals, who have a common goal, are directly opposed. In a role-set the person at its focal point may not be able to meet the different expectations of the members of his or her role-set.[9] For example, in universities that embrace participation, many conflicting demands are made on persons at the focal points of role-sets such as professorial heads of department. The head of department who is required to undertake administration, teaching and research is often placed in conflict because of the heavy demands made on him or her, especially those of administration, with the result that very often his or her teaching suffers. Promotion by publication can produce stress in members of staff who wish to promote teaching, or who are asked to develop new courses.

The headteachers of schools find themselves in much the same position. As Dunham points out, the Head 'is at the centre of all internal and external transactions of the school. In consequence he is continually having need to make rapid adjustments as he meets with pupils, colleagues, governors, parents, meals staff and anyone else concerned with the school like building contractors'[10] and yet most of the problems that have to be solved are relatively small. By and large, they are not strategic in nature. The trouble is that they are continuing, and because they are demanding, there is a tendency to develop skills in handling the trivial so that mistakes are made when dealing with the strategic – as, for example, trying to change the direction of the curriculum.

Within organizations there are many sources of conflict. They are frequently due to poor communication, which is often a function of the structure of organization. The organization can accentuate personality clashes and power struggles among its members, and external pressures dictated by customers can set them on the run.

Heller and Wilpert have gone so far as to argue that 'conflict may be a necessary and crucial ingredient of organizational life, if the mobilization of adaptive resources to changing conditions is to be ensured. For this reason management has to learn techniques for resolving organizational conflicts which cause the groups involved to make compromises which aim to help the organization survive.'[11]

Often industrial and commercial organizations require managers and sales staff to be away from home, and this can cause not only stress in the family but in themselves.[12] The importance of external factors, as they apply to conflict more generally between organizations, individuals and working groups cannot be underestimated. Undoubtedly, many of those involved in the 1984 miners' strike and the newspaper troubles at Wapping in England, which ended in 1987, would say that they were not the cause of the trouble. Rather it was the economic, social and work structure in which they lived that brought about the resistance to change.[13]

Role conflict is not always harmful and may occur without conflicting role expectations. This is very often the case with teacher–pupil interactions in the classroom, when sanctions are imposed on a particular pupil for a particular behaviour regarded as deviant. The class may not like them but, nevertheless, acquiesce because that is what is expected to happen. Similarly, management and labour may take different views about when dismissal of personnel is justified, for there is likely to be a conflict of interest and functions. However, everyone accommodates themselves to what happens because they have no other expectations of the situation.

Conflict, therefore, that takes place between role players in an organization , or sectors of an organization, may have either harmful or beneficial or, for that matter, no effect on the efficiency of an organization.

Conflict and Participation in Management

The notion that conflict is necessarily harmful has led to the general philosophy that worker participation in management will benefit industry. However, as McCarthy and Parker have pointed out, 'it is the outsider rather than the insider, who expects an absence of conflict as a precondition for situations which most people who live in them find relatively satisfactory and acceptable for most of the time'.[14]

Other insights suggest that participative styles of leadership may be more successful in some kinds of industry than others. It may, for example, be extremely difficult in organizations that do not find it easy to make profits. Heller and Wilpert,[15] who make this point, contrast the history of the railways since 1945 with food manufacturing and pharmaceutical products, for which there has been a considerable demand. As a result of a comparative study among managers in several nations, they came to the conclusion that managers use a variety of means to influence their subordinates, and that the means chosen were dictated by the characteristics of the task to be done. However, they also concluded that when managers are surrounded by persons with high-level skills, they are more likely to use participative methods of decision-making than if they are surrounded by people with low-level skills. Other studies have suggested that when managers think their job environment is uncertain and unpredictable, they may use more participative methods of decision-making with their subordinates.[16]

When the English were occupied with the continued failure of their cricket team to beat the West Indies, several journalists began to consider the management of the team. At the apex of the selection mechanism are three selectors. All of them are experienced but retired cricketers. One of them is appointed chairman by the cricket authorities. Below the selectors is a team manager, which is a recent innovation. The team captain, who is selected before the team is selected, joins the selectors for the purpose of selecting the other ten players. Alan Lee, the sports writer of *The Sunday Times*, argued that this regime did not invest the manager with the freedom and authority necessary for the creation of a single compact unit accountable to a single professional man (we might add, as is the case with football). Other journalists also wrote of the manager being too much on the side of the players and, Lee said:

> Under the present regime, Micky Stewart cannot be fairly judged as a manager. If his words often appear to be so much flannel and his hold on discipline dangerously slight, it may well be because he is still answerable to May. If he acts like one of the players it could be because he has no power to feel above them.[17]

(Stewart was the manager, May the chairman of the selectors.) This is reminiscent of foremen by-passing in industrial organizations, about which much was written in the 1960s.

In larger organizations, the shop stewards realized that foremen could not make decisions that were likely to affect the whole of the workforce, so they went to the level of management, which could. For example, a decision to change the timing of a tea-break in a section is likely to affect the whole works. In spite of rules that required workers to bring grievances to the foremen in the first instance, workers often approached shop stewards with their complaints.[18] The effect of this was sometimes to cause the foremen to become uncertain about their role because their authority had been undermined.

Related to this and other dimensions of the role is the fact that, independently of the country in which managers are studied, it is found that there is a great deal of skill under-utilization.[19] There is no doubt that under-utilization is a cause of much frustration, and is often not recognized by management, just as in the same way managers do not often realize the harmful effects of ambiguities in the roles they have defined for others.

Because conflict arises from the interactions individuals have with each other, it is important to understand the internal and external factors that influence an individual's behaviour, that is, personality, on the one hand, and role interaction on the other.

Role Ambiguity and Power

Ambiguity and role conflict can cause stress. Even if individuals do not suffer stress, they may react in ways that make the goals of the organization more difficult to achieve. As we saw in the last chapter, ambiguity can be a source of difficulty between people, for such ambiguity lies in the perception of the role that either the role player, or participants in the role-set, have of the player's role. The example of the cricket manager's role, given in the preceding section, illustrates both ambiguity and the potential for conflict.

Role ambiguity occurs when a person is deprived of information. This may be deliberate so as to isolate the person (role isolation), or it may be due to the fact that the appropriate information is not available. One of the consequences of the division of labour is that management comes to believe that broad information is unnecessary for most jobs. So, in 1970, one enquiry found that two out of five persons were not given sufficient information to do their job properly.

The consequences of role ambiguity may be profound for the individual. Uncertainty about the way in which our work is evaluated, and opportunities for advancement, can lead to deep frustration. The responsibility we have, and the expectations of others about our performance, may cause low job satisfaction, low self-confidence and a high sense of futility. Such factors may cause stress, which can lead to anxiety and depression.[20]

When a role is ambiguous it can be manipulated. One case study, quoted by Jaques, showed how patients in psychiatric hospitals were able to manipulate doctors, nurses and orderlies who were not clear about their accountability or authority.[21] In industry, a line manager can be taken out of the line and put in a functional task with the intention of getting the manager to resign, because the functional role cannot be carried out as it is not clearly defined.

Those who hold power but whose jobs are ambiguously defined can be ineffective. Jaques also cites the example of a vice-chancellor whose task was described in an official report on higher education thus: 'his role which probably, fortunately, is seldom spelt out in written constitutions. Yet it would be difficult to overstate its importance, particularly in a period of expansion, which calls for imagination and continuous initiative.'[22] Jaques goes on to say that 'what the report fails to note in this praise of vagueness is its inconsistency with the statement further down the same paragraph in the report that "governing bodies should give serious attention to improving their organisation" with regard to the variety and burden of work of the Vice-Chancellor'.[23] Such improvements, argues Jaques, cannot be 'achieved for a role which is imprecisely defined.'[24] Having recently been involved in an election by academic staff for the head of a university,

I can testify that much of the difficulty in getting to grips with the central issues were the differing role expectations that the electors had of the headship. In consequence, the candidates were forced to spend much time in their campaigns defining their perceptions of the role. Subsequent dissatisfaction arose with some electors from the fact that the perceived expectations, and expectations generated by the campaign, could not be met because the nature of the job (role-set) dictated emphases on other activities.

The Need for Job Description

Jaques does not argue that there are no advantages in ill-defined roles. At the same time the extreme example of the head of the university points up the value of job definitions that are clearly defined by the task requirements. Role conflict and role ambiguity tend to be greater at the higher levels in hierarchical systems of management, and when they cause work overload may become important elements in job stress.

The advantages of job definitions is that they can avoid mismatches between the capabilities a person brings to a job and the requirements of the task. A mismatch occurs when there are no or inadequate resources to do the task wanted, and/or the organization has not been adapted to allow the task to be done. In contrast, Jaques has pointed out that a mismatch also arises when the job is too easy because of an excess of resources. Similarly, if in cognitive terms a task is too difficult and beyond the capability of the individual, or too easy, there is a mismatch. This is not to say that all stress should be removed from the situation for, as in learning, some stress may be desirable. However, it is essential to know with whom one is dealing, for people respond to stress in different ways as research on the effects of school and university examinations show.[25]

Shaping Our Environment

Environmental shaping demands a high level of intelligence and, in particular, the inter- and intrapersonal skills of Gardner, or the social skills of Sternberg described in Chapter 2. The more articulate and educated we become, the more we are aware of our own philosophy and the more we will want to shape our environment. This is a particular problem for those who work in the media and who have had the advantage of an Oxbridge education. Their interpretation of events may well reflect their personal philosophy and thus, as we saw in the last chapter, influence their objectivity. This point is no better illustrated than by the differing interpretations given to their roles by two religious-affairs correspondents of the BBC, one of whom, Priestland, had been that organization's Washington correspondent.

Of the two, Edgar Brennan wrote:

> As the BBC's religious correspondent, Priestland saw the job very differently from his predecessor, Douglas Brown. Brown was always the traditional BBC reporter, observing, chronicling and interpreting, but keeping his own views and loyalties very much in

the background. Priestland saw his role, as he tells us everywhere, as 'to patrol the borderland between journalism and religion . . . between objectivity and commitment'. At times the commitment prevailed over the objectivity; despite his disclaimer of professional theological learning, he did not feel himself inhibited from lecturing the British Churches on what he felt was their theological backwardness. Disarmingly, he admits to 'pretensions of punditry'.[26]

Clearly, personality plays an important role in our ability to shape and control our environments. In some we will adapt, others we will try to shape. Heller and Wilpert[27] asked managers to describe the skill requirements of their job in terms of twelve attributes. These were knowledge of technical skills, close contact with people, knowledge of human nature, imagination, self-confidence, responsibility, decisiveness, tact, adaptability, forcefulness, intelligence and initiative. In Sternberg's theory, intelligence would not be included since these skills contribute to intelligence.

Equally, most of them are factors that, when equated together, would be called personality, or at least dimensions of personality. If we are to shape our environment, we have to understand how these traits are acted out by and in ourselves.

A beginning can be made with the subject of the previous paragraphs: conflict. Psychoanalysts are concerned with conflict within ourselves. Such conflict may create a tension that is a source of disintegration in opposition to the 'integration' we require. If we find ourselves disintegrating we will try to reshape our environment to restore within us that lost sense of 'integration' (provided that the disintegration has not become completely pathological). Stability and security demand consistency of behaviour and whether we are managers, teachers, parents, workers or pupils, we require consistent and controlled behaviour from those with whom we associate and, in return, we need to show a similar consistency. The problem is that sometimes we may be too rigid and in situations that demand change we find ourselves unable to adapt.

We have, therefore, to learn about ourselves. Reflective thinking should yield observations that will help us cope with other people and groups. For example, when do we embark on aggressive behaviour and what effect does it have? A person who has a strong need for affiliation is unlikely to adopt behaviours that would lead a group to exclude him or her from membership. A person who might otherwise respond to a request from a beggar might, if he or she is with his or her group, abuse the beggar.

We avoid embarrassing situations and to do this we use an ego-defence mechanism. The ego-defence mechanism used by the person who is forced to interact with the beggar is called infavoidance. Ego-defence mechanisms, according to Lazarus,[28] are learnt behaviours. They are mental devices that help us to cope with the mental stress arising from conflicting needs. There are many ego-defence mechanisms. Freud held that repression was the most important ego-defence mechanism. It is a form of self-deception in which the ideas and problems facing a person are chased away below the preconscious into the unconscious. Self-deceptions are common and help us to live reasonably comfortable lives – similarly with sublimation that, in its broadcast sense, is the redirection of a

Table 3.1　Questionnaire for use in negotiating-skills development training

---

SELF-APPRAISAL – BEHAVIOUR IN DISCUSSION

Please study your performance from the video playback. This is a private assessment so be perfectly frank in answering the questions – otherwise you are only fooling yourself.

In this discussion I tended to:	YES	NO
ask specific questions about the topic under discussion	☐	☐
try to score debating points	☐	☐
get irritated with an opponent	☐	☐
ask for clarification/facts about a point made by the other side	☐	☐
contribute helpful suggestions	☐	☐
admit I was misinformed/wrong	☐	☐
interrupt before a speaker had finished	☐	☐
opt out of answering an opponent's question on the grounds that I would appear to give way	☐	☐
criticize when I had not really got a real point to make	☐	☐
close the door to further argument	☐	☐
change my mind when my assumptions were shown to be faulty	☐	☐
keep quiet when I had nothing constructive to say	☐	☐
overrule the chairman/leader	☐	☐
prepare my case before the meeting	☐	☐
not listen to an opponent's argument because I disagreed with his or her case	☐	☐

**PLACE THIS SHEET INSIDE THE FOLDED SHEET 2
AND FOLD OVER THE RIGHT-HAND EDGE SO THAT THE ANSWERS
SHOW IN CUT-OUTS**

Table 3.1 (cont.) Sheet 2

Now compare your results and consider whether your
  contribution to the meeting was:

Potentially	Potentially	CORRECT ANSWERS
destructive	helpful to	
to your case	your case	

```
  —+——+——+——+——+——+——+—
  −3   −2   −1   0   +1   +2   +3
```

Because I was:

Bloody-minded   Co-operative
```
—+——+——+——+——+——+——+—
```

Quarrelsome   Benign
```
—+——+——+——+——+——+——+—
```

Rigid   Flexible
```
—+——+——+——+——+——+——+—
```

Intolerant   Tolerant
```
—+——+——+——+——+——+——+—
```

Closed-minded   Open-minded
```
—+——+——+——+——+——+——+—
```

Talkative   Silent
```
—+——+——+——+——+——+——+—
```

Dependent   Independent
```
—+——+——+——+——+——+——+—
```

Lacking in   Well-
information/knowledge   informed
```
—+——+——+——+——+——+——+—
  −3   −2   −1   0   +1   +2   +3
```

Now compare what you have written with your original
score

    − Points   + Points

Now attempt to define ways in which training could help
you improve your performance in discussion

Correct answers   (R)
Incorrect answers   (W)
Questions unanswered (U)

Score: $\dfrac{R - W}{5}$

NOW FOLD OVER THE
LEFT-HAND   EDGE
AND   ANSWER   THE
QUESTIONS

motive from a relatively unacceptable goal (however desirable as a need) to a more acceptable one. These defence mechanisms help us to control our behaviour. It is evident that individuals are capable of controlling their actions, although some under-control, that is, tend to act on the spur of the moment, while others, who are slow to make up their mind and carry out detailed planning of future actions, may over-control. There are many occasions when we wished we could have behaved as others do in certain situations. We would wish for more certainty, more direction, more firmness, more control, and so on. We would like to be less hot-headed or more able to perceive all facets of a problem. Regression, when we retreat to an earlier developmental level involving us in making a less mature response to the situation in which we find ourselves, is another well-known ego-defence mechanism.

While there is a lot of truth in the view that the dispositions of personality are deep and persistent, the evidence would support the case that we can develop skills that can direct and control our behaviour. Role-playing is a technique that has as its aim the achievement of these goals.[29] For example, the questionnaire in Table 3.1 was designed for use in training sessions for the development of negotiating skills. Trade-union and management representatives would be filmed during a negotiation. The video is then played back to the group, after which the individuals in the group respond to the questionnaire. Several sessions of this kind are intended to bring about more effective negotiating skills.[30] Such exercises have been introduced in life-skills programmes in schools.

Role-playing gives us an understanding of power. We cannot and should not shirk away from the issue of power for, as Hunt says, 'Role systems exist for interpersonal relationships, which depend on influence, which depends on power. Power is a resource, while its effect is influence. The effects of influence are co-operation, conflict, love, hate, fear, jealousy, and all those other emotions encountered in role systems.'[31] How do we exercise power and how do we respond to power? Do we try to create fear in one way or another by the use of coercive power? Would we, if we could, exercise remunerative power through the dispensation of rewards and/or patronage? Or do we rely on the legal power vested in the position we occupy? Are we able to use expertise as a means of power? Not every expert is able to exercise power. How do you respond to power? Do those whom you admire influence your decision? To what extent do you exercise and are influenced by charismatic power? And, finally, what do you do to acquire power?

That answers to these questions matter is illustrated by Cooper's investigations, which have led him to the view that men's style of management contributes to stress. Moreover, it tended to stop workers from producing at their best. Women were more likely to be the better managers of the future. He is quoted as saying that 'Stress at work is closely related to the amount of control people feel they have over their area of responsibility. British management – mostly men – are not, in general, too good at allowing their subordinates this kind of freedom, because they are too sensitive about their own power.'[32]

Role Behaviour, Role Analysis and the Organization

This chapter follows the chapter on perception for the reason that all human learning begins with perceptions. As we saw earlier, the perceptions we have of others are greatly influenced by our prior knowledge and experience, as well as by the environmental press in which we operate. We live in a variety of systems, the most important of which are those that embrace the family, friendship and work groups. In any system the basic unit is the role. Role-players are in exchange with the environment, and they try to shape or adapt the system in which they find themselves. In some circumstances they will find themselves in conflict with other role-players, and at other times, because of ambiguity, they may find themselves in mental conflict with themselves. Circumstances and the person will dictate the individual response to conflict and tension. By themselves they are neutral, and sometimes tension will be beneficial to the individual and at other times harmful.

This discussion has omitted several fairly obvious aspects of role behaviour. For example, it is a matter of everyday experience that role-players in State and semi-State organizations are able to hide behind their role definitions. Not only can this impede change but it can also be particularly painful to members of the public with whom they are involved. Unlike foremen by-passing, they can prevent queries they cannot handle from being passed upwards, especially when those individuals with whom they are dealing do not have the knowledge and/or drive to force the query upwards. Similarly, those in senior positions can delay decision by passing queries handed in at the top down the line. All this we understand from the television programme that gained world-wide popularity – 'Yes, Minister'. As that programme illustrates, the games we play in our role-sets apply to all walks of life. No one – politician, senior civil servant, manager, worker, student, husband and wife – is free of them.

Independently of the precise definitions given in the preceding sections, role is a word in common use. Sometimes it is used as an alternative to function. It is also used to describe institutional arrangements. Just as individuals in their groups can be described in terms of roles, so too can organizations and institutions. For example, an important and continuing debate in Britain relates to 'the relative roles of government and industry in education and particularly their attitudes in training for the use of high technology'.[33]

Sometimes we describe systems in terms other than role when the use of role would have given a better understanding. Role analysis, which takes into account all the parameters associated with a role and the role played, is a very powerful tool for examining an organization. It goes beyond the analysis of tasks. One such study is briefly described in Chapter 5. If we are to shape and control our environment, we need to understand how we perceive and develop and adapt our roles to meet the differing circumstances with which we are continually faced.

While adaptability may be regarded as a skill, our use of that skill depends on our dispositions. Nevertheless, we can be helped to develop this skill. To be able to adapt within an organization, we need to learn how our skills can contribute to the organization, and to understand how the skills of the 'others' in our role-set can best be utilized. To achieve this goal, we will require an understanding of how jobs can be designed or redesigned to serve better both the individual and the organization. The more we understand the principle of behaviour in organizations, the more we are likely to benefit from such exercises and the more we shall learn to help ourselves to change.

The view we take of why individuals are motivated to work underpins the judgements we make about organizational structure, the role of the manager and thus to the meaning we give the managerial role. It is with the 'nature' of roles at work and the ways they may help or hinder change that the next chapter is concerned.

Notes and References

1. Burns, T. (1966) On the plurality of social systems, in J.R. Lawrence (ed.) *Operational Research and the Social Sciences*, Tavistock, London.
2. See Heywood, J. (1984) *Considering the Curriculum During Student Teaching*, Kogan Page, London, Chap. 5; Hopson, B. and Scally, M. (1981) *Lifeskills Teaching*, McGraw-Hill, London; and for details of courses, Further Education Unit (1981) *Developing Social and Life Skills. Strategies for Tutors*, HMSO, London, City and Guilds of London Institute (1984) *The Certification of Pre-Vocational Education*, London, and Council Resolution 11:9:1983, *Concerning Vocational Training Policies in the European Community in the 1980s*, Commission for the European Economic Community, Brussels.
3. Bey, C. (1962) A social theory of higher education, in N. Sanford (ed.) *The American College*, Wiley, New York, NY.
4. These definitions come from Goldthorpe, J., Lockwood, D., Bechhofer, F. and Platt, J. (1970) *The Affluent Worker: Industrial Attitudes and Behaviour*, Cambridge University Press.
5. This paragraph is based on the research reports of the Royal Commission on industrial relations. See, for example, McCarthy, W.E.J. and Parker, S.R. (1968) *Shop Stewards and Workshop Relations*, Research Report no. 10, Royal Commission on Trade Unions and Employers Associatory, HMSO, London. See also note 15.
6. Role-set, role conflict and ambiguity were originally discussed by R.L. Kahn. See Kahn, R.L. (1973) Conflict: ambiguity and overload: three elements in job stress, *Occupational Mental health*, Vol. 3, no. 1, pp. 191–4; and Kahn, R.L. and French, J.R.P. (1970) Status and conflict: two themes in the study of stress, in J.E. McGrath (ed.) *Social and Psychological Factors in Stress*, Wiley, New York, NY, and Cox, T. (1978) *Stress*, Macmillan, London.
7. Mant, A. (1979) *The Rise and Fall of the British Manager*, Pan Books, London.
8. *Ibid.*
9. See Kahn, Conflict (note 6) and Kahn and French, Status and conflict, (note 6). See also Cooper, C. and Marshall, J. (1977) *Understanding Executive Stress*, Petrocelli, New York, NY. Intra-sender conflict exists when someone is asked by another to accomplish two objectives that are in apparent conflict. Inter-sender conflict occurs when a person receives contradictory instructions from two or more people. Inter-role conflict occurs when an individual has to take on incompatible roles.
10. Dunham, J. (1984) *Stress in Teaching*, Croom Helm, Beckenham.
11. Heller, F.A. and Wilpert, B. (1981) *Competence and Power in Managerial Decision Making*, Wiley, New York, NY.
12. Jaques, E. (1970) *Work Creativity and Social Justice*, Heinemann, London. See also Cooper, C. and Marshall, J. (eds.) (1980) *White Collar and Professional Stress*, Wiley, Chichester; and Syrett, M. (1988) How a posting overseas can put you under stress, *The Sunday Times*, Section E, 31 January.
13. See, for example, the study of a long strike in 1970 at Pilkingtons glass works by Lane, T. and Roberts, K. (1971) *Strike at Pilkington* Fontana, London, where this position is proposed.
14. McCarthy and Parker, *Shop Stewards* (note 5).
15. Heller and Wilpert, *Competence and Power* (note 11).
16. Mant, *Rise and Fall* (note 7) and Heller and Wilpert, *Competence and Power* (note 11).

17. Lee, A. (1988) Time to speak with one voice, *The Times,* 7 July.
18. McCarthy and Parker, *Shop Stewards* (note 5).
19. See reference 11. There are several other studies that indicate this to be the case.
20. See, for example, Dunham, *Stress in Teaching* (note 10); and Gray, H.L. and Freeman, A. (1988) *Teaching without Stress,* Paul Chapman Publishing, London.
21. Jaques, *Work Creativity* (note 12).
22. *Ibid.*
23. *Ibid.*
24. *Ibid.*
25. Heywood, J. (1989) *Assessment in Education,* Wiley, Chichester.
26. Brennan, E. (1988) Review of *Something Understood,* by Gerald Priestland, Arrow Books, London, in *The Tablet,* 9 July, p. 789.
27. Heller and Wilpert, *Competence and Power* (note 11).
28. Lazarus, R.S. (1963) *Personality and Adjustment,* Prentice-Hall, Englewood Cliffs, NJ. For a list of ego-defence mechanisms, needs and behaviours, see Heywood, J. (1982) *Pitfalls and Planning in Student Teaching,* Kogan Page, London.
29. Role-playing exercises and business games have been developed for all levels of the education system. Decision-making exercises have been developed for use in schools as, for example, by BP (British Petroleum), who published *North Sea Oil.* There are journals published on this topic, for example, *American Journal of Simulation and Games* (Sage Publications Ltd, 28 Banner St, London EC1V 8QE). There are also societies, for example, the Society for the Advancement of Games and Simulations in Education and Training (c/o Centre for Extension Studies, University of Technology, Loughborough, Leics. LE11 3TU). In Britain, the *International Yearbook of Educational and Instructional Technology* contains information on this topic. It is published annually by Kogan Page, London. Among the many books are Bulleid, H.A.V. (1977) *Brief Cases: Being Concise Management Case Studies,* Mechanical Engineering Publications, London; and Elgood, C. (1976) *Handbook of Management Games,* Gower, Aldershot (this includes a directory of British management games).
30. There are many inventories of this kind, for example, in Adair, J., Ayres, R., Debenham, I. and Despres, D. (1978) *A Handbook of Management Training Exercises,* British Association for Commercial and Industrial Education, London, Vol. 1 (the copyright of the exercises is purchased with the book); and Woodcock, M. (1979) *The Team Development Manual,* Gower Press, Aldershot. In the USA, the 'California Personality Inventory' is widely used, Gough, H.G. (1958) *California Personality Inventors,* Consulting Psychologists Press, Palo Alto, Calif.
31. Hunt, J.W. (1979) *Management People at Work,* McGraw-Hill, Maidenhead. Galbraith, J.K. (1984) *Anatomy of Power,* Hamish Hamilton, London, distinguishes between condign, compensatory and conditioned power. Condign power threatens with something that is physically or emotionally painful; compensatory power offers an individual or advantageous reward or payment; and conditioned power occurs when someone is able to change another's belief.
32. Spicer, J. (1988) Women 'are better managers', *The Times,* 6 January.
33. From Seward-Thompson, B. (1988) Sorting out the roles to the best advantage, *The Times,* 5 July.

4

EVERYONE A MANAGER

Introduction

The view we take of why individuals are motivated to work underpins the judgements we make about organizational structure, the role of the manager and thus the meaning given to service in the managerial role. The same applies to teachers and their evaluations of why students learn. Various stereotypes of workers (learners) are used to demonstrate these axioms, and from the evidence it is argued that there is no simple model that accounts for the motivation to work or learn. However, individuals behave in different ways, and at different times, according to the circumstances in which they find themselves. Accordingly, each model of the individual has something to add to our understanding of human behaviour and the reasons why some people adapt and others resist change. None of these models excuse management from providing a technology of production or learning that is a challenge to the worker or student. To do this requires considerable changes in attitude towards work and its organization among managers. Such change may be brought about by an understanding of the inherent capability in individuals for decision-making and the necessity for them to use management skills in every role and task they undertake. This argument is supported by a discussion of the nature of decision-making and the learning process. Everyone is shown to do managerial tasks, and a model of the individual as a manager is proposed.

The Rational – Economic Individual

If I were asked to say what it is that men and women do most, apart from sleep and work, I think I would answer very quickly and without much thought, 'gossip'. When we seek another job we often try to work out who the competitors are, particularly if we operate, as I do, in a relatively small group of university professors. Even if we don't do that, we are apt to spend much time with our colleagues wondering why this or that manager or teacher was appointed. Often there are unexpressed but uneasy feelings in our mind arising from the fact that we are not quite sure what the job demands anyway. We find it difficult to describe readily our mythical model of the manager. The more rarefied the job, say a university vice-chancellor, or the president of the USA, the more difficult it is to come to grips with the nature of the job. So, too, is the 'fall' of a senior man cause for gossip. In this respect men are no different from women, although the way in which women perceive men often differs considerably from the way in which men perceive women. More striking is the fact that the way we perceive the actions of workers in a strike situation is likely to be very different from the way in which we would perceive the same workers on the municipal golf course or in the bar. Our expectations vary as people change their roles. We associate one set of expectations with the work role, another with the friendship role, and so on. Our family has totally different expectations of us from those of our manager, or of our teacher, or of our colleague.

If we try to analyse our expectations in depth, we find we are thinking about the way in which a person will behave in those particular circumstances. Moreover, we draw conclusions about the way in which those concerned with that person and his or her behaviour should behave. These expectations are often biased and stem from the deeply held beliefs acquired during our lifetime. The 'pictures' associated with these beliefs we call stereotypes, and it is such stereotypes that often guide our behaviour in relation to our judgements about the performance of workers. In this respect, our views of why individuals work are important for they underpin the judgements we make about organizational structure, the role of the manager and thus the meaning given to service in the managerial role.

One of the important changes in values made as feudal society moved towards a free-market society was the idea that individuals could sell their skills. Just as there was a market for commodities, so there was a market for labour. This change of philosophy, which also heralded the advent of industrial organization, led to new relationships between employer and employee. As long as labour was plentiful, unorganized men, women and children could be bought and sold at will. Undoubtedly there was a great deal of injustice, and the development of industrial relations in Britain during the last twenty years has to be seen in this context, and more especially attitudes to change. Sir John Hoskyns, the Director General of the Institute of Directors has argued that the British and British law have matured to an extent where owner and worker can now treat each other with dignity and respect. When they do, companies will be successful. However, views about the reasons why individuals work run deep, and many managers undoubtedly believe in the rational – economical individual described by Schein.[1] Here is Schein's description, except that I have substituted 'individual' for 'man':

1. The individual is primarily motivated by economic incentives and will do that which gets him or her the greatest economic gain.
2. Since economic incentives are under the control of the organization, an individual is essentially a passive agent to be manipulated, motivated and controlled by the organization.

3. The individual's feelings are essentially irrational and must be prevented from interfering with his or her rational calculation of self-interest.
4. Organization can and must be designed in such a way as to neutralize and control the individual's feelings and therefore his or her unpredictable traits.

Schein also describes McGregor's theory X and Y.[2] I have changed the original wording from 'worker' to 'individual' in this summary of theory X:

> i) An individual is inherently lazy and must therefore be motivated by outside incentives.
> ii) The individual's natural goals run counter to those of the organization, hence the individual must be controlled by external forces to ensure his working toward organizational goals.
> iii) Because of his irrational feelings, an individual is basically incapable of self-discipline and self-control.

There is no escape from the fact that many owners and managers do react to individuals because they have such beliefs. Similar views are to be found among teachers about their students:

1. The student is primarily motivated by academic incentives and will do whatever gets him or her the greatest academic gain.
2. Since academic incentives are under the control of the institution, the student is essentially a passive agent to be manipulated, motivated and controlled by the organization.
3. The student's feelings are essentially irrational and must be prevented from interfering with his or her rational calculation of self-interest.
4. Institutions and their organizational (curriculum) arrangements can and must be designed in such a way as to neutralize and control their feelings and therefore their unpredictable traits.[3]

Extrinsic incentives, such as regular testing, may be used to encourage students. Chalk-and-talk methods of lecturing will probably be employed. Bonus payments may be used to encourage workers, and there is much evidence that individuals will work for economic incentives, and that payment schemes can be introduced that will have the effect of increasing output.[4] There is also plenty of evidence from the Industrial Revolution to show that before workers organized into trade unions they were badly manipulated. But neither eventuality shows that people are irrational. Consider the assembly line in which each worker is associated with the accomplishment of a small – to the worker, relatively unimportant – repetitive task. Here the technology, its designer and its manager have assumed that human beings should do such tasks. Is it unreasonable in these circumstances that a worker should take an instrumental attitude towards work? Workers who have had such diverse backgrounds as civil servants and small shopkeepers have been prepared to work on a motor-vehicle assembly line because it brought rewards that enabled them to play a significant role in their families. They worked in order to obtain the means to give them satisfaction outside their work.[5] The pressure to maximize their rewards in these circumstances makes sense. It is only irrational when it fails to take into account those pressures in the market that might eventually lead to the demise of the firm. It is in this respect that one can see in Britain a failure to learn, for the tendency in Britain (complicated by a large public sector) has been for relativities to play a large part in the wage bargaining at the expense of influence from the market, which influences the demand for products.

The implications of Theory-X attitudes for management, and indeed for teachers, are that managers and teachers must plan, organize, motivate and control without reference to the feelings and needs of the workers and pupils. It leads to a rationalist approach to management that is apparently still prevalent in many companies in the USA. Peters and Waterman, in their best selling book, *In Search of Excellence,* say its analytic approach, with its emphasis on quantitative techniques and factual data, has been to the detriment of excellence in many American companies, and for this they blame, along with many others, the American business-school curriculum![6]

Given production lines based on automation and numerous part tasks, and an instrumental attitude towards work, it is perhaps not surprising that managers should develop such attitudes toward work in spite of the fact that it has been shown that financial incentives do not, of themselves, guarantee more success, for the West Germans work hard for 36 per cent less inequality than the Americans, and the Japanese achieve more again, with 50 per cent less inequality in incomes.[7]

Dispositions brought about by belief in this model necessarily confirm 'us' and 'them' attitudes, and underlying these attitudes in Britain is the class structure, which some argue was the cause of Britain's industrial decline in the last century. Inspection of newspaper reports suggests that in Britain there is a strong element of 'us' and 'them' in industrial relations, which is desired. For example, in 1980 both the Confederation of British Industry and Trade Union Congress opposed the recommendation of a government committee report on worker participation in management, as well as proposals from the EEC that would lead to two-tier boards similar to those operated in Germany.[8] But research in behaviour in organizations has shown that even at the level of assembly work, the factors that influence the motivation to work are complex.

The Social Aspects of Work

Sometimes it is the social aspects of work that influence individual behaviour, as the well-known Hawthorne studies showed. From them, Elton Mayo was led to assume that individuals were primarily motivated by social needs, and would therefore be more responsive to their peer groups than to management.[9] In consequence, supervisors should try to meet an individual's social needs. The solidaristically oriented individuals described by Goldthorpe would belong to this category. This early version of the human-relations school of management was shown to be too simplistic, and eventually the model of social humanity it generated was replaced by other models, in particular, Theory Y and Self-Actualizing Man.

Alternative Faiths: Theory Y and Self-Actualization

Theory Y was proposed by McGregor as the opposite of Theory X, and as the true version of work behaviour. Schein[10] quotes McGregor's theory Y as follows (I have substituted person for man):

1. 'The expenditure of physical and mental effort in work is as natural as play or rest.' The ordinary person does not inherently dislike work: according to the conditions, it may be a source of satisfaction or punishment.
2. External control is not the only means for obtaining effort. 'A person will exercise self-direction and self-control in the service of objectives to which he is committed.'
3. 'The average human being learns, under proper conditions, not only to accept but to seek responsibility.'
4. Many more people are able to contribute creatively to the solution of organizational problems than do so.
5. At present, the potentialities of the average person are not being fully used.

It embraces self-actualizing beings in the most recent models. The idea of the self-actualizing individual had considerable influence on management, and teacher training embraces all an individual's needs. An individual is motivated to work as his or her needs are met; but the primary physiological needs have to be met before the secondary psychological needs – the needs for self-esteem and autonomy have to be met before self-actualization, when an individual is fully occupied and satisfied with what they do.[11]

The model of the individual that derives from this theory of the self-actualizing individual is in stark contrast to the rational–economic model. Now the individual seeks autonomy in the work that has to be done and, given an appropriate challenge, will be motivated to meet the new demand, and this will make the organization more effective. Given the chance, a worker will voluntarily integrate his or her own goals with those of the organization. The managers' task is, therefore, to arrange that the organization brings to the worker an environment and resources that will help the individual strive toward self-actualization. Barnes has argued against this hierarchical concept of need-fulfilment on the grounds that self-actualization (that is, to become everything that one is capable of becoming) is unlikely to be possible operationally. He argues that the safety needs overlap the higher needs because whenever one of these is threatened, so is the individual's safety.[12]

Studies of the jobs done by accountants and engineers seemed to support the Maslow model, but these were of professional people. They certainly supported the view that the meaning work has for the individual is an important factor in satisfaction, although they also showed more significantly that the things that caused dissatisfaction were not the same as those that caused satisfaction.[13] In any case, it may be that the worker with an instrumental disposition to work finds self-actualization at home in the family and/or in a hobby. It follows from the fact that individuals exist in a plurality of social systems that what is important to them at particular times, and in particular places, varies throughout the life-span. So when we try to understand a worker's behaviour and attitudes

> the critical question often is not the one so frequently posed of *what* are people really interested or most interested in or whether they are more interested in job satisfaction and intrinsic rewards than money and extrinsic rewards, but rather *when* are they interested in intrinsic rewards and *when* they are interested in extrinsic rewards.[14]

We have only to look at how our attitudes change through life to see that this is so.[15]

The Complex Being

The situation in school or university is no different. The motivation to study in the first year is different from that in a year in which we do not have to sit major examinations, or in systems of continuous assessment where it is self-evident that the pressures to study are different. Moreover, motivation in examinations is strongly influenced by the individual's emotional disposition, and there is no reason to suppose that this is not true of workers. The individual's reaction to any situation is complex, and the only model of the learner or worker that satisfied all conditions is, to quote Schein, 'complex'. My adaptation[16] of his model is as follows:

1. The learner (worker or manager) is complex: the individual is highly variable, and at any time has many motives, some of which are more important than others. Since an individual's motive patterns are complex, the individual's response to incentives will also change with circumstances.
2. The learner (worker or manager) is capable of learning new motives through his or her curriculum, work and institutional experiences. The psychological contract the individual makes with his or her peers, teachers and managers is the result of a complex interaction between perceived needs and learning (work) and institutional experiences.
3. The learner's (worker's or manager's) motives in different institutions or different sub-systems of the same institution may be different; the student (worker) who is alienated in the formal structure may find fulfilment of social and self-actualization needs in the student union, trade union or other parts of the extra-mural system, or outside the system altogether as, for example, in the family or in a hobby. If the curriculum or work is complex, in respect of perceived needs or apparent abilities, some parts of the curriculum (work) may engage some motives, while other parts engage other motives.
4. The learner (worker or manager) can become productively involved with the curriculum (work) and institution on the basis of many different kinds of motive. The individual's ultimate satisfaction in the institution depends only in part on the nature of personal motivation. The nature of the task to be performed, the abilities and experience of the learner (worker) and the nature of the teachers, administrators and managers in the institution, all interact to produce a certain pattern of work and feelings.

5. The learner (worker or manager) can respond to many different kinds of learning (work) strategy depending on his or her own motives and abilities and the nature of the task. There is no one correct learning (working) strategy that will work for all learners (workers) at all times.

There are many models of individual behaviour. Each of the models from which complex humanity is derived throw light on individual behaviour, and the actions of individuals as they react to particular management styles, and organizational structures. It is clear from all the books written on the topic – despite all the investigations that suggest individuals are badly managed – that many organizations continue to be ineffective for this reason.

Inspection of the rational–economic model of humanity shows it to have an affinity with those psychological theories that consider individuals to be impelled by appetites, drives and incentives. At the extreme they are also 'automaton' in their response to the world. Habits are easily ingrained. While we may react strongly against this view of humanity in the sense that it is perceived to be totally deterministic and a denial of the 'free will' to determine actions, it contains, nevertheless, an element of truth. There is, as we have seen, more than an elementary case for the rational–economic model, particularly in jobs where the worker is a machine-minder in an automated system. But people do act, and apparently of their own free volition, and sometimes the actions they take bring them into conflict with the work they do. Neither should we be surprised at this, for few individuals are entirely passive. We all want to have some control over what we do. Therefore, we should look to models of the individual that are active, not passive. Necessarily they will be based on analyses of what people do when they act, be it at work or play.

Individuals at Work

Work can be analysed in a variety of ways. We can observe what a person actually does and this we do in time-and-motion study. We can infer what a person does in solving problems from the process related to the activity area in which the problem is set. Thus we are led to argue from the process of engineering design that the engineering designer utilizes a particular set of problem-solving skills. The problem, as it were, dictates the cognitive set. Figures 4.1 and 4.2 show simple schematics of the processes of being an engineer and a scientist. The skills involved in these two activities are remarkably similar, yet most of us would have difficulty in accepting that this is the case. The fundamental activities of information processing and decision-making are overshadowed by the content to which they are applied, and the content of scientific analysis is different from that of engineering design.

Equally, we have difficulty with the view that decision-making and learning are identical processes. We tend to equate learning with something done at school. Yet learning is about the development of understanding and therefore the acquisition of new goals. We have to assemble new information so that it relates to

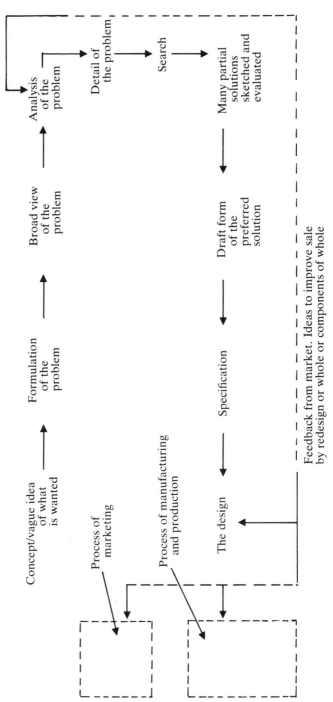

Figure 4.1   A model of the process of engineering design and manufacture (developed from a schema due to Krick E.V. 1966) An Introduction to Engineering Design, Wiley, New York, NY

and adds to existing frames of reference. Any decision-making exercise involves us in the same mental activity. The results of the activity, when analysed, are the new learning, which is placed in the memory store for future reference. The skills of decision-making and the skills of learning are the same, and the simplified cybernetic model of decision-making (see Figure 4.3) is included to illustrate this point. We can't help being decision-makers, yet I suspect that most of us do not think of ourselves as decision-makers even though we possess and continuously utilize these executive skills.

If it is true that our models of humanity influence our behaviour towards each other, then the idea that we all possess and utilize executive skills (see Chapter 1) should give us a different perspective of the worth (dignity) and potential of the human beings with whom we are in contact.

In an extensive study of an industrial organization, we attempted to analyse the work done by each engineer. The company called everyone in its engineering operation an engineer, so the term embraced a number of people who would not be regarded as professional engineers (for example, technicians, draughtsmen, contracts clerks, certain personnel in stores). Wages and salaries were measured against different grades (levels) of engineer.

We found that the 200 people in engineering functions performed about 450 operations of the type shown in Table 4.1, which relate to the stages of work in a development engineer's job. Some were 'small' and some 'large' in executive terms. We gave each of those in an engineering function this list of operations and asked them to tell us which ones they used in their jobs. With the results we were able to classify these operations into fourteen engineering activities.[17] We were also able to group individuals by the operations they used in their jobs and by this technique deduced twelve work types.[18]

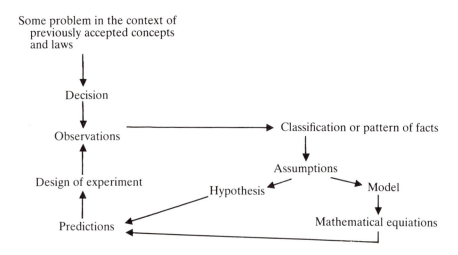

Figure 4.2   A simplified model of how a scientist goes about his or her work (from Heywood, J. and Montagu-Pollock, (1976) Science for Arts Students, A case study in curriculum design, Society for Research into Higher Education, Guildford

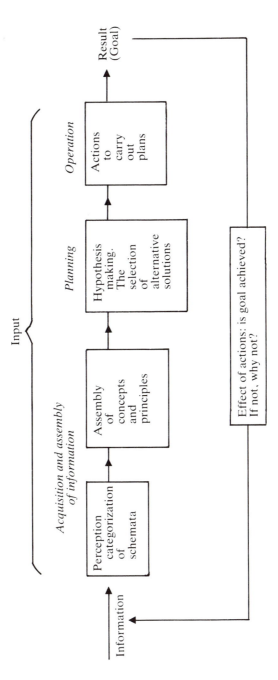

Figure 4.3   A model of the decision-making process (modified from a schema suggested by F. MacDonald, 1969) Educational Psychology, Wadsworth, Cal.

Table 4.1   The operations used in the stages in the work of a development engineer

Stage 1. Looking at the overall design outline	Assess general feasibility of design outline Identify changes in construction design
Stage 2. Carry out prototype testing	Interpret test reports supplied by technicians Request technicians to carry out tests Observe first running of prototype component Assess smoothness of running prototype component Increase loads on prototype component for test purposes Write progress reports Supply progress reports to customer Select level of testing appropriate to eventual usage Extrapolate from test results to save further testing Decide when basic specification has been first met
Stage 3. Carry out formal specification testing	Initiate formal specification testing Submit testing requirements to technician Discuss testing requirements with technician Specify test equipment to be used Ensure that necessary instrumentation is available Ensure inspector is informed of type-testing programme Observe type testing
Stage 4. Produce test reports	Add engineering comments to technician's reports Refer to test reports on earlier components Refer to test reports prepared by other firms Submit evidence from earlier test reports Submit evidence from test reports prepared elsewhere

It is also possible to show that these skills can be related to broad cognitive executive operations, or behavioural skills, as they have been called in education. In Table 4.2 the operations in one of the engineering activities have been re-grouped to show their dependence on a particular cognitive skill. The titles of these basic skills are chosen because they focus on the type of activity, that is, application, communication, diagnosis, evaluation and management. They could equally be given numbers. They are analogous to Gardner's intelligences in that they are not hierarchically ordered; neither are they discreet, although some individuals may perform better in one skill area than others. All of the activities can be re-classified in this way and while we did not find an activity, or a work type, that corresponded to the traditional stereotype of a manager, it can be shown that management skills enter into every job, independently of job level in the hierarchy. This finding is in line with others, especially of technicians, which show that they gain a knowledge of science and mathematics at the expense of management in their education. They are not, therefore, prepared for the jobs they have to do.[19] Our analysis shows that our understanding of traditional job types severely restricts our comprehension of the skills required to do jobs and, in consequence, the potential that individuals have for development into other jobs,

Table 4.2   A subjective analysis of 'activity 1' in terms of operations contributing to skills of application, communication, diagnosis, evaluation and management (direction and control)*§

Application
Use test reports from other firms
Use test reports on earlier components
Use Pert Chart†
Prepare rig for testing†
Simulate normal working conditions for component†

Communication
Discuss testing requirements with technician
Consult regarding cause of service fault
Pass report to another engineer
Notify designer regarding existence of fault
Advise production department concerning faults

Diagnosis
Identify deviations from specifications
Interpret performance graphs‡
Interpret test reports supplied by technicians‡
Confirm existence of fault by appropriate checks
Monitor investigations into fault diagnosis

Evaluation
Assess whether existing component meets customer specifications
Assess success of fault-removal attempt
Examine reports supplied
Assess validity of continuous budgets†
Assess customer's real-timing requirements†

Management (direction and control)
Initiate diagnosis of fault‡
Suggest modifications to testing specifications
Give advice to technicians on test results
Observe dismantling of part failure in service
Decide measures required to eliminate faults

Notes
* In 'Activity 1' there were 32 operations in all. These were assigned as follows: Application – 2; Communication – 5; Diagnosis – 11; Evaluation – 3; Management (direction and control) – 8.
† Operations taken from other derived 'activities' to make up groups of five operations.
‡ Illustrations of overlap between the behavioural groups in the table arising from the subjective nature of the method of assignment.
§ For a detailed discussion of taxonomies and their users in education, job analysis and training, see Heywood, J. (1989) *Assessment in Higher Education*, Wiley, Chichester.

requiring a higher level of performance in relation to people and machines. To put it in another way, our perceptions of what people can do impose limits on our view of their potential. It is this, as much as anything else, that leads to the under-utilization of personnel, which is so often found in industry. If we are to overcome this we need to have a different view of the way we use skills in the performance of tasks, and this will require a comprehension of the fact that managerial skills are used in every job or that every person is a manager.

Every Person a Manager

In Table 4.2, the executive skill is labelled 'management' with 'direction and control' following in brackets. This is because it is derived from the definition of management in *The Little Oxford Dictionary*. Thus, the operations in Engineering Activity 1, which seemed to indicate direction and control either of self or of others as well as self, have been grouped under management (direction and control). All of the other fourteen activities showed that some of their operations could be categorized as management in this way.

When I interviewed those in engineering functions, I was very impressed by the way in which, individually, they not only 'managed' but also had to 'manage' their jobs. They told me of how, by necessity, they had had to widen the scope of their initial brief through communication and co-operation with other people. The role definitions were inadequate and, in some cases, this seemed to have been an advantage. Often, in order to get a job done, a person would have to persuade another, over whom they had no authority, to do a job. For example, a person concerned with a contract that required the company to maintain a spare-parts store at the airport might have to organize the manufacture of a single specialist component to replace one that had been used. Because there was no production line, the contracts engineer had to persuade those who manufactured the company's products to slip this job in with their other duties. No formal system existed for this work, yet if it were not done, a contract might be broken. The contracts engineer had to develop his role to achieve this goal. In so doing, he used management skills. Other similar situations came to light in these interviews. It seemed that persons were appointed to roles they had to change in order to communicate. The organization was rather more a system of persons in relations rather than a hierarchical structure. It is in such experiences that feelings of responsibility are acquired. With regard to designers, we found in this and other studies that it was not so much status that they sought but responsibility. It was almost as if they had to justify to themselves that they were doing something worthwhile by measuring it in terms of responsibility.[20]

It is not unreasonable to suppose that the perceived activity of management is as much an attraction of the job as the salary. In our study, everyone was involved in direction and control and, hence, in management. Thus it is that the extent of job satisfaction may be measured by the degree to which individual needs for direction and control are satisfied. This in turn is as much a function of personality as it is of personal history, ability and interest. What is an acceptable goal to one person will not be to another: some want to be stretched, others want a strict routine. No two persons in a section will be exactly alike. In the same section there will be both aggressive people and timid people who, if they are taken outside the sphere they are capable of controlling, will have to be supported. Sometimes persons with high ability will find themselves in this situation.

A person is a psycho-social system. Within the boundaries of that system, most individuals wish to be 'organic', to use a term first suggested by Burns and Stalker.[21] They wish to be able to take actions and decisions as well as mature. The boundaries of these psycho-social systems arise as a function of the needs of the job and the needs of the person. When these are matched for each person in the organization, a hierarchical system becomes structured by individuals who are organic within their own system. The system itself becomes organic if it can respond to the needs of individuals. Both systems have to be self-adjusting. Within them every person is his or her own manager. The implications of this view are profound. Not everyone wants to be a 'manager' in the traditional sense, but they do wish to be given the dignity of a human being, capable of decision-making.

The idea that every person is a manager receives general approbation, yet when I put this forward as a significant model of humanity I was regarded by some as naïve. The reason for this is not hard to see, for the stereotype of a manager is not related to direction and control as described in the foregoing paragraphs. Management is thought to be the activity of a role in which the individual is authorized to get work done through an employed subordinate for whose work that individual is held accountable.[22] It is a view that assumes that management is an overt activity of control in a downward direction. In a hierarchical organization, instructions are handed down and communications sent up. A secretary may have no apparent control over people, yet the discretion he or she has as an intermediary is considerable. A cleaner can exercise considerable control over a manager's temper by the way in which he or she reorganizes the room. A skilled craftsworker exercises control over the product he or she is making. When we play our roles in the family, with our friends or at work, we exert direction and control, sometimes at a very high level of influence. Sometimes we are not aware that we have this effect. The workers in the Bank-Wiring Room (in the Hawthorne experiments) would not understand their 'unconscious' behaviour as management yet, as a group, they exhibited direction and control. We may argue that what happened was manipulation, but there is an area of behaviour where manipulation and behaviour are the same thing for the person so controlled.

In a democratic society that is increasingly well educated, the demand for participation and co-operation at work will grow. This requires organizations to behave as learning systems, for a high level of adaptability will be required. Not only will workers want to be involved, but they will also want to be more autonomous. This is not contradictory because the more autonomous a worker, the more effective that person's work is likely to be.[23] Heller and Wilpert have pointed out that if participation is to be effective, the skill level of the workforce will have to be high. It is for this reason that students, while still at school, should be exposed to a variety of learning techniques.[24] Moreover, at some time during the later stages of their schooling, they should have to negotiate a component of their curriculum for independent study.

Replacing a tap, cooking, planning a holiday are all activities that require the utilization of decision-making skills to which we draw attention only when a person is said to be managing. Because this is not recognized we do not try to develop these capabilities. Thus, in every role there is a 'management' (servant) component as well as a 'learning' (gift) component. At one time one will predominate, and at another time, the other. The roles we adopt, the perceptions we have and the attitudes we acquire, affect our performance. The trouble is that, for much of the time, these capabilities remain dormant and in consequence we do not acquire dispositions that help to prepare for and control change. Decision-making and problem-solving skills are of no avail if they do not generate action. Thus it is with the potential for action that managers are concerned, and in particular with the best organization of the means of involvement in the technology of production. The next chapter reviews in more detail some of the studies that have been done on the organization of work and their implications for the world of work and change in which we live.

Notes and References

1. Schein, E.H. (1965) *Organizational Psychology,* Prentice-Hall, Englewood Cliffs, NJ.
2. McGregor, D.M. (1960) *The Human Side of Enterprise,* McGraw-Hill, New York, NY. (see also note 3).
3. Throughout this text I have adopted the formularization of these models by Schein (see note 1). However in my (1977) *Assessment in Higher Education*, Wiley, Chichester, I modified them to demonstrate their validity to the learner and teacher. They have also been applied to the behaviour of principals by Kaiser, J.S. (1985) *The Principalship,* Burgess Publishing, Minneapolis, Minn. (see Chapter 1). I have generalized them to the 'person' or 'individual' in this chapter.
4. Lupton, T. (ed.) (1972) *Payment Systems,* Penguin Books, Harmondsworth.
5. See Chapter 3.
6. Peters, J. and Waterman, R.H. (1982) *In Search of Excellence: Lessons from America's Best Run Companies,* Harper & Row, New York, NY.
7. Thurow, L.C. (1980) *The Zero Sum Society: Distribution and the Possibilities for Economic Change,* Basic Books, New York, NY.
8. Lord Bullock chaired the committee: (1977) *Report of the Committee of Enquiry into Industrial Democracy,* HMSO, London.
9. See Chapter 5 for a brief discussion of the Hawthorne studies.
10. Schein, *Organizational Psychology* (notes 1 and 3).
11. Maslow, A. (1964) *Motivation and Personality,* Harper & Row, New York, NY.
12. Barnes, L.B. (1960) *Organizational Systems and Engineering Groups*, Harvard School of Business, Cambridge, Mass.
13. Herzberg, F., Mausner, B. and Synderman, B. (1959) *The Motivation to Work*, Wiley, New York, NY. From this study came the concept of satisfiers and dissatisfiers in job satisfaction. They are as shown in Table 4.3. The factors that give people satisfaction at work are by no means the same as those that cause them dissatisfaction. As Goldthorpe found (Chapter 2), 'the question of satisfaction from work cannot in the end be usefully considered except in relation to the more basic question of the meaning that work has for the worker' (Goldthorpe *et al. The Affluent–Worker* (note 3, Chapter 3)).

Table 4.3   Satisfiers and dissatisfiers

Satisfiers (motivating factors, elements that increase job satisfaction)	Dissatisfiers (hygiene factors, elements that diminish job satisfaction)
1. Achievement	1. Company policy and administration
2. Recognition	2. Supervision – technical
3. Work itself	3. Salary
4. Responsibility	4. Interpersonal relations supervision
5. Advancement	5. Working conditions

14. Daniel, W.W. and McIntosh, N. (1972) *The Right to Manage,* Macdonald & Jane's, London.

15. See, for example, Mant, A. (1970) *The Middle Aged Manager: A National Resource*, British Institute of Management, London; and Hunt, J.W. (1979) *Managing People at Work*, McGraw-Hill, Maidenhead.

16. Heywood, *Assessment* (note 3).

17. Youngman, M.B., Oxtoby, R., Monk, J.D. and Heywood, J. (1977) *Analyzing Jobs*, Gower Press, Aldershot. The techniques of cluster and statistical analysis are described in full in this book. The activities were (1) production of specifications; (2) organization of testing; (3) testing; and (4) quality monitoring. Together these formed a related cluster. The second cluster was (5) testing. The third related cluster included (6) customer liaison; (7) project supervision; (8) production scheduling; (9) long-term planning; and (10) contract supervision. The remaining related clusters included (11) organization of materials/methods; (12) facilitate manufacture; (13) design; and (14) draughting.

18. The twelve work types were (1) management and liaison; (2) product specification and development; and (3) project engineering, together grouped in the first related cluster. The second included (4) draughtsmen; (5) methods planning; and (6) design. The third related cluster included (7) technicians; and (8) quality and support. The fourth related cluster included (9) service functions; (10) manufacturing; (11) standards; and (12) contracts/sales. Again, inspection of the related clusters suggests that the technique had high validity.

The technique was applied by V. Flanagan to analyse the work of managers in the Irish Development Authority. Apart from demonstrating the general applicability of the technique, she derived a taxonomy for in-service training (M.Ed., Thesis, University of Dublin).

19. Clements, I. and Roberts, I. (1981) Practitioner views of industrial needs and course unit content, in J. Heywood (ed.) *The New Technician Education*, Society for Research into Higher Education, Guildford.

20. Monk, J.D. and Heywood, J. (1977) The education and career patterns of mechanical engineers in design and management, *The Vocational Aspect of Education*, Vol. 29, no. 72, pp. 5–16.

21. Burns, T. and Stalker, G. (1961) *The Management of Innovation*, Tavistock, London. This is also discussed in Chapter 5.

22. Jaques, E. (1970) *Work Creativity and Social Justice,* Heinemann, London.

23. Martin, S. (1983) *Managing without Managers. Alternative Work Arrangements in Public Organizations*, Sage, Beverly Hills, Calif.

24. Many texts explain brainstorming, and many exercises have been designed to develop this skill. See, in particular, Krick, E.V. (1966) *An Introduction to Engineering Design,* Wiley, New York, NY; and Carter, R., Martin, J., Mayblin, B. and Monday, M. (1984) *Systems, Management and Change: A Graphic Guide,* Paul Chapman Publishing Ltd., London.

There are several well-known books on thinking and learning as, for example, Abercrombie, M.L.J. (1960) *The Anatomy of Judgement*, Penguin Books, Harmondsworth; and de Bono, E. (1971) *The Use of Lateral Thinking,* Penguin Books, Harmondsworth. For general problem-solving heuristics, see Koen, W. (1985) *Definition of the Engineering Method,* American Society for Engineering Education, Washington, DC.

5

PATTERNS OF WORK

Introduction

In the last chapter we saw how the views we hold of why people work not only influence our attitudes to the way they should be treated, but also to the way work should be organized. We also saw how all jobs involve management when it is defined as direction and control. In this chapter we look at how organizational structures can influence work behaviour in order to understand better both our own situation as well as to design an organization that operates effectively. To achieve this goal, some of the major investigations of organizational behaviour are discussed briefly. Reference is also made to the organizational structures of some organizations regarded as highly successful. Some striking parallels are drawn between these studies and practices in classroom and schools.

Social Relations at Work

Reference is made in Chapter 4 to the Hawthorne studies, which led to the social model of humanity.[1] The authors of these studies were responsible for other important ideas relating to the methods used in such studies. The most important of these was the 'Hawthorne effect' (sometimes called the 'halo effect'). It describes the actions of people in response to the observer that cover up the reality of what would happen in the group if the observer were not there. This concept is now very much part of everyday awareness. For example, a journalist commenting on the failure of the English cricket team against the West Indies said the captain needed to create a Hawthorne effect! The Hawthorne experiments were built around observations of people at work. The one that led to our understanding of the Hawthorne effect required a group of girls to work under a variety of conditions. It was predicted that some conditions of work would improve productivity while others would reduce efficiency. In the event, all the changes that were introduced to reduce productivity had the opposite effect. Productivity kept increasing and they could not understand why. Eventually they established that the girls who had been selected for this experiment thought they had been specially chosen to help the investigator. So to help the investigator they increased productivity with every change in their work conditions.

The same kind of effect is observed in the classroom. For a variety of reasons, pupils respond with greater efforts to some teachers than to others, and these teachers might be entirely unconscious of their effect. In school, pupils go out of their way to respond in the way they believe teacher thinks is best. They must satisfy the teacher's needs as they perceive them, which is not always conducive to effective learning. Some student teachers try to create a Hawthorne effect.[2] In social science it is now well understood that research involving people is easily contaminated by the investigator.

The Hawthorne studies led to the general postulate that motivation, productivity and quality are related to the social relationships between workers, and thus to Mayo's model of social humanity. There were also findings related to organizational structure that were of considerable importance. These come from the Bank-Wiring Room study, which is summarized below.

Briefly, men who wired and soldered banks of equipment were, with their supervisors (fourteen persons in all), put together in a special room where they could be watched by a trained observer. After a period the observer's presence was ignored. Within the group, two sub-groups developed that were related to the front and back of the workroom. The workers at the front of the room felt they had more status than those at the back of the room because they believed they had a more difficult job to do. Some workers did not belong to either group.

The group developed 'norms' of behaviour, that is, unwritten rules about behaviour and performance. Thus they had norms about the amount of work that should be done in return for the pay they were offered. This, according to the observer, was well below that which could have been achieved, although their output satisfied the company. Anyone who worked at a rate above the norm was called a 'rate buster', while those who worked at a rate that would produce below the norm were called 'chiselers'. Deviations from the norm led to pressures on the deviants to get back in line.

It was also understood that those in authority (the supervisors) must not act officiously or take advantage of their authority position. An inspector who deviated had to be transferred to another department because of the pressures put upon him. The inspectors were regarded as no better than anybody else, and they acquiesced in the behaviour of the group as the consistency and output remained restricted. The group also undertook other activities that were contrary to company policy. For example, they exchanged jobs. Soldermen sometimes did wiring while wiremen did soldering.

The two status groups were characterized by productivity. The high-status group were high producers who thought the low-status group were social isolates. Neither dexterity nor intelligence tests correlated with individual output. But of greater interest is the mechanism that restricted output. The high-status group nagged the low-status group about 'chiseling'. This was resented by the low-status group who, in their turn, decided that the best way to get their own back was to reduce their rate of production, the net effect of which was to get the backs up of the high-status group with the same result.

This study illustrates the importance of social relationships at work. It also showed that there was an informal system of work that was as important as the formal. It is easy to deduce that change is not likely to be accomplished with ease in such circumstances.

The same is true of schools and classrooms. There is both a formal and informal curriculum: that is, the official statement versus actual practice. But there is also a 'hidden curriculum' because children learn a variety of ideas that are not related to the syllabus. For example, children learn how to get on with their peers as well as how to satisfy their teacher. Their peers may expect them to cheat or to refrain from achieving high marks. The same kind of processes are at work as those in the Bank-Wiring Room. The idea of the 'hidden agenda' is now part of everyday vocabulary. It is the 'hidden organization' that is the subject of so much gossip.

Behavioural research of all kinds tends to replace theories as its analyses become more refined. In so doing it can disregard recognizable dimensions of human behaviour. At some times, social man and informal (hidden) organization have significance in the understanding of organizational process. In this case we learn how worker can influence worker. In socio-technical systems theory, we learn how the social organization and productivity are influenced by technology.

Socio-Technical Systems

The concept of a socio-technical system derives from studies undertaken by the Tavistock Institute of Human Relations, which investigated the effects of three different systems of mechanization on the production of coal.[3]

Traditionally, coal-miners worked in small groups. A miner and his mate cut the coal, which was then removed in 'tubs' by labourers. Together they formed a group. Initially they were picked by the team leader who cut the coal, and clearly this had to be done on the basis of mutual compatibility. It led to the establishment of long-term relationships and deep emotional bonds that would include the care and welfare of a sick man in the group and/or his family. The coal-face was mined in small sections from which the descriptive term 'shortwall' comes. The better the section, the greater the return when a piecework system was in operation. Thus there was conflict and competition for the good sections.

When the cutting process was mechanized it changed, as you can imagine, the structure of the work group considerably. Instead of small coherent groups, forty or so men came under the supervision of one supervisor. Moreover, they were spread out over the length of the equipment, which was of the order of 180 m (200 yd), in conditions that were far from pleasant: considerable heat, dust and noise in a tunnel that was often no more than 1 m (3 ft) high and 2 m (2 yd) wide. Sometimes the miners were committed to a single and sometimes a part-task. Those who cut the coal gained the highest status, while the other small groups were differentiated by the particular tasks they did. Contrary to expectations, productivity was low and the quality of work poor. The investigators from the Tavistock Institute found a state of '*anomie*' (loss of meaning). The old emotional ties had been broken, and there were many difficulties in the way of completing the tasks they were given.

With the help of these investigators, the Coal Board redesigned their mechanical system for 'longwall mining' into a composite designed to make work more meaningful by increasing the number of tasks done by each miner, and by arranging the grouping of tasks so that emotional needs could be met. It increased productivity. Once again the social needs of humanity were shown to be important. But the study also showed that the technology of production also creates a social system. Thus, in any organization there is both a technical system and a social system. Moreover, technical systems can be designed in such a way that they either tend to impede or enhance the satisfaction of social needs.

An organization in this perspective is regarded as a socio-technical system. Classrooms may be analysed in the same way. Benches or desks that are arranged to face the teacher at the front of the class will produce a different teaching system from one where the desks are arranged so that the children can work in groups. It is much easier for children to work on their own in small groups. Teaching methods are limited when the desks are fixed so as to face the blackboard. Small-group work can help teachers when the range of ability in a class is very wide. It is also much more suited to project work that helps to develop executive skills. Just as different methods of production change the role of the manager, so it is that different arrangements of the classroom change the role of the teacher. The function of the teacher is to aid learning. Thus the teacher's task is to choose the instructional strategy that will best achieve the learning objectives to be obtained. The teacher becomes a manager or facilitator of learning. And the manager, instead of being the creator of work, the motivator and the controller, becomes the facilitator and sympathetic supporter, to quote Schein.[4]

The same is true of higher education. Much research shows that the lecture method is very limited when compared with small-group instruction. One American model goes so far as to suggest that the methods of instruction used in universities actively impede the cognitive and affective development of the students.[5]

The idea of a socio-technical system is a very different concept from that of informal organization, although informal organizations can exist in the socio-technical system as, for example, the organization that develops among students during break periods. Even so, the administrative arrangements for breaks (for example, supervisions, use of rooms) are part of the socio-technical system. An important consequence of this concept is that the designer of a classroom, or production unit, should take into account the effects of the technical system on the social structure of the organization. These studies also highlight the importance of the work group as a controlling agent in productivity, and this can be just as serious in the classroom when a peer group takes control. In particular, these investigations show how work can be restricted, and in this lies their importance in industrial relations.

Organizational Structure and the Work of Professional People

At the other end of the job spectrum there were several studies of people we commonly call 'professional' at work, and the factors that enhance or impede creativity and innovation among this group. In the USA, for example, it was found that there were more positive attitudes and output from engineers when their work was arranged in an open system.[6] In a similar study in Scotland, it was found that companies would more likely innovate if they were organized in an organic, as opposed to a mechanistic, way.[7]

The mechanistic type of organization described by Burns and Stalker is similar to that of a bureaucracy.[8] In a bureaucracy every person (official) is subject to impersonal orders that guide their actions. They operate within a framework of rules that have been specifically established for this purpose. Their actions have to conform with these rules; thus they have to have a specified sphere of competence in which obligations, authority and obedience are strictly defined. They conduct their business by means of written documents. Because they are unable to operate outside of this framework, communications between them and the public are often accompanied by friction. Not knowing the rules, the public are unable to determine whether anything can be done, or even to know whether the official, with whom they are dealing, has it in his or her power to refer the matter to higher authority. Officials, in their turn, can hide behind the prescribed rules for their role. There is thus considerable antipathy toward the bureaucracy of government. It is generally thought that it is difficult to innovate in such organizations.

Burns and Stalker found that most of the companies they studied were organized in this way. In these mechanistic organizations, there is a specialized differentiation of functional tasks. Each task is pursued by the persons involved with techniques and purpose, more or less distinct from those of the concern as a whole. So the reconciliation of these distinct performances has to be accomplished by a supervisor. Groups of performances have also to be reconciled, and this is achieved by a hierarchical structure of control, authority and communication. In such organizations the location of comprehensive knowledge is at the top. It will be appreciated that there is inevitably a minimum interaction between peers.

Schools are typically organizations of this kind. But Burns and Stalker also found organizations in which individual workers understood their role in terms of the general aims of the organization. Such systems were organized so that every one contributed to the common goal of the organization. Individual tasks are related to the total situation of the company, so they have to be adjusted and continually redefined as they interact with each other. To maintain this situation, control, authority and communication are allowed to derive from the mutual relationships between the group rather than from the contractual relationships of specified roles to be found in a bureaucracy. In such organizations, the head is not omnipresent. Burns and Stalker believed that organic systems of this kind were more open to innovation than mechanistic systems.

My impression of the highly innovative company in the aircraft industry we studied in Chapter 4 leads me to enter a caveat to that theory because it seemed to be moving towards an organic framework – although it still operated within a broad mechanistic framework. It seemed to be midway between the two. As one authority puts it, 'real-life organisations tend to occupy intermediate positions in the grey areas between one extreme and another.'[9]

It seems that leadership is important and may cause innovation in a relatively mechanistic organization. For example, although MacMahon in Ireland found the theory to hold as between two schools of a mechanistic type and two in the organic mode, he also showed that the principals were key figures in the changes that took place.[10] Also, had there been changes within the system – such as in the examination syllabuses – all organizations, however structured, would have been forced to participate, even if with some difficulty.

Inspection of the differences between the mechanistic and organistic systems shows that a person would be required to make a radical change in his or her role if he or she were to move from one system to another. This would have to be accompanied by a substantial change in attitudes if the person is to adapt to the new role. There is probably some truth in the view that individuals are more comfortable in a mechanistic system than they are in organic systems. Children, when they reach the age of 11 or 12, like the rather more structured teaching they receive in secondary schools as compared with organic systems that characterize many primary-school classrooms. There is a high level of security attached to highly structured roles. In less structured roles, a high level of adaptability and flexibility is required. New attitudes have to be learnt and this is difficult. This gives some idea of the problems that are likely to be encountered in the introduction of more flexible organizations, such as a semi-autonomous working group. We have to get used to working in more open, as opposed to more closed, systems.

Open versus Closed Systems

An open system is one that is in exchange with its environment, whereas a closed system is one that has no exchange with its environment. A closed system will eventually die, whereas the open system maintains itself because it is able to export and import 'material' from the environment. This description of biological or thermodynamic systems[11] may be applied to organizations. An industrial or commercial organization is in exchange with its market. If it does not respond to the market it will die. Within the market it also has to choose how it competes. Will it compete with the same type of 'good' companies over a range of products, or only in product areas where it has a technical advantage?

The way in which the senior management of an enterprise views the environment may also condition their attitudes within the organization. Barnes described the attitudes of management and a particular section of a company in the electronics industry.[12] This company not only had to operate in a highly competitive way but also had to meet the goals set by its parent organization. The pressures on the general manager were for low prices and high quality with the effect that engineering management believed that productivity was much more important than quality. This meant that developmental work in the department investigated did not have high quality, even though it seemed that developmental work was required.

Barnes shows how the chief engineer and supervisor were placed in middle-man roles. Management and business values (practical engineering and productivity) were stressed to their subordinates, whereas to their seniors, in contrast, they emphasized the value of the scientific approach to engineering to their supervisors, thereby reflecting the views of their staff. On the one hand, the supervisor 'stresses scientific principles and deplores production engineering's knob twisting approach. On the other hand, he builds up subordinate resistance by asking them to turn out more "quickies", to get out into the factory, and to be less scientifically rigorous'.

In contrast, Barnes described another company in the same business that was also highly competitive but making products in which it had a technical advantage. It is not surprising to find that in this company technical and scientific knowledge was valued, and that the attitudes throughout the organization were different. The field engineer, who was the equivalent of chief engineer in the first company, did not present one face to the engineers and another to management. There were no pressures on him for productivity and practicality. The pressure that came through, if it can be called a pressure, was management's encouragement of individual development. Officials at the top of the organization put down company success to the informality that spread across the organization. So the field engineer, in responding to this, arranged for his subordinates to have high autonomy while at the same time ensuring interaction between them and himself so that a system of mutual influence was created.

As things stood the second company was more efficient than the first. Barnes put this down to the organizational structures of the company. The first was a relatively 'closed' system, he stresses the term relatively, while the second was relatively 'open'. The first discouraged performance while the second encouraged performance. In the first the engineers thought they should be doing engineering development whereas the pressure was on them to worry about production. In the second there were no explicit pressures for productivity and practicality of the knob twisting kind.

Of particular interest is the fact that the organization of the first department seemed to highlight the different value dispositions between the individuals in the group.

Those who were oriented towards the values of science (for example, truth and knowledge) tended towards relatively low non-work activities, low interactions and low mutual friendships. Those who wanted to attain promotion, acceptance and prestige within the organization tended towards relatively higher interactions, high interaction and high mutual friendship. Barnes called the former group 'professionals' and the latter group 'organizationals'. The third group he called 'socials' or those who wanted popularity and acceptance by the high-status groups. They were characterized by high non-work activities, high interactions but low mutual friendships.

In the second department, there was much more mixing between the grades, and there was a higher level of participation in non-work activities. The two structures influenced the way in which individuals in the departments behaved and worked, and they, in their turn, were influenced and reinforced by that mode of work. The open-system was more effective than the closed-system.

Open Systems in the Production Line

We are told that by the year 2000 many people will be working from home. This will mark a return to cottage industry. It is particularly true of methods of production. Williamson pointed this out, and remarked that batch-production methods were inferior to the small workshop of the nineteenth century.[13] Rank Xerox has created a system of home-based networks that have greatly reduced overheads.[14] It is not surprising that the entrepreneurs of the industrial revolution should have adopted assembly-line procedures because the small workshop in which everyone knew what everyone else was doing ensured high-quality work, since faults were easily spotted and quickly corrected. This is not so in the modern assembly line in which, because of the many part-tasks that have to be done, there is much less commitment to the goals of the organization.

Williamson drew an analogy between the small workshop and the human cell. Cells in living organisms do not increase in size but duplicate themselves as the organism grows. 'If an abnormally large cell does occasionally form as they sometimes do, the cancerous growth with which they are associated may result in the death of the organism.' His message for large-scale traditional batch-production methods in which there are lines of milling machines, lathes and other automated devices is clear. Errors, he argued, can go undetected until the final stage of manufacture, and because no one sees the total process of manufacture of an artefact from start to finish, wasteful work planning goes undetected unless there is a serious failure in manufacture. He went on to suggest that 'cellular' manufacture should replace conventional single-unit manufacturing enterprises. People and machine tools would be grouped into specialist cells manufacturing one category of component or a very limited range of components. At first sight it seems that the people would be just as limited as in traditional systems, but it is clear from his description of cellular organization that in such cell systems they have more responsibility. He wrote:

> Each component is classified in such a way that it is issued into the cell most appropriate for its manufacture. Such specialisation would bring its advantages: on the human side, in familiarity with the components, resulting in more detailed know-how, and a higher concentration of skill: and on the machine tool side, in the ability to use simpler machine tools specially suited to a limited range of components, supplemented by appropriate specialised tooling. An operator in a cell could use more than one machine tool, and in general there would be more machine tools than operators.[15]

Since the 1960s there have been many attempts to organize industrial and commercial organizations along these lines. These organizational structures have been variously called 'group technology', 'autonomous work groups' and 'cellular organization'. Of these, perhaps the most publicized are those developed by Volvo and Saab.[16]

All of these re-organizations stem from the view that the more a person is involved in their work, the more they will be committed to the achievement of the organization's goals. Thus cell structures relate more generally to the idea of job enrichment and self-actualization.

Job Enrichment and Job Satisfaction

Job satisfaction, as we have seen, has to be looked at from the point of view of the attitudes the worker brings to his or her job. From this it appears that a distinction has to be made between satisfaction with the actual job and satisfaction with their present employment. The two may not be associated in any direct way. It is with the job that we are concerned. Taken together, the studies reported in these chapters suggest that management should

1. provide a worker with adequate elbow room;
2. give opportunities for learning on the job and for going on learning;
3. design work for an optimal level of variety;
4. arrange the environment so that workers can and do get help from their workmates; and
5. help workers to obtain a sense of their work as contributing to social welfare.[17]

The principles have been found to apply to learning in the classroom.[18] Notice how the fourth and fifth points relate to discipline.

The Swedish vehicle-manufacturing firm, Volvo, expressed these principles in internal documents used to describe a new engine plant designed for group technology thus:

> The possibility of having influence on his own work situation is of vital importance for the individual's job satisfaction and motivation. An increased participation also means a better utilization of the experience and initiative of the employee. Participation is a right which conveys, simultaneously, an obligation of responsibility. The basis for increased participation is the willingness of each leader to utilize opportunities for delegating and joint consultation.

If groups of this kind are to be successful, the workers will have to develop higher-level skills in the areas of technical competence, human relationships and self-assessment.

Team project-work in school is designed to achieve this objective and is much encouraged. The *Technologie* programme in the junior-cycle French curriculum is based on the project method.[19] The children, from the age of 12, market research a product, which they can make. The class is split into several groups responsible for managing, making and learning. For example, it is decided to manufacture 100 small electronic alarms to meet market demand. The children will order the components, fabricate the box, wire up the electronic equipment and learn the principles of electronics at the same time. This project method is carried through the whole junior cycle. Each project is substantive in terms of the time deployed.

It may, with some justice, be claimed that this is a preparation for work and life. The group work I saw suggests to me that they are likely to experience the same problems of motivation that are experienced in industry, unless they are carefully managed. It is possible even at this age for students to take over from the teachers responsibility for the project, but this would require a very substantial shift in perception on the part of the students.

In the study reported in the last chapter, it will be recalled that the school pupils felt that pupils in their first year should be treated as Theory X.

When individual projects are undertaken, it is often the practice for students in schools and colleges to negotiate the topics with their tutors, and there are a few courses in higher education where students also negotiate the procedures for assessment. Increasingly in higher education, students are being encouraged to develop skills in self-assessment.[20] The relevance of this to the development of positive attitudes towards quality should be self-evident. During the last decade, there have been many attempts in schools to run mini-companies, especially for those who are not pursuing academic studies in the senior cycle of education.[21] Much, however, is lost if the students do not rigorously evaluate their experience of running their own ventures in the light of the available knowledge of human behaviour in such situations. For this purpose, they need to develop skills in self-assessment, and these it seems are the most difficult to develop. Work in Ireland has suggested that young students in mini-companies are likely to benefit from a formal course in management studies prior to the mini-company activity.[22]

It is not without significance that these are the kind of principles the Japanese put into practice when they establish factories abroad as, for example, the Toshiba plant in Plymouth, or the much advertised Datsun car plant at Sunderland.[23] It is significant that non-union companies in Britain that meet these objectives seem to be among the most efficient.[24] The need for more flexible organizations is widely recognized and matrix organizations have been felt by some to meet this need.

Matrix Organizations

'Each era of management evolves new forms of organisation as new problems are encountered.' So writes the author of a recent study of Marks and Spencer.[25] Matrix organizations, which have evolved during the last decade, are designed for both flexibility and easy decision-making. They are able to reconcile several conflicting objectives, especially when a company has to respond to two sectors simultaneously, or when uncertainties in the market create a demand for large amounts of data, or when there are strong restraints on resources.

In engineering, matrix organizations can handle several projects simultaneously. Their teams combine both function and line tasks. The project manager acquires experts when they are required. When the experts' task is finished, they go to other parts of the organization where they are needed. Some managers report to two bosses and this is a characteristic of matrix organizations. In this dual command-control situation, managers have small formal authority but a great deal of responsibililty. Power is shared equally between project needs and the people requirements of the organization. Matrix organizations are intended to be highly adaptable. The company we investigated in the aircraft industry had many of the characteristics of a matrix organization.

Administration can be operated on a matrix basis in large educational institutions. A major difference between companies and schools is the time-scale of adaptability. It is relatively short in companies as compared with educational institutions.

Learning and Change

There is generally a need in industry and the classroom for increased worker and student participation. However, such changes may not be brought about without substantial changes in management, union and worker attitudes. Such changes may be understood in terms of the manager arranging the organization to receive the gifts of the learner (worker) and this, as we saw in the last chapter, is a skill that may be learnt. It is with the potential for change as seen from the perspective of the organization as a learning system, that the next chapter is concerned.

Notes and References

1. The Hawthorne studies are described in many books. See, in particular, Brown, J.A.C. (1980) *Social Psychology of Industry,* Penguin Books, Harmondsworth; and also Pugh, D.S. (ed.) *Organisation Theory: Selected Readings,* Penguin Books, Harmondsworth.
2. See Chapter 1 of Heywood, J. (1984) *Considering the Curriculum During Student Teaching,* Kogan Page, London.
3. *Ibid.*
4. *Ibid.* See articles by Emery, F.E. and Trist, E.L. in Emery, F.E. (ed.) (1969) *Systems Thinking,* Penguin Books, Harmondsworth.
5. Schein, E.H. (1965) (1972) *Organizational Psychology,* Prentice-Hall, Englewood Cliffs, NJ.
6. Heywood, J. (1988) *Assessment in Higher Education,* Wiley, New York, NY.
7. Barnes, L.B. (1960) *Organizational Systems and Engineering Groups,* Harvard School of Business, Cambridge, Mass.
8. Burns T. and Stalker, G. (1961) *The Management of Innovation,* Tavistock, London.
9. Sadler, P.J. (1969) *Designing an Organisation Structure: A Behavioural Science Approach,* Ashridge Management College, Berkhamstead.
10. MacMahon, J. (1976) M.Ed. thesis, University of Dublin, Dublin.
11. Von Bertalanffy, L. (1966) The theory of open systems, reprinted in F.E. Emery (ed.) *Systems Thinking,* Penguin Books, Harmondsworth.
12. Barnes, *Organizational Systems* (note 8).
13. Williamson, D.T.N. (1971) *Trade Balance in the 1970s. The Role of Mechanical Engineering,* National Economic Development Office, HMSO, London. Historians might take a less sanguine view of cottage industry. It was open to a great deal of exploitation. Nevertheless, the principle remains.
14. Networkers are people who work from home or a local network office, using a micro-computer to transmit and receive from head office or plants. They work on as broad a range of skills as possible. Rank Xerox's 54 networkers provide the company with a range of services spreading through marketing, market planning, market research, business planning, financial analysis, operational research, pensions, safety, security, public relations, training and many more.

    The Chairman of Rank Xerox points out that much travelling time is saved: considerable costs are saved. He says:

    > Invariably, every time people think about reducing costs, they will straight away ask: 'how can we reduce people?' It is a very unusual use of the word productivity because what is being reduced is the productive element of the organisation in favour of keeping the sterile, unproductive, inflationary pattern. Thus

reducing overheads through networking is one possibility. The main objective of networking is to keep people not lose them.

Hornby, D. (1986) Can we teach ourselves to change?, *The Royal Bank of Scotland Review*, no. 151, pp. 14–21.

15. Williamson, *Trade Balance* (note 13).

16. For descriptions of developments in a variety of organizations, commercial and industrial, large and small, in group technology, see Argenti, J. (1972) *Management Systems for the Seventies*, Allen & Unwin, London; Burbridge, J.L. (1975) *The Introduction of Group Technology*, Heinemann, London; Butteris, M. (1975) *Techniques and Development in Management. A Selection*, Institute of Personnel Management, London; Gorman, L. and Molloy, E. (1972) *People, Jobs and Organisations*, Irish Productivity Centre, Dublin; and Ranson, G.N. (1972) *Group Technology*, McGraw-Hill, Maidenhead.

17. Emery, G. and Emery, M. (1975) Cuts and guidelines for raising the quality of working life, in D. Ginzburg (ed.) *Bringing Work to Life*, Productivity Promotion Council of Australia, Cheshire, Melbourne.

18. Heywood, J. (1982) *Pitfalls and Planning in Student Teaching*, Kogan Page, London.

19. Murray, M. (1986) Recent developments in the school curriculum in France, in J. Heywood and P. Matthews (eds.) *Technology, Society and the School Curriculum: Practice and Theory in Europe*, Roundthorn, Manchester.

20. Heywood, J. (1988) *Assessment in Higher Education*, Wiley, Chichester.

21. Successful mini-company schemes have been run in schools in America, Britain and Ireland. The idea of the American Junior Achievement Project has also been used in Ireland, but many school schemes now operate under their own propulsion. The students contribute to the basic capital and receive a return on their investment from the products they choose, design, manufacture and market. *Young Citizen* (1984) The mini-company scheme in schools, no. 23, pp. 1–6. For more recent work, see Murray, M. (1989) Thesis, University of Dublin.

22. Belbin and Belbin describe work done at the Centre Universitaire de Co-operation Economique et Sociale at Nancy, in adult training that began in 1964–5 and through which many students have passed. Self-assessment is at the focus of the programme, which includes self-evaluation of evening sessions, at the end of each term, and the end of the year. It is hoped that the students will, at the end of the year, be able to counsel themselves to repeat the course, withdraw from training, enrol for a higher course, or enrol for full-time study. This is achieved by evaluating their own progress throughout the year.

The daily session begins with a forty-minutes lecture and finishes with a forty-minutes group activity controlled by an assistant. In between, a twenty-minutes period is devoted to self-assessment. In this period, a short-question test is set to see if the students understand the principle they have tried to convey. The correct solutions are given and the students correct their work using the following criteria:

- Failed to understand the text of a question.
- Made an error of calculation.
- Misused a formula or used a wrong formula.
- Forgot something.
- Made an error of reasoning.
- Failed in some other way.

The assistant marks the questions and makes notes if a student wrongly diagnosed the reason for an incorrect reply. The lecturer is given an analysis and can take appropriate action if this is thought to be necessary. The students receive their answer sheets back. Belbin, R. and Belbin, R.M. (1972) *Problems in Adult Retraining*, Heinemann, London. For a recent review of developments in self-assessment in higher education, see Heywood, *Assessment* (note 25).

22. Murray, Thesis (note 26).

23. Bailey, J. (1984) The best of both worlds, *Industrial Society*, pp. 10–13.

24. Newman, N. (1980) The joint industry solution, *Management Today*, April, pp. 60–5.

25. Tse, K.K. (1985) *Marks and Spencer. Anatomy of Britain's Most Efficiently Managed Company*, Pergamon Press, Oxford.

6
INSTITUTIONS AS LEARNING SYSTEMS

Introduction

There are increasing trends in participative work at all levels, and legislation is being introduced to increase the information provided to workers. For participation to be successful, investors will need to understand the factors that cause the life and death of organizations, and both managers and workers will need a better comprehension of how wealth is created. The framework of such an understanding should be laid in school, otherwise it may never be obtained. In this chapter an organization is viewed as a learning system. Manufacturing enterprises have to work at the frontiers of manufacturing technology if they are to survive. It is because of this that they differ from academic institutions, although the same pressures for survival have caused some universities in England to become much more oriented towards the needs of industry.[1] Successful organizations are likely to spend a great deal of money on research and development but most of it will be concentrated on product innovation that takes place in small steps rather than from the results of basic research. The purpose of research is both to understand and to change the limits.[2] Industries die if they fail to adapt to the market. Moreover, beliefs about the market influence behaviour throughout the organization, as do beliefs about worker behaviour. Small groups may be organized in such a way that they are either 'open' or 'closed' to learning, and therefore to adaptability. The particular approach of quality circles used in Japan is described. It is argued that the same principles apply to the inhibition and enhancement of learning in the classroom.

Participation at Work and in Management

Since the mid-1970s, there has been considerable discussion about worker's roles in management in both industry and commerce.[3] This has gone under the name of 'participation', which is somewhat unfortunate since – as the previous chapter suggests – there are a variety of levels of 'participation'. The cell techniques of production are a method for increasing involvement in the job and 'participation' in the determinants of the job that one has to do. The idea of the Japanese quality circle, which has swept through education and industry in the USA, is a method of participation in which all the workers in a small unit of the organization find and solve problems related to that unit. Participation is more generally taken to mean management of the company. There have been demands from blue-collar workers for an equal influence in management decision, and Pope John XXIII, in an encyclical as early as 1961, supported such demands when he wrote that 'the present demand for workers to have a greater say in the conduct of the firm accords not only with man's nature, but also with recent progress in the economic, social and political spheres'.[4]

For participation to be effective, it has to be recognized that workers have an intellectual contribution to make and that for this to be achieved they need to have high levels of skill and knowledge. This applies as much to very small organizations as it does to the large. To employ a university undergraduate to advise and to watch customers in a shop for a six-hour period without letting him or her manage the cash desk is to ensure a quick turnover of labour that cannot be in the interests of the shopkeeper.

There is plenty of experience of participation in West Germany, where legislation ensures that companies are organized to allow workers to participate in the major decisions of management. The shareholders meeting elects a supervisory board that includes representatives of both the shareholders and employees. This supervisory board appoints the management board that runs the company. The supervisory board meets quarterly and approves the accounts. The works council meets once a month with the employer. It elects an economics committee, which deals with such things as managers and capital investment as well as with production and sales. The European Economic Commission has proposed legislation for the whole community in respect of the information to be disclosed to workers and of their rights in regard to participation.

British management structures are criticized because, while the board of directors runs the company, and the shareholders have (at least in principle) some say in its management, those who work to produce the profits have no say in its management. This came about because entrepreneurs obtain their funds for development initially from persons willing to invest in their activities (shareholders), who then have the right to elect the board of management. The profits of the enterprise are used to pay these shareholders interest on their investment (see Chapter 7). Beliefs about the potential of a company dictate the price at which these shares can be bought and sold on the stock market. Great confidence in a company usually causes the price of shares to rise. Loss of confidence causes the price of the shares to fall.

All of this happens independently of the worker and shopfloor activity. Yet while many workers may not know what is happening to the shares of their company on the stock market, it is clear that they have a direct interest in these activities since the rise and fall of share prices exerts powerful psychological pressures on the board and thus on company policy. It is equally clear that the shareholders have a strong interest in the performance of the workforce. At the same time, it is widely believed that since the shareholders provided the capital and thus the initial means of acquiring wealth, then they should be the only persons who should have a say in the conduct of the company. Unfortunately, their interests are in the profits and, if they see that money is to be made from the sale of the company, or by re-investment of their monies in another company, then instability may arise. The recent experience of the London and New York stock markets supports this view.

In Britain, 1986 was a climax year to a series of policy changes brought about by a Conservative government. The overall objective was to reduce monopoly, limit restrictive practices and, in consequence, increase competition throughout industry. In 1986, restrictive practices were removed from the stock exchange at the same time as the stock market was computerized. The social structure of the stock market was altered fundamentally.

The year preceding these changes had seen merger activity reach a new peak. Subsequent to the introduction of the 'new' stock exchange, the market was shattered by the Guinness affair. Guinness, an international drinks company, had bought another large drinks company in a fierce takeover battle. It was subsequently found that during the takeover, Guinness (with key persons in its merchant bank and brokers) had kept the price of Guinness shares high by methods that were illegal. The shock of the revelations caused the City to stop and think, and subsequently a bid for the world-famous glass manufacturers, Pilkington, by another large but technically unrelated company failed. Since then, merger mania has continued. In Europe, the takeovers of the British-owned Rowntree chocolate enterprise by the Swiss owned Nestlé and the Rover Car Company by British Aerospace have brought home to industrialists that the 1992 changes in the European Economic Community will have a powerful influence on industry, which could be for the better or for the worse. It has heightened the debate about the interests of industry as opposed to the interests of the financial institutions in mergers.

Mergers provide a test of shareholder understanding and commitment. Given that they may, and often do, choose to support companies that will strip the assets, which might be badly needed in a country, and, given that the 25 best industrial performers (which also happen to be the giants) have been badly supported by the stock market,[5] it is not surprising that workers should be suspicious of merger deals in which they have no say. All the evidence supports the view that the stock market is not influenced by advances on return in capital since, although at relatively high levels, the real share price of the industrial giants declined. Growth in sales rather than efficiency in the employment of capital is frequently the stock market's indicator of success. Because shareholders have so little commitment to companies, there can be irresponsibility in respect of long-term national development. So it is that there are political groupings who believe that industrial and commercial activities should be closely controlled by government. In these circumstances, it is not surprising that they should not receive the support of the workers or that the theory of merger benefits should be unacceptable. And in

Britain, the confused policy relating to mergers re-inforces such views.[6]

The position is no different in the USA. The anti-merger group has now found a major ally in Lee Iacocca. In a recent book, *Talking Straight*,[7] this controversial industrialist, who saved the Chrysler motor company from bankruptcy, describes how the projected takeovers of US Steel and the Goodyear tyre company worried him because they were Chrysler's biggest companies. Iacocca argues that the effect of the Reagan administration's *laissez-faire* attitude was to bury American anti-trust legislation. In so doing, it made an environment in which corporate raiders thrived. The myth they create in the financial market is that they are doing the company a good turn. Iacocca describes how Sir James Goldsmith told the boss of Goodyear, Robert Mercer, that the company's assets were under-performing and undervalued. He would change that by giving a different direction to the company. Iacocca quotes Mercer as follows:

> He thought that our aerospace division was a recent diversification. But we'd been in that business since 1911. He didn't understand what we were doing in chemicals. Yet the chemical business supplies synthetic rubber and other chemicals so that we can manufacture rubber products across a vast spectrum.
> He then questioned our involvement in the energy business not realising that there are seven gallons of oil in each passenger tyre we produce.[8]

Iacocca asks us to imagine what it would be like to have a business of that dimension run by someone with so little knowledge of its operations.

To fend off the bid, Goodyear had to take on a debt of $2.6 billion. The raiders made a profit of $93 million. The expenses for the advice given to Goodyear were £50 million. In no way did this raid improve the productive capacity of the company, and it deflected large sums of money away from research and development.

Iacocca's book (in contrast to his first) has been severely criticized as the work of a braggart by Ivan Fallon in his review in *The Sunday Times*. Sir James Goldsmith has replied, also in the same newpaper,[9] and argued that Goodyear had to do what he was proposing. In the terms of the particular issues raised here, there have been many similar criticisms of mergers and asset strippers.

It seems clear that there is a fundamental conflict between the needs of industry and the short-term profits required by the financial institutions. While some large corporations undoubtedly need a shake-up, there is no doubt that they can do it for themselves, as ICI did, if they recognize the limits of present products (see below) and the need always to find new markets. Fortunately, it now seems to be understood that, in some cases, mergers are harmful. They raise questions of social as well as financial responsibility. They can be a substitute for investment, which is risky and takes time. Sometimes they can cause unemployment without a corresponding improvement in efficiency, especially where there is pressure to close parts of a business that are not so profitable. In so far as chief executives and managers are concerned, the fear of mergers may lead to short-term pre-occupations rather than with the strategic planning necessary for research into new products. Companies will not undertake long-term research if they are threatened by takeover, a fact that worried a House of Lords committee in the

UK.[10] Thus there is a need to develop strong long-term commitments between the investors and their companies. To achieve this, boardrooms would have to be recast so that the large shareholders would be directly represented. But their representatives, just as those of the workers, would have to be prepared to operate at a level of detail to which they are presently unaccustomed.[11] As a start much more information is required.

Iacocca believes that existing regulations in the USA are not capable of dealing with the problem. He suggests a limit on the number of junk bonds that can be purchased. This would cut off the most-used supply of money. He also suggests a waiting period of a year before the stockholder receives the privilege of voting. This would cause some measure of commitment. Doubtless much more will be heard of these issues in the coming years.

Information and Participation

There is, therefore, a strong case for participation, and a beginning has been made in the UK through legislation intended to provide better information about institutional affairs. Information is not participation, and it is still possible to omit essential items from the information given. For example, it was shown that only in 12 of 120 pension funds was the actuary's report and the breakdown of investment made available automatically to members.[12] Such information is highly technical and few of the members might understand it in its entirety, but that is no reason for not making it available. More interestingly, it was found that most of the arbitrators on the 1982 list of the Advisory, Conciliation and Arbitration Service felt that extensive disclosure of financial information would make little difference to the award the arbitrator would make.[13] This is understandable given the negative attitudes to participation in Britain by both employers' associations and trade unions, who rejected the proposals of a government committee.

Within nationalized industries in Britain, there have been major attempts at participation as, for example, in the Post Office. This experiment showed fundamental differences between the unions and management to industrial democracy. The nominees of the union appear to have had very little influence on policy because of the hostility of management.[14] This situation was exacerbated by the unions who were unable to challenge management because of lack of knowledge and credibility within the board.

One way to overcome this might be to make the workers shareholders in a way that enables them to share in the profits of the company as, for example, in ICI. In the privatization of State institutions, assets have been transferred to employees on favourable terms. For example, in the 1986 British Telecom sale, limits were put on the number of shares that could be purchased at the time of the sale. This was done to encourage the small shareholder.[15] It has also been argued that the workers' ownership of privatized concerns may go towards compensating them for the rigours of competition,[16] and that such organizations can be successful is illustrated by the privatization into worker-manager ownership of National Carriers from British Rail.

In recent years, profit-sharing has been fostered by changes in taxation. Since the majority of individuals are home-owners, so they should be intellectually able to participate in profit-sharing. It is also argued that profit-sharing introduces an automatic flexibility into the wage system since it creates a closer identity between the goals and interests of the workers and the profit-related performance of the company.[17] One way that has been suggested to link extra pay to performance is that a certain part of an individual's tax should be free but related to work performance. In Britain this idea received the support of Redwood, who had been a member of the Prime Minister's policy unit. Payments of this kind fluctuate with performance, so in times of recession – although pay rates would be reduced – workers would not be laid off except in very exceptional circumstances.

Levels of Involvement and Learning

In the preceding paragraphs, different ways of participation in the management of organizations have been described. They represent different levels of involvement. The more distant the involvement, either of shareholders or workers, the more problems there are for the organization. Since learners learn only what they themselves do, if workers are to involve themselves successfully in a company, they will have to learn much more about how it works. It is from learning that we derive the knowledge with which to wield influence. The purpose of participation should be creative development, and for many this will be uncomfortable. It is unlikely to be accomplished without conflict, but at least such conflict should be purposeful.

From the foregoing it is clear that the divorce between investors, management and workers is great. There is plenty of evidence to suggest a relationship between poor managerial performance and poor earnings among managers.[18] Therefore it would seem that, whereas managers and workers need to understand the factors that create wealth, investors need to understand the factors that lead to the life and death of organizations. This is why the following chapter has been included. It should be, in my view, a requirement that all students acquire such understanding within their schooling. We begin, therefore, with a discussion of the life and death of organizations viewed from the perspective of learning.

The Manufacturing System

A manufacturing enterprise may be organized so as to produce precise specifications for a product that has been designed by someone else. Marks and Spencer obtain their goods from such enterprises. Sometimes companies that undertake tasks of this kind are very small as, for example, the exhaust-manufacturing enterprise mentioned later. Other companies, on the other hand, have the basic idea for the product, develop it, manufacture it, install it and maintain it. This was the case with the aircraft electrical-component firm that was the subject of our investigation.[19] All companies operate in a variety of role systems (see Chapter 3). Among the important systems in this aircraft firm were the idea system and the financial system that supported the idea system. Working in the open system of the market, the company was particularly vulnerable to the whims of government defence policies, and had, therefore, been interested in new-product development. These new products did not fail even though, during our investigation, this department was run down. During our study, the company went through a merger and re-merger as a result of a fundamental re-organization in the parent company. Nevertheless, it met many criteria for excellence suggested by such authors as Peters and Waterman.[20] Its major problem was, and is, the need to survive in a changing market that has seen, in particular, a considerable reduction in defence contracts. Our purpose here, therefore, is to consider its idea system.

The Organization as a Learning System

The S-curve is a learning curve and it describes the effort put in to improving a product or process, and the results the company obtains from that investment (see Figure 6.1, curve (a)). It will be seen that this curve parallels my learning curve of

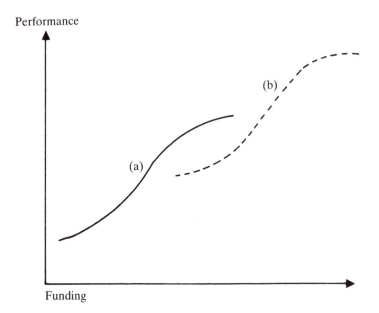

Figure 6.1   Richard Foster's S-curve is also a learning curve of the development of a technological product. Curve (a) may be compared to curve (a) in Figure 6.2. Curve (b) may be compared to (d) in Figure 6.2, and finally with (e) in Figure 6.2. The important difference between the two in Foster's model is the relationship between increasing/continuing investment in a technology and its performance

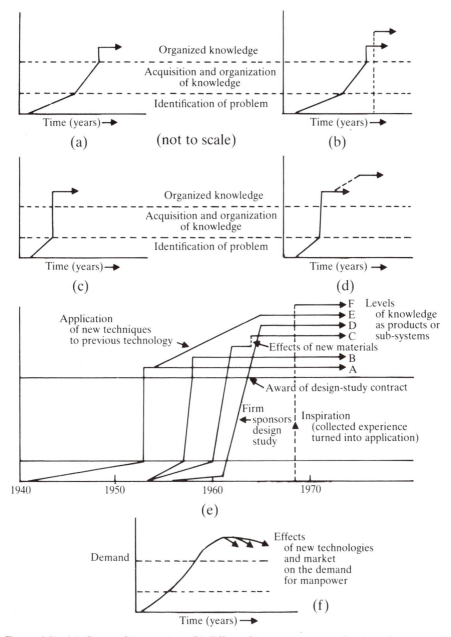

Figure 6.2   (a) Curve of innovation; (b) Effect of instantaneous application of organized knowledge; (c) Acquisition of knowledge by patent; (d) Application of new materials, devices or techniques to present technology; (e) The pattern of innovation in the company of this study (approximately to scale); (f) Illustration of rate of change of demand for manpower as a function of the learning/innovation curve (Source: International Journal of Electrical Engineering Education, *Vol. 12, p. 229)*

innovation (Figure 6.2(a)), and that each new adaptation (Figure 6.2(e)) represents an additional cost. In Foster's model, a new-product process starts a new S curve (Figure 6.1, and curve (b)) and in this respect Foster's model adds an important dimension to mine. Figure 6.2 shows that from the acquisition of an idea the company goes through the same processes of learning as individuals, except that the phases take place over a long period of time.

We have shown how the problem was formulated, and how the information collected by the purchase of a licence from the USA led to the quick structuring of knowledge.[21] We have also shown how the demand for particular kinds of knowledge, and therefore personnel, changed as the problem-solving cycle progressed. Those engineers capable of innovation were not necessarily effective in tasks related to the care and maintenance of the product within the market. The demand for manpower relates to the stages of the problem-solving.[22] The progress of the cycle is from relatively unstructured knowledge to the highly structured knowledge associated with the finished product. There is continuing feedback from the market, and the product is adapted to meet the needs of the market, which in turn is influenced by changing technology. It is the equivalent of the literature search in post-graduate research. Adaptation involves skills in the formulation of alternatives and the evaluation of their effectiveness. Relatively simple changes in design or hypotheses in research can bring about substantial changes in the system or plan of action for research. Because much engineering is visible it is possible for the experienced but unqualified person to make suggestions for change that can have a profound effect on future development. This poses a dilemma for the professional trained as a scientist, for it brings him or her into conflict with the art of engineering. It is for this reason, among others, that training in perceptual learning is so important. Adaptation to the new knowledge demands substantial re-learning on the part of individual engineers and craftworkers.

Given that the more experienced we are with learning, and hence the greater our adaptability, it follows from research on adult learning[23] that schools have an essential role to play in the development of attitudes associated with adaptability and flexibility. Adults who had some knowledge of learning how to learn, learnt more easily than those who had no such knowledge. This means that it is important that every individual should have a knowledge of learning before they leave school, and understand how learning influences adaptability and is, in turn, influenced by the environment. Just as the significance of perceptual learning (Chapter 3) is emphasized, so are the techniques of instruction for these. Other investigations have shown that instructional strategies are important, and discovery learning has been successfully used in training and retraining.[24]

It is a striking feature of the profiles and assessment schedules being used for the evaluation of student performance in school that none of them indicate if a student understands what learning is and what it is to learn. It is the components of the process that are assessed. How we learn remains one of the best-kept secrets of the educational system, yet if we do not broach these problems, how can individuals expect to adapt? So it is that educationalists have to be as much concerned with the

Table 6.1 Partial derivation of a taxonomy of work behaviour derived from typical industrial situations in which managers and workers were in confrontation due to W. Humble. (*Source*: Heywood, J. (1989) *Assessment in Higher Education,* Wiley, Chichester.)

Ability to adapt

The ability

- to perceive the organizational structure, its formal and informal relationships, its social and technical systems, its value systems and languages;
- to understand the technical, human and financial aspects of the system or situation;
- to perceive the different thought processes involved in the solution of human and technological problems;
- to reflect on one's own (self) attitudes and needs in terms of the actions required to obtain goals that keep the organization alive; and so on.

Ability to control

The ability

- to know the key areas of management;
- to understand how skills should be organized for use;
- to understand his or her own knowledge requirements in relation to his or her needs for communication, competence and excellence;
- to understand a situation and know (1) what people ought to be doing, (2) whether they are doing it effectively, (3) what climate needs to be created to get the job done effectively;
- to get action;
- to discriminate between relevant and irrelevant information; and so on.

Ability to relate to people

The ability

- to understand the rights, responsibilities and obligations of those involved in the activity;
- to understand and to predict the effect of his or her behaviour on a situation;
- to evaluate his or her actions;
- to understand the attitudes and values of people in all parts of the organization;
- to create the feeling that the job is important; and so on.

---

domain of action and emotion (affective) as they are with the cognitive, as the outline taxonomy relating to adaptability and control shows (see Table 6.1). This is why there is so much interest in experiential learning.

The Market and Research and Development

The market is a major stimulus to learning, and thus the main cause of adaptation. There is no substantive evidence to suggest that the situation now is any different from that in the Industrial Revolution. One or two significant inventions among thousands of other inventions made in the eighteenth and nineteenth centuries were the key to future developments. Similarly in this century, one or two inventions, such as the silicon chip, have caused major changes of direction. Once the direction is established, the process is of development in small steps. During the history of the aircraft-component companies, there were only one or two innovations that could be said to have had a dramatic overnight influence. During the Industrial Revolution, the key innovations greatly increased the rate of change, but it was over a fairly lengthy period. So it is at the present time: the chip has revolutionized the computer industry and, in its turn, it is beginning to influence every home. At the same time invention and innovation, for the most part, still follow the same pattern, in which there is a long time delay between the innovation and its practical implementation.[25] This view is supported by the fact that in America, where a ready response to innovation is expected by the 'foreigner', journalists writing about the American response to robotics take an opposite view and suggest that the US strategy is – 'conservative' and under-capitalized – more especially when it is compared with that of Japan. Invention continues to be, as it was in the Industrial Revolution,[26] primarily a response to economic demand, and that is why so many inventions fail, in particular, some that are science based. The microcomputer industry mirrors the situation found in the Industrial Revolution in that there are many new entrants to the field but few survivors. It is different in the sense that the multinationals have a command of the economy of a kind that was not available in the eighteenth and nineteenth centuries. They are the inheritors of that revolution and their command is the international market in which Japan is now emerging as the major force in a great many sections of manufacturing activity. The kind of markets in which the British now have to compete is quite different from those they built in the Industrial Revolution. Yet, as the Japanese have so often shown, it is possible to obtain a major hold in markets where American technology had the lead as, for example, in high-capacity semi-conductor memories.

The investigation in the aircraft-component company also threw some light on the nature of research and development in the company. It is often argued that companies do not do enough 'R' and 'D', and it seems that the 'R' is about pure science and its potential for application.[27] This investigation illustrated certain key differences between academic and industrial research. An industrial organization does not, by and large, work at the frontiers of 'truth' (pure knowledge). Its purpose is the achievement of business aims. Industrial organizations do, however, work at frontiers of manufacturing technology. We tend to understand by research, backroom work at the frontiers of pure knowledge. It is evident, however, that that is not the kind of research that creates wealth in the short run. Japan's five major electrical manufacturers spend around £860 million a year on R and D and employ 28,000 people, yet only 4.4 per cent of this money is spent on basic research. Their R and D is geared to product innovation.[28] As more than one writer has said, they have an ability that ought to be copied in England. And that is quite simply 'to copy' or 'borrow' and produce at the right price for the market!

The Death of Industries

There is, in the high-technology business, much coming and going. Companies are born while others die. Some survive for a long time, others die almost immediately, and this depends on the rather trite axiom of having the right product at the right time. The skill of the entrepreneur is to ensure that his or her product meets those requirements. In this respect it is of no passing interest to consider what makes for success in the fashion and cosmetic industries, for it is a market requirement that they should change, and both respond to and generate new fashions. We shall return to this theme again and again in the chapters that follow.

During the last decade, we have seen severe challenges to the American car manufacturers and the decline of both the coal and the steel industries in Europe and the USA. These in particular have been the victims of substitution as the plastics industry has grown, as well as by competition from cheaper products from abroad, and especially the Far East in respect of steel.[29] The more general effects upon the rational economics of unemployment and social conditions thereby created are profound and, as we shall see, the difficulties in making adjustments to such large changes are considerable. Such changes affect all countries, and Japan is no exception. In an attempt to reduce its railway workforce by 120,000 it has also been faced with industrial unrest, so the Soviets are happy to report![30] Having said that, there would seem to be no escape from the view that the response to changes in western markets to Japanese entry has been slow. Thus, from the behavioural research point of view, the outcome of the American response to Japanese intervention in semi-conductor production will be of considerable interest.

Sometimes companies allow their experience to direct their activities. Companies tend to learn a particular point of view. Kolb investigated an organization faced with change, where he found that the engineers were unable to deal with major organizational problems. What had been the organization's strength, its engineering expertise, had become its weakness. Because engineering had flourished at the expense of the development of such other organizational functions as marketing and the management of human resources, the company was struggling with, rather than mastering, its environment, and finding competition difficult.[31] This supports the view that companies need to understand that they have to learn continually.

In a British response to maintain learning, the Department of Industry has encouraged joint ventures between English and Japanese companies. Trevor asked, if it is a fact that the competitive edge of Japanese companies is so strong in certain fields, is it futile to talk of trying to catch up? His answer was clearly 'No', although he thought much needed to be done. The companies he investigated had weaknesses of either a technological or financial nature (with the exception of one). Any company that is weak can be exploited by any other organization, let alone the Japanese. In a novel use of the terms 'hardware' (machinery, technology and products) and 'software' (the organization of production by management), Trevor concluded that when the Japanese went abroad they looked at all aspects of the productive system in that country and took the ideas back to Japan. It did not matter where it came from or if, in the situation in which they appraised it, it worked. What mattered was whether they could use the idea to become more competitive. They continue to be on the look-out for ideas that will make them more competitive. If this is what the writer to *The Times* meant when he suggested that the British should copy, then it is clearly a game that anyone can play. However, Trevor's major point is that the Japanese do not develop their 'hardware' and 'software' separately. The failure in Britain, and in the USA, has been to bring the two sides together and, in support of this thesis, he drew attention to the fact that the two successful British companies among those he investigated were those who had adopted Japanese industrial knowledge and put it to their use.[32]

Both large and small industries in Britain failed to learn in the market and therefore to adapt. They did not change their goals and, as Jay has pointed out, this led to the demise of the cotton industry, for the perception that an industry has of its goals dictates its actions:

'We spin and weave cotton' was their dominant thought, and all ideas had to spring from there – they had to be ideas for selling the cotton the factories were producing. But, 'We spin and weave cotton' is a statement produced by looking inwards . . . If they had looked outward, at their market, they would have come up with a different statement, namely 'People wear clothes'. In that case they would have been integrating with knitted goods and man-made fibres from the start, instead of desperately diversifying into brick-making and cake shops at the finish.'[33]

The financial director of Unilever, speaking to the Confederation of Irish Industries, asked why Irish industry continued to concentrate investment on the ever-more efficient production of low-margin commodities, of which there is a surplus, at the expense of product innovation, which would provide the high-margin products consumers want.[34]

Beliefs about the market also have an influence on behaviour in the organization. As we have seen, attitudes towards management and, in turn, of management towards worker, stem in part from the goals of the organization, and in part from views about how people work. This is no better illustrated than by the two electronics departments described in the last chapter. One, the first, had its potential for learning limited by its structure, which was a closed-system. The more successful company was relatively 'open' and encouraged learning through its structures, even if it was not aware that that was what it was doing. Thirty years later, we would talk about how company culture blocks innovation. A survey of British industry found that innovation was rated as no more than fairly important by 48 of 200 directors. Its other findings are little different from those of the Burns and Stalker investigation, also of thirty years ago. The chief factors that hindered or promoted innovation were company culture, staff involvement, market forces, resource allocation, communications and leadership.[35]

It is clear that in responding to their environment, all organizations have to adapt to new circumstances and, as such, develop distinctive learning styles. We shall consider this point again, particularly as it relates to Foster's[36] theories in the last section. Organizations contain within themselves factors that impede change, that interact with managers and workers to produce a resultant opposed to change. One way to tackle this problem is to employ specialist change agents from outside consultants.[37] Another way is to create a learning situation within the company. This is what the Japanese do by means of quality circles.

Japan had a reputation for cheap and nasty copying, which was depriving it of overseas markets. To remedy this defect, a number of major companies decided to promote quality and reliability throughout the workforce by involving the workers themselves in problem-solving and decision-making. To this end they made it possible for their workers to join together in small groups to solve the problems with which they were faced. These groups are quality circles. Of the principles underlying this approach, probably the most significant and most challenging was the idea that these work groups should be voluntary. The other principles of operation are as follows:

1. Most people have the ability to solve a wide range of problems.
2. Only a few of the abilities that people have are used at work.
3. Given the opportunity, individuals will use their talents to solve problems.
4. Given training, individuals will be able to organize their work.
5. Work problems are best solved at the work place.

There is nothing novel about this model of the worker. It is enshrined in McGregor's Theory Y and Maslow's self-actualizing being. What was different was the technique for bringing it about on an almost national front. As defined by Robson, a quality circle is a small group of volunteers who work with the same supervisor and who meet together once a week for an hour to identify, analyse and solve problems related to their own work. It is not done in a haphazard way and training is provided in problem-solving and finding.[38] During training, the participants in the circle are encouraged to win. Everyone is encouraged to win: there are no losers. Everyone is encouraged to enjoy the quality circle, and there is no obligation either to remain a member or for the group to persist.

The circles receive training in organized problem-solving. This meets the dictum that the learner will solve problems better or develop the skills of critical thinking better if he or she understands how problems are solved. In 1960 Saupe listed some steps in critical thinking to meet this goal (Table 6.2).[39] Notice that these are the same as those for decision-making shown in Figures 4.1, 4.2 and 4.3.

Table 6.2   Some steps in the process of critical thinking (after J. Saupe, in *Evaluation in Higher Education* (1961) Houghton Mifflin, Boston, Mass., 34)

1. Ability to recognize the existence of a problem.

2. Ability to define a problem.

3. Ability to select information pertinent to the problem.

4. Ability to recognize assumptions bearing on the problem.

5. Ability to make relevant hypotheses.

6. Ability to draw conclusions validly from assumptions, hypotheses and pertinent information.

7. Ability to judge the validity of processes leading to the conclusion.

8. Ability to evaluate a conclusion in terms of its assessment.

It is not surprising to find, therefore, that training is given in brainstorming in quality circles to show the group how to generate ideas. The methods for analysing problems are very similar to the techniques for lateral thinking advocated by de Bono,[40] and others concerned with the development of problem-solving and divergent thinking. There is an important training session on presenting to management, and other sessions on working together, and solving problems that the groups create for themselves. It follows from perceptual-learning theory that the most effective learning systems are those that can tolerate differences of perspective.

Skill Development and Self-Assessment

There is nothing new in all this – education syllabuses are littered with statements of objectives that purport to meet the same goals. For example, Table 6.3 shows a set of skills we would expect undergraduates to develop while in university, yet they were designed to meet the requirements of history, social and environmental studies for pupils in the age group 8–13. Why isn't it that, in these circumstances where much is apparently done to foster such skills, they are not developed? It has been argued that students in US colleges rarely reach high levels of critical thought because they are not trained to do so: the lecture and tutorial methods that prevail are geared to the giving and receiving of knowledge.[41] In England and Ireland it has been shown that, unless there is a direct link between the objective, the assessment procedure used and the instructional strategy, it is unlikely that the objective will be obtained. Thus it is that most statements of objectives have no influence on teaching and learning since a systems approach is not used to bring them about (Figure 6.3(a)).[42] The same can be said of the management-by-objectives approach, which was commonplace in industry during the 1960s (Figure 6.3 (b)).[43] Both required the active participation of the learners for success. And this view is supported by Kolb, who from a different analysis of organizations concluded that 'learning should be an explicit objective pursued as

Table 6.3   Abilities to be developed in history, geography and social studies (Schools Council Project, 8–13. Reproduced by kind permission of W.A.L. Blyth. See Blyth, W.A.L. (1973) *Place, Time and Society 8–13*, Collins, Bristol, for a description of the project)

The ability to:

1. *find* information through reading, listening, observing;

2. *understand* and *interpret* pictures, charts, graphs, maps, etc.;

3. *organize* information through concepts and generalizations;

4. *communicate* findings through an appropriate medium, e.g. orally, graphically, pictorially or in writing;

5. *evaluate* information; and

6. *test* hypotheses and generalizations, and *question* the adequacy of classifications.

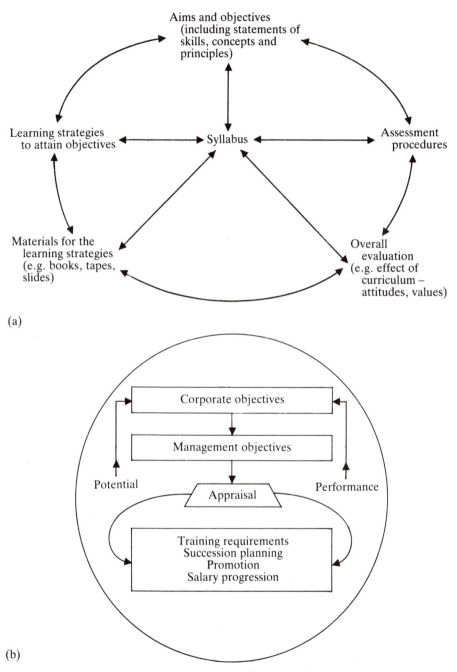

(a)

(b)

Figure 6.3 A simplified model of the relation between aims, objectives, assessment, evaluation, learning strategies and syllabus to be compared with the model for management by objectives in Figure 6.3(b) which is based on Turner, B.T. (1969) Management Training for Engineers, *Business Books, London*

consciously and deliberately as profit or productivity' by managers.[44] Moreover, he argued that managers should set aside time to critique and learn from important meetings and decisions. Self-assessment is something managers, teachers and students are rarely trained to do, although, as we have seen, there is increasing interest in this aspect of learning.

Self-assessment requires the development of the skill of self-reflection.[45] In this respect it is of more than passing interest to note that Heirs is of the opinion that the major factor that contributes to good management is the way in which managers think, not during decision-making, but before decisions are made.[46] Managers must be thinkers not doers. They have the task of managing a 'thinking team'. This is entirely consistent with the view that in participative organizations, everyone is a learner, for learning and decision-making are but different aspects of the same mental process. What differentiates individuals one from another is the ability to act on their learning.

Nowhere is self-assessment more essential than in a matrix organization, for objectives and accountabilities have to be established for both individuals and the team. In their turn these individuals of differing opinions and backgrounds have to learn to communicate and to work with each other. Thus it is that individuals need skills in debate and sensitivity towards others to accept that competence and knowledge should be the cause of decisions, and to accept that a team is more than a group of individuals.

If education is about preparation for life and work, then formalized group work of the kind undertaken in quality circles needs to be part of the everyday curriculum. Because such groups are small in number they will necessitate more resources. Any effort in this direction will, however, be largely wasted if it is not accompanied by substantial changes in management and teaching practice. For Heller and Wilpert showed, even the long-term viability of changes in job design is also doubtful, even when workers are allowed to participate in them, if 'they are not matched by congruent beliefs and practices at the policy-making levels in the apex of the organisational pyramid.'[47]

Retrospect and Prospect

(Chapters 1–6, 7–10 and 11–12.)

In this chapter I have used an investigation I and some colleagues made of a component manufacturer in the aircraft industry to describe organizations as learning systems. My model shows that innovations and organizations go through the same phases of learning as we do when we are problem-solving and decision-making. There is no difference in the process – both are goal-seeking endeavours. The model also shows how progress is generally made by a continuous flow of small adaptations. The same was true of developments in the Industrial Revolution.

I have shown elsewhere how such curves can be used to predict the type of workforce an organization is likely to need, and have used it to explain the difference between official workforce forecasts in the UK and actuality.[48] The model also shows what happens to the organization when a sudden discontinuity, such as a new invention, is introduced. In effect it starts a new curve of learning for those immediately involved, and probably for the whole organization.

In Chapter 2 I drew attention to the effects of experience on learning, and that ultimately experience could inhibit innovation. The examples given in support of this view came from the studies we made of this company. Discontinuities are important because they provide that *'choc des opinions'* that is so necessary a stimulant to new learning by anyone or any organization. I have also tried to throw some light on the difference between pure research and the kind of research required in industry, but I have not followed this through to suggest that the key difference is one of attitude.

From studies of many organizations, Richard Foster, a director with McKinsey's, the consultants, has shown how these learning curves have practical significance in business forecasting. He argues that successful companies are successful because they understand the dynamics of competition. The three ideas he advances to explain these dynamics are the S-curve, the attacker's advantage and discontinuities.[49]

The S-curve is a learning curve that describes the effort put into improving a product or process, and the results the company obtains from that investment (Figure 6.1). Thus in my curve, each new adaptation represents an additional cost (Figure 6.2). Foster shows that during the first phase of innovation, a great deal of money has to be invested for little apparent return. As knowledge is structured, investment has to be increased substantially, and at the top of the curve more and more is put in for less and less return. As Richard Foster puts it, 'Ships don't sail much faster, cash registers don't work much better, and clothes don't get much cleaner'.[50] He supports this thesis with many brief case studies, as he does the other two concepts – the attacker's advantage and discontinuities.

It is a characteristic of many companies that they continue to invest when they are at the limits of what is possible with a particular technology. When they are persisting with investment for little return, they are at the mercy of competitors, or as they are more appropriately called by Foster, attackers. These attackers will be looking at alternative technologies using a different knowledge base. Foster calls the period of change from one group of products or processes to another with a new knowledge base, a 'discontinuity'. The new product or process starts a new S-curve.

Foster argues that if companies are to survive attacks they must recognize the limits of the particular technology they are using. Thus a major role for the application of science in technology is the prediction of the limits of the particular technology in use. In this way, companies will learn to develop new knowledge bases earlier. This is an important facet of technological literacy.

If this is related to the problem of merger mania, it will be seen that social responsibility requires that all those who own companies should be technologically literate. Simply put, this means, to quote Foster, that

> Top management has to develop a language and a facility for talking about and directing technology. We don't hear about technology in the board room, except for some

progress reports that we pretend to understand or criticise, because we don't have a language or conceptual framework for managing technology. There have been several theories proposed to help management 'link' technology with the market by charting a company's strength in a particular technology against its market potential, but the link is often only visual and superficial. Indeed there is no understanding of the linkage.[51]

Foster's purpose was to establish a linkage and language for management in an era of discontinuity.

Because they lack the language and the right questions, they can't answer the beg questions: How much trouble is my company really in? Does this new product or process represent a real threat? What is the long term verdict? In the middle of the competitive battle when there is smoke on the field and people and products are falling over that is what they need to know.[52]

Prospects

' "Read me and get rich", "Read me and know the future". Who could possibly resist the siren calls of the business writers?' so writes Likierman at the beginning of a review that covers a number of such publications.[53] The fact is they make a good read and presumably reinforce the beliefs of some executives and niggle others. Perhaps even a few take them to heart and try to do something about their own situation. Likierman makes similar points – 'Each [he says] will provide some insights, each will give some food for thought'.[54] Yet, we look for action, so where is the hope for action?

Likierman reminds us that most of the books are American, and that only some American experience translates to our culture. He also says that what is good for someone running a small-service business will be irrelevant to a middle manager in ICI, and vice versa. This I believe is open to question. So much of my own work in learning subjects shows that it is differences in content that cloud the communality of first principles. Managers search for their identity in culture and in so doing limit their flexibility. Common to many reports from either side of the Atlantic is the view that the educational system should be helping students of all levels of achievement to become adaptable.

One of the major roles education has played since the end of the Second World War is the reinforcement of articulation. British youngsters are becoming much more like Americans in their articulacy, notwithstanding the level of their intelligence. They make demands, they believe they can think and as education continues to develop their thinking powers, so they are likely to make increasing demands on society and their employees. Thus it is that over a long period of time we may anticipate that every level of business style management will be expected to be more participatory. Since every job, however small, contains within it the skills of management (Chapter 5) there is a base on which to build. But that construction has to begin early, for if participative management is to be successful, both workers and management have to have common goals. Such goals are not merely economic and financial but embrace the wider society in which we live.

The trouble with many management theories is that they have concentrated on the interaction between the individual and organizational structure at the expense of any formal study of industry and wealth creators, or of the way individuals and organization interact with the wider society of which they are sub-systems. It cannot be expected that management and workers come together to pursue common goals unless the values they have are shared by the wider society, for organizations respond to rather than create the value systems within which they operate. Thus for participation, workers, management and owners have to have a shared view of the social role of the organization in the economy, which means that a *sine qua non* of their knowledge base must be an appreciation of the different approaches to the political economy. It is within this context that they must come to a view about the role of the organization in wealth creation and thus of profits.

The chapters that follow consider these issues. Chapter 7 is concerned with wealth creation and the role of profits in the development of an organization. Chapter 8 is concerned with those practices within organizations, and more generally in society that impede the effectiveness of organizations and societies to achieve their goals. It is, therefore, concerned as much with the professions as it is with trade unions. Chapter 9 is concerned with how the values in society, or what has above been called culture, create the environment in which organizations work. This is extended in Chapter 10, which considers the problem of unemployment and relates to the economic debate that has pursued politicians since the end of the Second World War.

Chapters 11 and 12, which conclude the book, return to the issues of leadership and education. Those readers who consider the book to be in two parts might like to read Chapter 11 at this stage.

Notes and References

1. *The Times* (1985) Special report on the university of Salford, pp. 15–19, 27 June.
2. Foster, R. (1986) *Innovation: The Attacker's Advantage,* Macmillan, London.
3. Bell, D.W. (1979) *Industrial Participation*, Pitman, London; Heller, F.A. and Wilpert, B. (1981) *Competence and Power in Managerial Decision Making,* Wiley, Chichester; and Wall, T.D. and Lischeron, J.A. (1977) *Worker Participation: A Critique of the Literature and Some Fresh Evidence*, McGraw-Hill, Maidenhead.
4. Pope John XXIII (1961) *Mater et Magistra*, Catholic Truth Society, London.
5. Luffman, G. and Reed, R. (1984) *The Strategy and Performance of British Industry, 1970–1980*, Macmillan, London.
6. Merger acquisitions should shake up enterprises in which the assets are under-priced and under-utilized, and improve management that is incompetent. At the same time, the activities of speculators and investors during the takeover battle put a price on the company. In theory the activity in the market should put a price on the organization involved which reflects its usefulness as a resource. An efficient-merger should lead so the argument goes to a more efficient allocation of resources (financial in the first place) throughout the economy. Unfortunately, 1986 showed that prices in takeover battles were the subject of 'dirty tricks'. Many of the deals ignored the code of conduct and this has led to calls for legislation to prevent conflicts between professional conduct on the part of advisers and the desire to make easy money. A new word came on the scene from the USA: Arbitrageur. It was associated with Ivan Boesky, and it is suggested that arbitrageurs created complex networks of disinformation. By creating unfounded rumours about takeover bids, arbitrageurs can manipulate share prices to their own ends. A company that has a number of divisions and whose shares are liquid is open to this kind of manipulation. It is hoped

that there will be a return to the state of affairs where a merger will be made on its merits rather than on wheeling and dealing.

One of the difficulties in Britain is that policy in respect of mergers is very much dependent on the political party in power. Moreover, those policies may not always be clear. For example, it is held that for research to be done effectively in the electronics industry, firms need to be large. For example, General Electric (GE) in America sells £24.1 billion per annum, Hitachi £16.1 billion, Philips £13.1 billion and GEC in England £5.8 billion. Yet in England, GEC was refused permission to make a takeover bid for another English electrical giant, Plessey, in 1986. This means that Britain does not have a large electrical enterprise.

One reason for the opposition to the merger was the attitude of the Ministry of Defence. It argued that the merger would reduce competition for defence contracts in Britain. It was also argued that GEC was the product of mergers that, at the time, were beneficial but that recently it had managed its research and innovation badly. It had failed to compete with Boeing in the development of early-warning aircraft. GEC had also created a cash mountain that it had not used (£1.7 billion) and that was not being used to create new technology.

At the beginning of 1989, GEC – together with Germany's largest firm, Siemens – made a joint bid for Plessey. In return, a consortium involving Plessey sought to purchase GEC with a view to breaking it up into parts. But it failed. At the same time, the GEC/Siemens inquiry was referred to the Monopolies and Mergers Commission which in turn proposed that the merger should be allowed subject to certain restrictions (20 April 1989).

It should be noted that any break up of GEC would have had profound implications for the level of employment in the regions.

7.   Iacocca, L. (1988) *Talking Straight*, Sidgwick & Jackson, London.
8.   *Ibid.*
9.   Goldsmith, Sir J. (1988) *The Sunday Times,*
10. House of Lords *Committee Report on Public Support for Research, The Times,* 8 Jan. 1987. Among other things it was proposed that companies should be required to disclose their research expenditures in their annual accounts.
11. There was virtually no day free of discussion of these matters in the business columns of *The Times* between October 1986 and February 1987.
12. Schuller, T. and Hyman, F. (1983) Information participation and pensions: strategy and employee related issues, *Personnel Reviews,* Vol. 12, no. 3, pp. 26–30.
13. Towers, B. and Wright, M. (1983) The disclosure of financial information in pay references at arbitration. Survey, discussion and conclusions, *Industrial Relations Journal,* Vol. 14, no. 4, pp. 83–91.
14. Batstone, E., Ferner, A. and Terry, M. (1983) *Unions on the Board,* Blackwell, Oxford.
15. Brittan, S. (1984) The politics and economics of privatisation, *Political Quarterly,* April/June.
16. Peacock, S. (1984) 'Privatisation in perspective' *Three Banks Review,* Vol. 144, pp. 3–25.
17. Weitzman, M. (1984) *The Share Economy,* Harvard University Press, Cambridge, Mass.
18. Crockett, G. and Elias, P. (1984) British managers; a study of their training, mobility and earnings, *British Journal of Industrial Relations,* Vol. 22, no. 1, pp. 34–46.
19. Youngman, M.B., Oxtoby, R., Monk, J.D. and Heywood, J. (1977) *Analyzing Jobs,* Gower, Aldershot.
20. Peters, J. and Waterman, R.H. (1982) *In Search of Excellence, Lessons from America's Best Run Companies,* Harper & Row, New York, NY.
21. Gledhill, J.H. (1966) Recent developments in electric power generation, *English Electric Journal,* Vol. 21, no. 6, p. 35. See also a brief description of the firm in Langrish, J., Gibbons, M., Evans, W.G. and Jevons, F.R. (1972) *Wealth from Knowledge,* Macmillan, London. Their study was carried out before ours when the firm was the special products' group of the English Electric Co.
22. Heywood, J. (1974) Trends in the supply and demand for qualified manpower in the sixties and seventies, *Vocational Aspect of Education,* Vol. 26, no. 64, pp. 65–72.
23. Belbin, R. and Belbin, R.M. (1972) *Problems in Adult Retraining,* Heinemann, London.
24. Jones, S. (1969) *The Design of Instruction,* HMSO, London. Other works, which are much more recent, are given throughout his text.
25. Jewkes, J.D., Stillman, J. and Sawyer, R. (1960) *The Sources of Invention,* Macmillan, London.
26. Lilley, S. (1970) *Technological Progress and the Industrial Revolution,* 'Fontana Economic History of Europe', Fontana, London.
27. During the week ending 21 February 1987, *The Times* carried three major articles on expenditure on research and development. It argued that Britain spent less on R and D than its competitors. The

Prime Minister was asked about this in the House of Commons. She said that the figures were not true. *The Times* disputed this on 21 February. The trouble is the term 'research'. Do companies include product innovation as research expenditure? The demand for more money to do research may lead to expenditure on research that leads to Nobel prizewinners, at which the British are excellent, and not to product innovation.

28. Clarke, C. and Banks, P. (1982) How to tackle Japan, *Management Today*, February, pp. 50–3.
29. Foster, *Innovation* (note 2).
30. Report in the Soviet railway paper, *The Whistle*. See also Chira, S. (1984) Fiscal problems threaten to derail Japan's highly prized train system, *International Herald Tribune*, 29 November.
31. Kolb, D. (1974) (ed.) *Organizational Psychology. A Book of Readings*, (2nd ed.) Chapter on 'Management and the learning process', Prentice-Hall, Englewood Cliffs, NJ.
32. Trevor, M.H. (1985) *Japanese Industrial Knowledge. Can it help British Industry?*, Policy Studies Institute, Gower, Aldershot; and Trevor, M.H. (1983) Japanese approaches to personnel, *Business Graduate*, Vol. 13, no. 3. (special issue on Japanese management and management education).
33. Jay, A. (1967) *Management and Machiavelli,* Penguin Books, Harmondsworth.
34. *The Irish Times* (1988) Editorial, 27 February.
35. Deloitte Haskins & Sells Management Consultants (1988) *Innovation: The Management Challenge for the UK*, PO box 198, Hillgate House, 26 Old Bailey, London. Summarized by G. Golzen in *The Sunday Times*, 24 January, 1988.
36. Foster, *Innovations* (note 2).
37. Bennis, W.G. (1966) Theory and methods in applying behavioural science and organizational change, in J.R. Lawrence (ed.) *Operational Research and the Social Sciences*, Tavistock, London.
38. Robson, M. (1982) *Quality Circles*, Gower, Aldershot. Gower Press markets a complete training practice for quality circles.
39. This list is also discussed in Heywood, J. (1982) *Pitfalls and Planning in Student Teaching*, Kogan Page, London.
40. de Bono, E. (1971) *The Use of Lateral Thinking*, Penguin Books, Harmondsworth.
41. Perry, W. (1968) *Intellectual Development in the College Years*, Holt, Reinhart & Winston, New York, NY.
42. From Heywood, J. (1984) *Considering the Curriculum During Student Teaching,* Kogan Page, London.
43. For a discussion of management by objectives, see Turner, B.T. (1969) *Management Training for Engineers*, Business Books, London. The diagram in Figure 6.3(b) is based on Turner's model.
44. Kolb, *Organizational Psychology* (note 35).
45. Heirs, B. (1987) *The Professional Decision Thinker: Our New Management Priority*, Sidgwick & Jackson, London.
46. *Ibid.*
47. Heller and Wilpert, *Competence and Power* (note 3).
48. Heywood, J. (1974) Trends in the supply and demand for qualified manpower in the sixties and seventies, *The Vocational Aspects of Education*, Vol. 26, No. 64, pp. 65–72.
49. Foster, *Innovations* (note 2).
50. *Ibid.*
51. *Ibid.*
52. *Ibid.*
53. Likierman, A. (1988) Follow your own business guru, *The Sunday Times* 3 April. Reviews: Waterman, R. (1988) *The Renewal Factor*, Bantam Press, London; Peters, T. (1988) *Thriving on Chaos,* Macmillan, London; Drucker, P. (1988) *The Frontiers of Management,* Heinemann, London; Sculley, J. (1988) *Odyssey: Pepsi to Apple*, Collins, London; and Maisonrouge, J. (1988) *Inside IBM*, Collins, London.
54. *Ibid.*

7

WEALTH

Introduction

'No one', writes Garraty, 'wants to settle for less than he now has. This is a human characteristic much strengthened, as I have just indicated, by continuous infla- tion.'[1] Most people wish to be better off than they are now, and there is a strong sentiment among the peoples of the world that governments, in particular, and voluntary agencies more generally, should help those who are worse off. To achieve these goals the western industrialized nations increase their wealth by the continuing creation of capital in relatively free markets. Those in the eastern bloc plan the creation of wealth on the basis of a different economic ideology – the right to a job is more important than the right to freedom.[2]

In this context, wealth is, by definition, the assets of individuals, organizations or a country (limited to their monetary value in the market). If I own a house that will sell on the market at £50,000, then I have an asset that is worth that amount. If I have to pay off a mortgage of £20,000, then I have an asset worth £30,000. For many of us that asset will not be realized until we are dead! Moreover, many of us would regard it as a necessity and not wealth. Our perceptions of wealth vary considerably. Individuals, even house-owners in the lower socio-economic groups, do not, on the whole, perceive themselves to be wealthy. They regard the person with a Rolls-Royce as the wealthy one. Yet in theory in the capitalist world it is open to anyone to enter the market and create wealth. A person might, for example, find it possible to buy wooden or plastic poles and brushes separately, but in sufficient quantity to make it profitable for him or her to join them together and sell them as brooms at a profit. Another person may have a permanent job by day and undertake car maintenance or painting by night. Both these individuals earn additional money with which they can increase their assets. Of course, they have a choice, for they could spend it on a holiday, or they may have to spend it on medical fees. In neither of these cases do they increase their assets. Nevertheless, in undertaking the basic tasks of making and selling they are demonstrating skills of entrepreneurship. In most cases, however, the asset – creating ideas – will demand more money than the entrepreneur has, as well as a more sophisticated market. It is with the cycle of entrepreneurship that this chapter is concerned.

The Entrepreneurs: Raising Funds

Entrepreneurs have many characteristics that distinguish them from other individuals,[3] among which is the ability to raise money and sell ideas or products. Some entrepreneurs have high stakes, and some low. In the USA, those with proven managerial and engineering skills have higher stakes than shopkeepers, craftworkers, estate agents and insurance brokers, as measured by their ability to attract funds. The higher-status groups could attract 'venture capital' involving very large sums, whereas the smaller enterprises found it more difficult to raise funds.[4] Both high- and low-status entrepreneurs experience similar difficulties in attacting funds, especially venture monies, and for the same reasons.[5]

Rejuvenating Enterprises: Buy-Outs

Apart from the financing of new enterprises, many enterprises need additional funds and some of these may be in difficulty. An approach that now finds some favour in the finance world to the redevelopment of enterprises is the purchase of an organization by its employers (buy-outs). The members of an organization may club together to purchase their company, if they can raise the capital. By 1988 buy-outs in the UK had passed the £3 billion mark in a period of six years.

A major goal of the privatization of State organizations, such as British Airways and British Gas in Britain, was to encourage employees either to purchase shares in the organization, or to buy the organization as a going concern.[6] In consequence, there were several successful ventures of which the National Freight Corporation is perhaps the best known. There continues to be interest among employees in buy-outs. However, it is, as Oakeshott points out, non-quoted companies and in the peripheral subsidiaries of quoted companies that the best chances of extending employee ownership exist.[7] A novel approach to employee ownership was adopted by a well-known form of domestic gas-heating appliance manufacturers, Baxendale, who put the share holding in an employee trust. It is expected that there will be a modest growth in employee ownership in the future. Such developments are sufficient justification for the inclusion of studies in entrepreneurship in the school curriculum, which provide both for a limited experience of actual entrepreneurship, and an understanding of the way companies work in the market.[8] School projects very often, like ordinary companies, put the emphasis on the product rather than the market. They cannot be expected to produce entrepreneurs.

The Product, the Market and Survival

One of the problems of the mini-companies that are now a familiar activity in schools, is that sometimes their products have little reality in terms of a market.

Given that the students are learning the skills of entrepreneurship, this may be permitted so long as they understand the needs of the market and recognize that, in the real world, family and friends will not so readily come to their aid. They also lack the competition the market gives and this, as Foster shows, is the key to developing skills.[9]

Many more inventions are made than ever survive the rigours of the market. This was as true of the Industrial Revolution as it is of the small-computer market today.[10] This failure to survive is very often due to a lack of appreciation of the market. An inventor, or for that matter a writer, may have a product or book which to him or her is perfect. However, he or she may not be able to persuade a manufacturer or a publisher to take up his or her product. His or her perceptions of the market, and the perceptions of those who deal in the market, are different. Many entrepreneurs in Britain and the USA do not appraise the market potential of their products and, in consequence, 'come up with a product rather than a business'.[11] Thus it is that we are concerned with the creation of a business in this chapter.

A business orientation demands that the sales of the product will support the overheads and business needs both now and in the future. A technically beautiful product may not be what the market needs. The popular and academic literature is full of stories of American and British firms in which superior technical ability leads to excessive product orientation at the expense of market considerations.[12]

The attitude that needs to be developed is one of 'service', and this is but a simple development of the notion of the manager as servant discussed in previous chapters. It is an inherent part of Japanese business philosophy. In providing a service to the customers, the Japanese also believe they provide a service to society.[13]

Thus, at the beginning of the learning curve of innovation, the entrepreneur needs to establish the market potential of the product or idea, and this will include its size and growth, and the ability of the entrepreneur to provide a continuing 'service'. In doing this the entrepreneur must establish the areas of risk and estimate the potential reasons for success and failure in the market.

The Areas of Risk

All areas of the market are a risk, since they are all open to competition. It is important, therefore, that the entrepreneur understands exactly what he or she intends to do in the market. It does not matter whether it is an idea for a service, patent, licence or artefact, it will either be in competition or create competition in the market. The key appraisal that has to be made relates to the ability of the product to take a competitive advantage over other products.

There are, for example, considerable risks in taking a new product to the world market. The Sinclair electric car did not find a place in the market, except as a fun vehicle for which there was no demand. Concorde, the faster-than-sound aircraft, did not meet market requirements. It was too small and the number of seats had to be adjusted as a function of payload. It was also ahead of its time. Sometimes it pays to be second, even when entering a section of the world market with a new product. Philips, the Dutch electrical giant, introduced the filter-coffee machine into Japan and within a year they were competing with every major Japanese manufacturer only to find themselves with only a third of the market. Subsequently, the Japanese machines made their way to the western world where they are now in most retailers. The more simple a product and the more success it has, the more likely it is to attract new entrants to the market. High-technology software is just such an example.

An entrepreneur has to appreciate the pitfalls of cost-cutting when a device or idea is introduced in direct competition with a similar product, for the entrepreneur may not produce an item that is marketable. In the small-computer market, some cheaper models, which exploited the same functionality of the brand models, often did not contain those features that would add to their value in the market.[14] In general, it is likely to be a mix of factors that lead to success. McDonald's fast-food services have modern technology supported by reliability and service, but they had the advantage of being first in the market. It is also possible to put large organizations into temporary difficulties if the product is right. For example, the mail-order houses in Britain took 50 per cent of the photographic-print market, and caused such large retailers as Boots to drop their prices.

Acquiring Capital

Given that the potential entrepreneur can face up to this, the agenda for planning the next stage is to acquire capital (in other words, the money to be put into the business). Capital may be acquired from one's family and friends, especially if the venture is small. It may be through a loan in the form of a contract or through the selling of shares at an agreed price between the seller and buyer (equity capital in Britain and the USA). In this case, the investor will be lending money to obtain a return on his or her investment through the money invested in the company rather than on interest received from lending money. Because the investor is able to buy and sell shares at the market price, it will be possible, if the company makes a profit, for the investor to sell the shares at a higher price than that given at the time of purchase. As we saw, this ability to make money from shares necessarily limits the commitment that a shareholder has to the business. It also determines the objectives of the financial market in Britain and the USA, and this may be at odds with the needs of industry. For example, the purpose of the capital market, writes Ball, is not 'to allocate funds but to price them. . . . The function of the capital market is to determine an economic price for a security or securities offer, after taking into account the appropriate degree of risk that should be attached to their prospective returns'.[15] In contrast, Tobin, a Nobel prizewinner in economics, writing about the efficiency of the American financial system, confesses

> to an uneasy Physiocratic suspicion, perhaps unbecoming in an academic, that we are throwing more and more of our resources, including the cream of our youth, into financial activities remote from the production of goods and services, into activities that

generate high private rewards disproportionate to their social productivity. I suspect that the immense power of the computer is being harnessed to this 'paper economy', not to do the same transactions more economically but to balloon the quantity and variety of financial exchanges.[16]

Earlier in the same article he points out that the headquarters of banks would take huge risks with loans to foreign countries but not allow their local branches to help new entrepreneurs.

The happenings on the London and New York stock exchanges would serve to re-inforce his fears. As we have seen, the morality of some dealings has been questioned, and the effectiveness of legislation questioned. Tobin's comment is certainly support for Iacocca, whose views on mergers were described in the last chapter. Associated with the debate about morality, although at some distance from it, is the question of size.

Changing Attitudes to Big and Small

Just as attitudes to merger change from time to time, so do attitudes to size. The two are by no means the same. In Britain there was a trend for industrial organizations to merge into conglomerates. Now there is a trend away from such organization, although one or two trusts continue to prosper.[17] One of the reasons for this was that some of the largest financial institutions had to be rescued in the 1970s because they had diversified by lending unwisely to property developers. It is no longer believed that economies of scale coupled to diversified activity necessarily lead to efficiency. Yet, as we have seen, it is still the large companies that use their capital most efficiently and are thus the most important to wealth creation in Britain.

Management has come to believe, and this is in keeping with the Japanese view, that their strengths lie in what they do best. But this has to be qualified by the fact that if there is no response in the market, then the company may die. It is the problem of the narrow focusing brought about the excessive experience and, as Foster shows, reliance on the same technology. Companies have to be outward looking in order to create new S-curves.[18] The life and death of the cotton industry in Britain is a monumental example of this point. Often it is the entrepreneur/innovator who, when he or she moves into new fields, fails. The Sinclair electric car is an example of this point.

In taking over new business areas, which they do not necessarily understand, management has to respond to the demands of the new areas into which they were merged rather than to the demands of existing activities they understood. For example, the troubles of the cotton industry cannot be totally explained by competition from overseas. The industrial structure created by mergers in the 1960s militated against its ability to respond to the market, and it has not been possible to replace those who had an entrepreneurial flare in existing organizations. While a large multinational company can close down non-profitmaking sections, this does not mean that it will be successful. Given the number of small enterprises in Japan, Blackburn's remark that the cotton industry was more profitable when it was fragmented is not without interest; neither is his comment that it is the specialist medium-sized companies that are successful.[19]

Since the finanical institutions exert considerable control over the future of companies, any response to the demand that they become more responsible must be accompanied by a demand that they ensure that companies can acquire capital to do what they do best. Both the American and British financial systems have been criticized because within them the cost of acquiring capital is too high.

Capital Financing

In America and Britain, the trend has been to finance capital from equity (in other words, shares), whereas in Japan the method of financing is through long-term loans at much lower rates of interest and therefore far less costly.[20] Because ordinary Japanese shareholders do not receive a good return on the capital they invest, companies find it difficult to raise capital through the market (equity capital). In consequence, they borrow money through loans from banks. This gives the banks a central position in the conglomerates. Trading companies help the banks to lend money. The trading companies borrow at a low rate of interest and lend at higher rates. As security they take over the merchandise of their clients for whom they buy and sell. These trading companies are intermediary organizations, and they operate at a variety of levels within the system of distribution and production. They can act as both wholesaler and exporter. Thus it is that the trading company is the pivot around which the manufacturer operates. Income to the bank, which is at the centre of the system, is also generated by savings, insurance companies and pension funds.[21]

Ball has argued that there is no inherent difficulty in the British financial system for the banks to provide long-term loans.[22] Indeed, medium-term loans for the smaller business are already being provided (see below). He argues that the unwillingness of companies to undertake long-term loans at fixed rates of interest has much more to do with the uncertainty about the real cost of borrowing over long periods than it does with the provision of the facility. Companies want stability. Ball draws an important distinction between finance and investment. He argues that 'the criticism that financial institutions fail to invest enough in British industry' implies 'that inadequate finance is available to industry to carry out the rewarding projects they have in mind'.[23] It is industry that invests.

A government committee, the Wilson Committee, found that there was no evidence to suggest there was a lack of finance for such projects. If anything, the banks were becoming closer to industry, although financial support for smaller companies is limited and this is a matter of concern in other countries as well.[24]

Under Capitalization

Very often a small business will start with a share capital of £200. One hundred pounds of this may be in the name of the owner, while the other £100 is put in the name of the owner's spouse. They become the sole directors of the business.

Certain legal advantages with regard to debt occur in Britain if a small venture is made into a private limited company. Unfortunately, the history of invention is littered with stories of inventions and inventors who were short of cash, and so many countries have organizations that sponsor inventions. In England, the National Research and Development Corporation supported the Hovercraft venture. However, the largest drive in recent years in Britain has been to improve the financial system in which small businesses operate.[25] These have included medium-term loans by banks, leasing and special-project finance. A noticeable shift toward bank financing has taken place and it marks a drift away from the capital market. The stock exchange also established an unlisted securities market.[26] It has been argued that while the involvement of the clearing banks has been encouraging, small business could be helped much more by reductions in interest and taxation rates.[27]

Although there is some doubt about the role of small business in the American boom of 1983–4, there is no doubt that politicians believe that small business is important to the economy.[28] They have only to look to Japan to find a model, for in Japan 80 per cent of the workforce is in businesses of less than 300 personnel.

Large enterprises can also suffer from under-capitalization. According to Cohen and Faris, 'the value of starting off in a small way varies according to the market, but on the whole it is usually wrong.'[29] They argue that this is because it will take higher advertising and large investment in plant. The entrepreneur who has no previous experience of handling money may put the whole venture at risk if he or she is unable to control large expenditures. At the other end of the market, the entrepreneur who wants to live off the business will seek his or her funding through the usual sources:

> History shows that most inventions from the steam engine to the computer have been the brain child of one person rather than a huge organisation. But it also shows that it is the enterprises with essential managemetn knowledge of marketing and manufacture – and not the inventor alone – which have turned inventions into great businesses.[30]

It is these skills the bank or the market will judge when they decide to make a loan or buy shares in the market.

The Business Merry-go-round

This title comes from the theme of a film called *The Balance Sheet Barrier*,[31] in which the flow of money in an enterprise is a merry-go-round between the money going into the business and the money going out.

Fixed Assets

In the cycle of events, once the business is running it will be possible to take some of the money from the profits for further investment. This money is the 'reserves'. Further capital may also be raised by the issue of more shares, which will be taken up by investors if they believe it will make the enterprise more profitable. Thus money used to start and maintain the business (that is, the capital) is obtained from shareholders, bank loans and that part of the profits put back into the business.

These form one side of that technical paper called a balance sheet, and this capital is used to run the company. The other side of a balance sheet shows how the money was spent, for example, on fixed assets (land, buildings, plant machinery, vehicles, etc.). Working capital comprising (1) current assets (raw materials, work in progress, finished good debtors and cash at the bank), (2) current liabilities (creditors) and investments, are also an expenditure of capital.

A company may use some of its profits to invest in other enterprises. It may eventually obtain sufficient numbers of shares with which to purchase an enterprise. In Britain it has been argued that the nationalized industries are less effective than they should be because they do not have the powers of investment open to private companies.

As indicated above, the entrepreneur has to buy permanent fixtures and fittings, such as plant and machinery. He or she may buy or rent the buildings on a long-term lease. Such institutions as banks and insurance companies often erect large buildings as a capital investment. They utilize some of the space themselves and rent the remainder. Multiple chain-stores often purchase the site and buildings, particularly when it is in an advantageous position in the main street. This gives an added value to the site and building. Items such as plant, buildings and machinery, which have to be kept, are called the *fixed assets*. While some assets, such as building and land, tend to appreciate in value, other assets, such as plant and machinery, depreciate in value. Household goods are particularly good examples of depreciation. Cars, refrigerators, televisions, begin to lose value from the time they are purchased. Most householders do not seem to put aside money for their replacement. Eventually, the machine breaks down and they replace it by means of a hire-purchase or credit-sales agreement. A well run company will not take this approach. It will ensure that the 'true' value of its equipment is written into the balance sheet. This means that it will allow a substantial sum for depreciation. At the same time, it will put aside money for future investment in new (replacement) equipment. Many economists argue that a major reason for Britain's industrial decline from 1945 was the failure of industry, not merely to replace its old equipment, but to invest in new equipment, although it is evident from tables by Barrett-Brown[32] that the decline had set in during the previous century.

Operating or Working Capital

A company cannot begin without capital to provide for the raw materials, labour and overheads required for continuous activity. So some of the money borrowed is put into the organization to make it work – hence the term *operating* or *working capital*. In a balance sheet no direct mention is made of labour costs. This is because they are incorporated into the price of goods on the shelf. The cost of raw materials in the factory is included because it is an asset. Similarly, work in progress is an asset. If goods have been delivered and not paid for they are also an asset. The persons owing money are called debtors. The current assets in relation to working capital therefore include:

1. raw materials
2. work in progress
3. finished goods
4. debtors
5. cash-in-hand and at bank.

But the company may also owe money for raw materials, stationery, electricity, gas, and so on. The persons to whom the company owes money are the creditors. The total working capital at any given time is the difference between the current assets and the current liabilities.

Problem of Stocks

Effective management ensures that while there is a continuous supply of raw materials there is not an over-large stockpile. Companies can get themselves into a position where the stocks are too high when compared with sales. This can happen and is possibly more serious with finished goods. Stocks of finished goods have to be depreciated. Books that remain in a publisher's warehouse are not an asset, even though their effective purchase price may be high. It is extremely difficult to sell novels after the first rush of enthusiasm on publication. If the stock remains after a year or two, it is unlikely to be sold. Small shopkeepers run into this difficulty. They cannot purchase sufficient stock to keep the price down because their turnover is small. Often they purchase items that are seldom bought because 'locals' rely on them for these 'odd' things, which cannot be purchased in many supermarkets. Small builders get into financial difficulty if they purchase stocks that cannot be used. If they then have insufficient liquidity (cash) with which to purchase materials to finish the job and/or to pay for the labour, then the job will not be completed and they will go bankrupt.

Stocks are a major problem for businesses in periods of recession. If their forecast sales are small, and their stocks reasonably large, they will tend to cut back production and use up their stocks. In consequence, when the boom in sales that follows a recession occurs, they find themselves unable to meet demand. Customers change to their competitors and the business finds itself struggling to retain its market position.

The total sum of the assets equals the total sum of the capital and reserves. In the balance sheet it shows that a company could meet its liabilities if all those to whom money is owed can be paid off in full. When this is not the case, an organization will have to go into receivership.

The balance sheet does not, by itself, explain the significance of restrictive practices. It does explain why the working capital should be kept as low as possible and, by implication, it shows the importance of the market.

The Price Mechanism

No company is a closed system. It is open not only to the market, but to those factors in society, such as governments, that influence the market. In a perfectly free market, price is determined by the supply and demand for a good. When a good has scarcity value, the price will rise. When there is an excess of supply over demand, the price will fall. Thus in theory, when there is a state of perfect competition, the price will be determined at the value where supply equals demand. It is argued that the consumer is best served by a free market. Monopolies cause prices to be artificially raised because they have complete control over the good to be sold. Because of this, public-service monopolies in Britain, such as coal, electricity, gas and water, come under considerable public scrutiny because of their pricing powers. The point to be made here is neither about perfect competition nor monopolies – it is simply that if a good is not in demand, stocks will grow and working capital will increase. Therefore, companies have to be ready to adapt to market conditions. This may mean new methods of production that, if they are opposed by the operation of restrictive practices, may bring the company to the brink of bankruptcy.

There is, it seems, a tendency to forget that it is not only the products of industry that create markets. They, in their turn, depend on an efficient workforce and create a labour market. Sometimes extraordinary prices are paid for people as, for example, when the London finance market became international in 1986. Some persons with particular expertise were bought and sold for hundreds of thousands of pounds. The price individuals and institutions are prepared to pay for ideas, products and people, places values on them that, in themselves, are indicative of social values. In Britain, sports men and women are said to be insufficiently valued when compared with those in eastern Europe or the USA. Nevertheless, some soccer stars have become millionaires, a fact that should be contrasted with the very poor salaries paid to engineers. The influence of values can be very profound on some kinds of institution. If, for example, the students seeking admission to university cause a drastic redistribution in the subjects demanded, some subject departments can be put in jeopardy, as was the case with Russian in Britain where the number of departments in universities had to be halved. The value that individuals place on education or, say, social welfare, determines the stance governments take towards the development of these services and thus to taxation – a point that does not seem to be widely understood. Such values are not absolute, and goods and services can be overvalued or undervalued in terms of their social-benefit cost. Such goods as education and health are invisible and not included in national balance sheets, although their efficiencies, particularly if they are State run, can be called into question. The term 'invisible' is normally used to describe the wealth generated by the financial institutions (for example, insurance, banking). They make a significant positive input into the British trade balances of the western nations and Japan.

The newest, and probably most interesting market, is the rapidly developing market for information, which has been created by the information-technology explosion. 'Stored information is an asset, the increasing potential of which is causing rapid changes in the world economies of information use and making available more information to more people.'[33] It is difficult to value information (and its flow), although it is clear that it has immense value and may be subject to the monopoly powers of such corporations as IBM, who control the machines and networks. A price mechanism is clearly developing and its production process is open to the same kind of financial analyses as a small company.

Costing the Production Process

Although many production processes involve labour in complex organizations, they are, in accounting terms, reducible to very simple operations. Table 7.1(a) and (b) illustrates this point. In this example, the progress of the materials from their input to the production line is traced through two operatives concerned with the assembly or machining of the finished product, and one who is concerned with packaging. The cost-per-day work is shown in Table 7.1(a) and the sum for a week

Table 7.1 The principles involved in the calculation of the costs of a simple product, such as an exhaust system (a) in a day; (b) over the week. It relates to the system shown in Figure 7.1

(a)	£
Raw materials (part finished goods)	250
Operator 1	20
Operator 2	20
Operator 3	15
Overheads	50
	355

(b)	Monday £	Tuesday £	Wednesday £	Thursday £	Friday £	Total £
Raw materials	250	250	250	250	250	250
Operator 1 (manufacturing)	20	20	20	20	20	100
Operator 2 (manufacturing)	20	20	20	20	20	100
Operator 3 (packaging)	15	15	15	15	15	75
						1,525
Overheads						50
						1,575

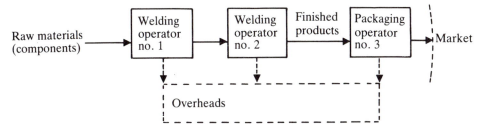

Figure 7.1 A simplified diagram of the production process. In this case, it is assumed that simple exhaust systems are being produced. It does not show the support services (e.g. clerical)

(five days) of the same operations is shown in Table 7.1(b).

In Figure 7.1, the overheads are shown in a hatched box because they will be constant whether the company produces goods on one day or five days during the week. The raw materials may be partly finished goods. For example, quite simple operations could be used to butt-weld a silencer to an exhaust pipe.[34] Many small companies support the motor industry in this way.

If we now put an additional sum of £100 to include profit on 50 exhaust systems, we see that the overall additional sum obtained in a week is £500. The total cost of the finished articles is then £2,075 or around £8 each, to which eventually will be added wholesale and retail prices. We can see at once that if there is a dispute that halves the output for a day, there will be a drop in profits. This is why unofficial stoppages, of which there were thousands in the 1960s and 1970s, are so damaging.

But their additional sum is not all profit. After taxation, which is substantial, dividends are paid to the shareholders. The remainder is the retained profit. This retained profit is not received by shareholders or the Inland Revenue. It is that sum which is put into the business to make it grow, and it is the growth of business that is the creation of wealth, in other words, the addition of assets. Working capital keeps the business in operation. Profits make it grow.

The Past State of an Enterprise

Information about past performance is important both to predictions about the future and to the adjustment of prices. Such information is to be found in statements of income and expenditure. Income is primarily derived from sales and investments. In the expenditure statement, a differentiation has to be made between the costs of 'distribution labour', 'manufacturing labour' and 'admin-istrative labour'. If these labour costs are unacceptably high, the entrepreneur will seek to substitute them by machinery that will do the same job. Technology necessarily puts people out of work in some jobs although it may create jobs elsewhere. *It is for this reason that it is necessary for employees at all levels to remain adaptable.*

The Future Prospects of an Enterprise

A company has always to be able to pay its creditors. These will include its workers to whom it will owe wages and salaries. It has, therefore, to make profits. If it does not, it may not be possible to pay its workers. In times of recession, companies sometimes have to borrow from the bank in order to pay their workers. It is important for them, therefore, to know the effects of future orders. For this purpose a cash flow projection is cast. This predicts income and expenditure (taking into account weekly or monthly balances) for the weeks or months of the year.

The value of this projection will be seen if the following problem is considered. A customer says that he wants 2,000 exhaust pipes in eight weeks. Payment will be made when all are received. To achieve this goal, the company would have to find some method of financing production during the eight weeks. Borrowing money from the bank might not be worthwhile if the interest rate is too high. In this case it might be better to turn the order down or arrange for the customer to make earlier payments. It also shows the dangers of fixed-price contracts, particularly during periods of inflation. Rolls-Royce ran into this difficulty in 1970. It led to the company being put into receivership. Bargaining by the buyer in these conditions leads the seller to offer the goods over a period of years for a fixed price. In this case, a number of aircraft engines were offered to an American aircraft manufacturer for a fixed price. High-development costs, together with the beginning of inflation, caused Rolls-Royce to default. The receivership was arranged with the government so that the company remained in business.[35]

But forward planning is also about having a strategic plan, and the idea of such planning should begin with the enterprise. Very many entrepreneurs fail to answer questions about either what they will do if they come in for heavy competition, or their strategy for expansion if the business is successful.[36] It is clear from the Japanese experience that a manufacturing enterprise should seek to develop its range around core components and systems rather than seek entirely new artefacts.

Manufacturing and Wealth

Even with increasing use of high technology, manufacturing is the main activity through which jobs are directly or indirectly created. Large manufacturing enterprises support a great many small enterprises. The greater the investment in manufacturing, the more jobs will be generated. These axioms remain true in Britain despite the success of the financial markets and the shift to service industries. Jones has said of the largest firm in Britain, ICI, that it would require an additional six million tourists (40 per cent more than at present) to replace that company's contribution to the balance of payments. British service exports are less than one-half British manufacturing exports: moreover, the share of world-service exports fell by 20 per cent as compared to 9 per cent for manufacturing throughout the world.[37] Kaldor also points out that manufacturing is not only stimulated by technology but also generates it as well.[38]

Profits, Investment and the Creation of Wealth

In this chapter we have considered the importance of wealth and how wealth is created. Our view is that if the world population is, in general, to get better off, it is necessary to create more wealth and to assist the developing countries to achieve this goal. Attention was drawn again to the questions raised in the previous chapter by the merger mania, about the difference between the objectives of industry and those of the financial markets. The fears of a Nobel-Laureat were described.

One purpose of this chapter has been to show the role of profits in an industrial enterprise. The same principles apply to dealing in the financial markets, especially in foreign exchange. In the UK many people feel that profits are not respectable. This is particularly so among teachers. The Conservative government, which was concerned to develop positive attitudes among school pupils to industry, introduced technology as a compulsory part of the school curriculum.[39] If it had as an underlying purpose a positive disposition to wealth creation, which was a major objective in the government programme, then its curriculum change cannot be said to have been successful. There is little or no mention of entrepreneurship or the market in the texts, and there was certainly no mention of the market at a conference on research into the teaching of craft, design and technology in schools, which I attended.

In Ireland there was much opposition to the inclusion of statements about wealth creation, or mention of profits, in the discussion document on science, technology and the school curriculum.[40] A major reason for these difficulties lies in the fact that relatively few students are exposed to practical economics during their schooling. This is in contrast to Japan, where economics is a practical subject.

However, during in-service training (designed to help teachers develop school curricula in this area) we have found that once the teachers have seen the video, *The Balance Sheet Barrier*, they see that profits are, of themselves, morally neutral.[41] It is what you do with them that matters and, as we have seen, this is a key issue in the controversy over mergers, and therefore very much a matter for the content of the curriculum in schools.[42]

It is equally clear that if companies are to be run effectively, workers and management have a common goal in ensuring that companies make profits. At the same time, they will want to ensure that they are properly used. The lesson to be taken from Foster's study, described in the last chapter, is that investment in the same product is ultimately self-defeating. Workforce and management have to seek out new ideas and adapt the company to those ideas. Simply to respond to the forces of competition may lead to death.

Managers and their workers have, therefore, a common interest in the internal effectiveness of their organizations. Mant has argued that one of the differences between companies in England and Germany is that much of the energy that should be spent in running the enterprise in English companies is spent in internal fighting, whereas the fighting the Germans do is in the market place.[43] This is a matter to which we will return in Chapter 10. Before that, however, Chapter 8 presents an examination of restrictive practices that inhibit internal effectiveness, and both companies and the professions are considered.

The attention given to the relationship between stocks and forecast sales in the foregoing paragraphs draws attention not only to the influence but also to the trade cycle through which all markets go. If the State is to prosper, it relies on the wealth created by business and industry. It has, therefore, to create the environmental conditions in which commercial and industrial organizations can work effectively.

Notes and References

1. Garraty, J.A. (1978) *Unemployment in History: Economic Thought and Public Policy*, Harper & Row, New York, NY.
2. For an introduction to economics in the Eastern Europe, and more especially Yugoslavia, see Barratt-Brown, M. (1970) *What Economics is About*, Weidenfield & Nicolson, London.
3. Miller, H. (1960) *The Way of Enterprise*, Institute of Economic Affairs, London.
4. Thackray, J. (1984) The US entrepreneur's new clothes, *Management Today*, November, pp. 58–66.
5. Cohen, R. and Faris, R. (1983) How to find venture capital, *Management Today*, April, pp. 74–8.
6. Oakeshott, R. (1985) The beginnings of an employee-owned sector, *Lloyds Bank Review*, no. 155, pp. 32–44; and Coyne, J. and Wright, M. (1982) Buy-outs and British industry, *Lloyds Bank Review*, no. 146, pp. 15–31.
7. Oakeshott, The beginnings (note 6).
8. See Chapter 5, notes 26, 27 and 28.
9. Foster, R. (1986) *Innovation: The Attacker's Advantage*. Macmillan, London.
10. Deane, P. (1973) Great Britain, in C.M. Cipolla (ed.) *The Emergence of Industrial Societies*, Fontana, London; and Isaac, D. (1985) The mixed micro-economy, *Management Today*, March, pp. 76–9 and p. 124.
11. Cohen and Faris, How to find (note 5).
12. Kolb, D. (ed.) (1974) *Organizational Psychology: A Book of Readings* (2nd edn), Prentice-Hall, Englewood Cliffs, NJ; Foster, *Innovation* (note 9); and Morland, R. (1983) Closing with Japan, *Management Today*, May, pp. 60–3.
13. Morland, Closing (note 12).
14. *Ibid.*
15. Ball, Sir J. (1984) Institutional investment, *Lloyds Bank Review*, no. 154, pp. 1–12.
16. Tobin, J. (1984) On the efficiency of the financial system, *Lloyds Bank Review*, no. 136, pp. 15–29.
17. Rybczynski, T.M. (1982) Structural changes in the financing of British industry and their implications, *National Westminster Bank Quarterly Review*, May, pp. 25–6; and Llewellyn, D. (1985) The changing structure of the UK financial system, *Three Banks Review*, no. 145, March, pp. 19–34.
18. Foster, *Innovation* (note 9).
19. Blackburn, J.A. (1982) The vanishing UK cotton industry, *National Westminster Bank Review*, November, pp. 42–52.
20. Gregory, G. (1984) Japan's winning capital asset, *Management Today*, June, pp. 74–8.
21. See note 2; Morland, Closing (note 12); and Haitana, K. (1976) *The Japanese Economic System*, Heath, Lexington, Mass.
22. Ball, Sir J. (1984) Institutional investment, *Lloyds Bank Review*, no. 154, pp. 1–12.
23. Ball, Institutional investment (note 15).

24. Rybczynski, Structural changes (note 17); Llewellyn, Changing structure (note 17); and Vittas, D. (1986) Bank's relations with industry: an international survey, *National Westminster Bank Review*, February, pp. 2–13.

25. Bolton Report (1971) *Small Firms,* HMSO, London.

26. Rybczynski, T. M. (1984) The UK financial system in transition, *National Westminster Bank Quarterly Review,* November, pp. 26–42.

27. Jarrett, M. and Wright, M. (1982) New initiatives in the financing of smaller firms, *National Westminster Bank Quarterly Review*, August, pp. 40–52.

28. Thackray, US entrepreneur's (note 4).

29. Cohen and Faris, How to find (note 5).

30. *Ibid.*

31. *The Balance Sheet Barrier* (A. Jay), Video Arts, London. One of the best introductions to business is this film, which stars the actors, John Cleese and Ronnie Corbett. There is an accompanying booklet written by Anthony Jay, who has also written the scripts for the following films, as well as the associated booklets: *Cost, Profit and Break-even* and *Control of Working Capital* (also Video Arts). In the same series there are *Depreciation and Inflation* (Emile Woolfe) and *Budgeting* (J. Hemingway).

    The section in the main text employs the same terminology used in *The Balance Sheet Barrier*. However, not all balance sheets are presented in this way, and the reader may find the International Labour Organization's book on the balance sheet helpful.

32. Barratt-Brown, *What Economics is About* (note 2).

33. Palliser, Sir M. (1986) Chairman of a committee of the British Invisible Exports Council. Report of committee quoted by P. Large in the *Guardian*, 4 April, p. 22.

34. Carpenter, N. (1972) designed a business game for engineering students at Liverpool University around the manufacture and sale of exhaust pipes. It included a training exercise. Details from the Department of Industrial Studies, University of Liverpool, Liverpool.

35. Gray, R. (1971) *Rolls on the Rocks: The Story of Rolls Royce*, Panther Books, London.

36. Cohen and Faris, How to find (note 5).

37. Jones, Sir H. (1986) Quoted from his BBC Television Dimbleby Lecture by R. Elgin, *The Sunday Times*, 6 April.

38. Kaldor, Lord (1985) Letter to *The Times*, 29 October.

39. The Education Reform Act 1988, HMSO, London.

40. Curriculum and Examination Board (1987) *Science, Technology and the Post-Primary Curriculum,* Government Publications, Dublin.

41. See note 31.

42. Carter, C.F. (1971) *Wealth: An Essay on the Purpose of Economics*, Penguin Books, Harmondsworth; and Kindleberger, C.P. (1980) Responsibility in economic life, *Lloyds Bank Review*, no. 138, pp. 1–11.

43. Mant, A. (1979) *The Rise and Fall of the British Manager,* Pan, London.

8
RESTRICTIVE PRACTICES

Introduction

We show in Chapter 7 that wealth creation depends on the efficiency with which market needs are met in design, quality, cost and delivery. Companies that cannot deliver a product the market wants at the right price will fail. In a competitive climate, the companies that meet these requirements succeed – those that don't, fail. Companies can be organized to optimize their efficiency but often they are prevented from doing this by practices imposed on them by the workers, or managers, or professionals. Management has often acquiesced in these practices for the sake of peace.

Societies, too, also operate restrictive practices. For example, there is a continuing debate about the role of import controls among the industrialized nations. Trade is by no means free. The first section of this chapter considers this issue. There is support for import controls and considerable opposition to a free-currency market. The prevailing opinion opposes such views and believes that all countries should behave as open systems. Among the arguments for import controls are that they protect the internal market; against this is that they lead to retaliation abroad, which could limit exports to the extent of job losses. There is, in the western world, a continuing fear of those advocates of isolationism in the USA.

A second section deals briefly with bureaucratic controls that maintain dying industries. These subsidies are thought by some to be wealth consuming; they are a reminder of the concept of social costs as compared with economic costs. The dominant view in the western world is that privatization leads to greater efficiency. A major problem for the western world is the cost of agricultural subsidies.

There are just as many restrictive practices among professional people as there are among trade unionists. Some may be justified, particularly where they are intended to aid human life, as in medicines. The professions claim the right to self-regulation. In Britain, education, status and professionalism are closely related. A group of institutions, sometimes called the semi-professions, seek to enhance their status by increasing the standard of educational qualification required for entry. A case study is included that briefly describes the history of engineering education in Britain. It is argued that the net effect of the increasing demand for qualifications is to transfer the potential for mobility to the educational system. The career route chosen sets the limits of mobility.

It is argued from the experience of engineering that the creation of a qualifying institute for managers is unlikely to confer any major benefits on industry. The role of the regulatory bodies in law, accounting and medicine is being questioned, with a view to introducing more competitiveness.

In Britain, the effects of trade union legislation have been to reduce restrictive practices and to make it possible for management to combat strikes. An important feature of this legislation were legal restrictions on secondary picketing. American observers have found much the same about union practices and conventions in the USA.

It is too early to say if there are permanent shifts of belief taking place among trade-unionists in Britain. The resistance to change is very great, as a number of disputes in 1988 showed. The indications are that changing patterns of employment are forcing change in industrial relations, where workplace bargaining is tending to take the place of collective bargaining. Other developments include flexible work schedules and work-sharing.

In learning terms, institutions and their employees have to be 'ready' for change. Restrictive practices are impediments to learning and thus to change.

Import Controls

Nations, such as Britain and the Republic of Ireland, rely on exports – both visible and invisible (banking, insurance, etc.) – for their economic viability. Because they adopt a relatively free-trade position, consumers in Britain and Ireland are able to buy goods from all over the world. In spite of the evidence from Japan that it is competition in the home market that provides the base for their export drive, there is no equivalent 'Buy British' syndrome. In the UK,[1] consumers are not, as in Japan, motivated patriotically, and this would seem to be the case in the Republic of Ireland, where there is substantial legitimate buying in Northern Ireland as well as smuggling! It is for this reason that it is easy for foreign competitors to break into and subsequently destroy markets in the British Isles. The immediate effect of purchasing products from overseas is to increase the volume of imports (including raw materials and energy) purchased. If the sum spent on imports is larger than the sum received for exports, then there is a trade deficit. Wealth may be used up in these circumstances. In consequence, the government may be forced to put up the rates of interest in order to reduce consumer spending. When, however, the balance of trade is in credit, and the income from exports is greater than that for imports, the conditions for wealth creation are favourable. Very often in Britain the overall balance is held in the black by the invisibles, for manufacturing often does not hold its own. The deficit position also describes a situation where there is a lack of demand for goods.

Since fewer goods will be introduced, there is less money for the government to tax and to re-invest. In the happy position of a balance of payments credit, there is demand for the goods being manufactured. The company increases its income as more goods are produced, and the government is able to take a greater slice in taxation. The same applies within the home market. If consumers purchase foreign goods at the expense of home products, they reduce the available income to the government (in the form of taxation). Increases in imports have the effect of reducing national wealth, if they persist. The export of money may also have the same effect if it arises from speculation on the international market as, for example, when interest rates are high in the USA. It earns for the home country when it is invested in an enterprise in another country.

There is in Britain considerable opposition to a free-currency market since it is believed that it takes up funds that would otherwise be invested internally. Many also support the idea of import controls on such goods as textiles, which are subject to 'dumping', in other words, the import of similar products at very cheap prices by foreign competitors. Import controls, it is contended,

1. protect newly founded industries;
2. counteract the effect of subsidies to the exporting industry in the exporter's country;
3. protect essential industries;
4. cushion industries that are declining.

There is an argument between economists about the effect of import controls on jobs. Those in favour of such controls believe they necessarily save jobs. Those against argue that if a company has to fight in the market it will usually be in a position to invest in new equipment to carry out the battle. Such machinery is likely to be labour saving if it is to provide greater productivity. In that case jobs will be lost. They also argue that to keep companies that would otherwise fail is to exacerbate inefficiency, the net effect of which may be to increase the costs to the consumer. In Britain, these were among the philosophies that differentiated the two main political parties during the 1980s. At the same time, there was considerable pressure in Britain and the USA to bring controls on Japanese exports because the Japanese markets were not open to their imports.

Such views have to be seen within the perspective of an open world system, where restrictions on one product by one country may lead to retaliation by another in an entirely different area of manufacture. In the USA, there is a fear of isolationist policies. If the USA were to restrict imports severely it could be very damaging to several west European economies. Of course, this account is considerably simplified. Many other factors have to be taken into account, such as the rate at which a country's currency trades in the international market (usually it's value in dollars).

One economist argues that none of this matters, because the international free-currency market is here to stay.[2] In consequence, previously held economic axioms no longer hold. It is difficult to see how the developments in the City of London and New York can be reversed.

Bureaucratic Controls

The trend towards privatization of State-controlled agencies stems from the belief that they will perform better in the private sector because they are not subject to bureaucratic controls. A State agency that benefits from subsidies is thought by some to be wealth consuming. However, in the sense that their employees are consumers, then such industries may create wealth. The question that has to be answered for each set of circumstances is whether the available resources would have been better invested in newer industries rather than in declining industries, since the wealth-creation powers of the former will be much greater than the latter. Such decisions are political as well as economic. It would seem to be essential to maintain a basic steel industry and railway network if only for strategic purposes. The open system works to a limited extent because the consumers also have the vote. Prices in the public sector are not completely inelastic.

Until recently, the British pharmaceutical industry was artificially supported by pricing in the National Health Service. Now only a limited range of drugs is approved so that the costs to the service are reduced. It remains to be seen if these limitations reduce research and development in the pharmaceutical industry, which it is claimed they will do. More generally, the view that the health service should be maintained for all is questionable. Free health care is limited in Ireland, for example, to people in lower-income groups. Those in higher brackets still pay part of their tax to the State to support the scheme, even though they receive no benefits. For them, a private-subscription scheme is available. A reasonable standard of care seems to be available. It is significant that welfare provision in Japan is relatively poor.

In sum, the prevailing view is that privatization leads to greater efficiency because of competition. The stock market in Britain would regard the privatization up to 1988 as a success.[3] However, the consumer might think that the privatization of British Telecom and British Gas simply changed one monopoly managership for another. British Telecom has been severely criticized for the service it provides its customers.

Perhaps the best-known subsidy is the agricultural subsidy (Common Agricultural Policy) of the European Economic Community. But as Lord[4] has pointed out, food and, in particular, rice, is highly subsidized in Japan. Apart from the fact that subsidies can artificially increase production, the effect of price support, which is the form the subsidies take, is to increase the price of the food to the consumer. It is argued that the effect of making agriculture open to third-world economies would be to increase their foreign currency earnings considerably. Many commentators view the way the western nations handle their agriculture as nothing short of scandalous.

Education, Semi-Professional People and the Search for Status

While we often criticize trade unions for the operation of restrictive practices, we forget that all the professions engage in restrictive practices of some kind or another. They often use education for this purpose.

Entry to a profession is tightly controlled by academic requirements that may or may not have relevance to actual practice. Society ascribes more value to some professions than to others. Thus it is believed that one way for a group to increase its status in society is to enhance the standard of the educational qualifications required for membership in that group. This is particularly true in Britain where, unlike the USA, membership of a professional association outside of medicine is linked closely with academic qualifications. In this respect the recent history of the British engineering institutions is of some interest because they have had, and continue to be, concerned for their status, and this they see as being intimately related to education and productivity.

In 1945, in a report on higher technological education, it was argued that the part-time technical college route that produced most of Britain's engineers, was inadequate for the task. Engineers, it said, should have a greater scientific background, although this should be oriented towards industrial design and manufacture. Their training should be full time, and the sandwich – co-operative – system was recommended. By 1959, ten colleges of technology had been established, which offered degrees on a sandwich or full-time basis. Some of these courses were for University of London degrees, others were for a Diploma in Technology, which the Ministry of Education said was equivalent to a degree. To ensure that this was so, the ministry created an organization to accredit the award.

Despite the considerable number of students on these courses, educationalists argued that Britain was short of qualified scientists and technologists, and in this they were supported by the professional institutions. Arguments that there was no shortage of qualified engineers and scientists were ignored. The professional institutions argued that the shortage of engineers was due to the low status the profession had in the eyes of the public. Therefore, they argued, it was necessary to obtain a qualification that would have high status. In the early 1960s, persons approved for membership of one of the fifteen chartered engineering institutions received the title C.Eng. (Chartered Engineer). Evidently this did not, at least in the eyes of the professional institutions, have the desired effect, for they have continued to argue that there is a shortage of engineers and that this is due to the low esteem in which engineers were held. Their arguments were supported by the view that the major reason for Britain's poor productivity was the failure to produce highly but relevantly qualified engineers, and early on they found support for this view in an official report on engineering design.[5]

To understand this situation, it is necessary to refer briefly to the Industrial Revolution and its influence on the development of educational practice. Engineers were traditionally recruited from the shopfloor and obtained such education as they could from part-time study. In contrast, scientists began to obtain their education in universities although, as Lilley has pointed out, its applications to industry were not taken too seriously so that by the end of the nineteenth century, Germany had gained a lead in the chemical industries.[6] However, by the 1950s the science-based industries were used to making a distinction between scientists and technicians. Graduates were employed as scientists. It was difficult for a person on a technician route to become a scientist. Technicians in these industries had a different status from those in engineering. The stereotyping of the person in a white laboratory coat handling test-tubes in a servant capacity to a scientist or a medical doctor approximated to the truth. It was virtually impossible for a medical laboratory technician to change courses and become a doctor. There was no way out of these technician careers.

In contrast, it was still possible to obtain professional qualifications in engineering by part-time study. Recruitment was by apprenticeship. A good firm would pick the best for technician-type activities and encourage them to pursue further study through night school and/or release on one day per week to college. The more able of this group could expect to acquire the qualifications necessary for professional membership of an institution by part-time study over seven or eight years. It was this approach to the study of engineering that was held to be inadequate. However, firms were not dissuaded from this method of employment and continued throughout the 1950s and 1960s to recruit from this source as well as the universities. Nevertheless, it became increasingly difficult for unqualified persons to enter research and advanced development: designers and draughtsmen began to find their careers limited, while entry to production and manufacturing in many firms continued to be dependent on recruitment from the shopfloor (see below). This was true of the firm we investigated, and since it was a highly innovative firm, that study cast some doubt on the thesis that performance and qualification are necessarily related. However, this may have been due to the fact that the firm was engaged in small-batch, high-quality product manufacture.

In 1961 the Ministry of Education initiated a series of changes that ultimately led to a semi-profession of technicians.[7] Marshall drew attention to the effects of educational structures on social mobility as early as 1939, when he wrote that:

> It is important to notice the effects of these changes on social mobility. An organised profession admits recruits by means of an impartial test of their knowledge and ability. In theory they are selected on merit, but it is merit of a particular kind which usually must be developed and displayed in a particular prescribed way. A narrow road leads into the profession through certain educational institutions. How far this favours social mobility depends on whether those institutions are open to the masses, so that merit can win recognition in all classes. Granted the broadening of the educational ladder is typical of modern democracies, the system of examination is more favourable to mobility than one of arbitrary appointment or casual promotion. But the chance to move comes early, during school days. Once it has been missed and a career has been started at a non-professional level, the whole system of formal qualifications makes movement at a later stage well-nigh impossible.[8]

The same is true of Japan. Selection is done within the system of schooling. All children receive the same educational programme until around the ninth grade, when they enter high schools of varying prestige. Selection is by means of highly competitive examinations. Selection to high school is by ability so that high schools acquire prestige within the system by the ability levels they attract, and this is re-inforced by the status of the particular universities and colleges they feed. Some high schools have the task of preparing their students for university, and others the more difficult job of coping with the less able and less well adjusted through – as in the case of Britain and Germany – the teaching of practical skills.[9] Thus, Japanese students are routed in high school, and the jobs available to them are a function of the high education achieved. Competition for life is undertaken in school. It is a meritocratic system that legitimizes the prevailing bureaucratic hierarchies, and that helps to mould individuals into accepting their future roles. Thus it is that social inequalities persist and are aided by the structure of education. The meritocratic principle is being threatened by the development of some private schools, which have managed to gain pre-eminence in schooling through examination success. They now make it possible, like the English public schools, for persons to buy educational advantage. In Tokyo, reports Rohlen, a drive to end the stratification of public schools had the effect of strengthening the élite public schools. The same sort of thing has happened in Britain where there has been a backlash against comprehensive education.[10]

Marshall, whose paper was originally written in 1939, correctly predicted that one result of these social and educational changes would be the lengthening of the period of formal education. Unemployment has forced governments in Europe to introduce a variety of courses (pre-employment, Technical Vocational Education Initiative, Vocational Preparation Training Programme, Youth Training Scheme) – all of which have the effect of lengthening the period of formal education. One major manufacturer in Britain, Pilkington Glass, no longer employs young persons below the age of 18. It believes every school leaver (at 16) who does not enter higher education should participate in a two-year Youth Training Scheme.

Some industrialists argued that the educational policies of the British government in the 1960s placed them in a straitjacket. In effect they were a restrictive practice. In the company we studied, it influenced the attitudes and motivation of draughtsmen and technicians, for these policies prevented them from moving into the professional engineering route. They could no longer expect to become assistant engineers. In the future it is likely that they will be seen to have been a special group affected by the long period of time it takes for legislation to cause a major structural change in the social and education system.

The creation of a sub- or a semi-profession of technicians narrows the road into the main profession. It remains to be seen if there will be serious dissatisfaction among those who do technician work if they find their mobility is severely restricted. If individual competitiveness is transferred from the economic to the educational world, the drives firms need to maintain their efficiency might be impaired. Clearly, what has happened to the worker in terms of the restrictions placed on him or her by the technology of production could happen to the technician by the restrictions placed on him or her by the socio-educational system, although changes within the last two or three years suggest that the system is becoming a little more flexible.[11]

This issue serves to support Lilley's view that the collapse of the British initiative in the Industrial Revolution was due to the class structure of British society. The fact that in neither Japan nor the USA, qualifications are not linked closely to membership of professional associations suggests that the development of the British engineering associations was a response to this class structure. Their qualifications were the vehicles by which engineers qualified because they could not get them through universities. However a Fellowship in Engineering has been created in the image of the Fellowship of the Royal Society, which is the most prestigious society in Britain, but it is unlikely to obtain the status which engineers seek.

More significantly, the regulations can be in conflict with the actual needs of industry as dictated by the jobs that have to be done. One study of technicians showed that many of them incorporated managerial tasks into their work, for which they had received little formal education. But in other areas they had been over-educated (for example, maths and science).[12]

Many comparisons have been made with the situation in Germany. Engineers have high status in Germany, and it is argued that engineers in Britain should be regarded 'unambiguously as a profession', such as law and medicine.[13] Professional stakes is a reflection of the class system that afflicts Britain. By and large, engineers are not drawn from the sectors that feed the bureaucracy and financial systems in the City, although the advent of technology in the City of London has brought persons with skills in handling technological devices from other sectors into its ambit.

In Germany, social status is not measured by personal refinement, education and breeding but by income and power. 'So German managers can afford to capitalise on income and power to justify self assurance. What you make of your social status in Germany is less controlled by social indicators. You can display income and power more freely and less self-consciously.[14]

In Britain, the semi-professions, such as those in para-medicine, have followed in the footsteps of the engineering institutions – that is, they have sought to raise the status of their profession by increasing the level of educational attainment required for entry into that profession. More often than not, this has been to the level of a university degree.[15] The effect of this is to restrict entry to the profession.

Central to the engineering issue is that of management in industry, for not only is the quality of management regarded as poor, but managers also have a status problem. Middle managers in the USA would seem to have a similar problem as large companies are made less hierarchical.[16] In Britain, the Council for Management Education and Development has proposed that an institute with a royal charter would lay down qualifications for managers in the same way as for accountants and engineers. However, if newspaper reports are anything to go by, this proposal has not engendered much support among managers. Peters, of Peters and Waterman fame is reported as saying to British managers that

I despise the word professional – what we need are 'amateurs'. Golzen reported that Peters went on to remind his audience that 'amateur' came from the Latin for love, he said we need managers who love innovation, quality and people. Those qualities, he has found, characterise the management of medium-sized firms – the fast, adaptable 'gazelles' that are most likely to survive in an era of rapid change because they are 'big enough to afford to innovate, small enough not to screw up'.[17]

In response, it was suggested that there was room for a foundation course in transferable skills, separate from company and culture-specific competencies, which is, of course, what life-skills programmes in schools are all about.

It is difficult to see how such an institute would resolve the problem of status. It has not done so in the case of engineering. An employer can employ anyone that he or she likes in an engineering function. No employer is likely to turn down a budding entrepreneur because he or she lacks qualifications. Both engineers and managers would improve their status if they were paid more. But they would become more significant if more of them were on the boards of British companies. Unfortunately, the road to the board is through the City.[18] This means that such status is not perceived to be a possibility and, in consequence, they do not seek a training that will give them executive responsibility. It may also be a consequence of the stratification between qualifications that those who enter engineering do not have a disposition for such activity. Professionalization of management might have the effect of maintaining their positions in middle management so that the persons who have to take the risk decisions continue to be the same kind of people as now.

The Professions and Restrictive Practices

It will be seen that one of the reasons why engineers and managers are unable to acquire status in British society is that they have no means of operating restrictive practices that the population at large would accept as reasonable. In a sense, and although they lack the opportunities for high pay that are open to engineers and managers, the relatively new para-medical professions are able to operate restrictive practices that give them some sense of status.

One mark of the professions in Britain is that they are self-regulating and have such organizations as the Law Society and the General Medical Council, which look after their interests. These bodies have been criticized for looking after their own interests rather than those of the public, whom they are established to serve. The 1987 Conservative government was criticized because, while it had tackled the problem of restrictive practices in the trade unions, it had not tackled those among the professions. The Law Society and the Bar came in for particular comment. The volume of criticism led the President of the Law Society to make a strong plea for self-regulation on the grounds that 'If the standards are no longer self imposed, then I suggest that the willingness of members of professions to participate in their regulation' may disappear'.[19]

Some degree of regulation is clearly necessary – the questions are, 'How much?' 'By whom?' and 'Do these organizations act in public or self-interest?' There is a feeling in Britain that they tend to act in their own rather than in the public's interest. Competition, it is thought, might bring better service and reduce costs.[20]

Professional versus Business Values

In the study reported by Barnes, it was shown that the more open the organizational system, the less the attention paid to status. It was also shown to be more efficient. Moreover, the 'open' department was not as well qualified as the 'closed' department! Motivation and opportunity offset to some extent levels of qualification. Organizational structures may be greater inhibitors of change than formal qualifications.

The same study highlights the importance of the value systems within certain organizational contexts. Apart from the desire to do science in the Barnes study, the values of the professional person who is employed can be in conflict with his or her employer, as was shown by the debate about 'Star Wars' (the Strategic Defence Initiative) in the USA in 1986. But at an operational level, the conflict might be quite different and the possession of a scientific approach unnecessarily impede adaptation. The problem is evidently to get a balance between the two. McClelland describes the work of an investigator who, to his surprise, found

> that the greater the technical capability of the company – the more industrial engineers it employed – the sooner it learned of the innovation, but the later it adopted the new technique. It is hard to pinpoint just which of the professional values mentioned earlier impede progress in this instance, but one could guess that the engineers felt responsible enough to their profession to be cautious, to insist on evidence a non-professional would not be so likely to demand, to want to approve only what they could really understand. Let me stress the obvious fact that such values are in no sense bad. They are necessary to the professions, in fact they help define the professional role.[21]

For some individuals, the professional system is of considerable importance. Thus, even within a bureaucratic orientation, there is likely to be a solidaristic grouping of people who are very active in their professional institutions. This is as true of academics as it is of engineers and others working in industry and commerce. Coping with this plurality of social systems is a learned process involving both flexibility and adaptability.

There is clearly a problem, the solution to which depends on executive management and professionals providing themselves with a much broader understanding of how science can contribute to business, on the one hand, and how business operates in the competitive environment of the world, on the other. That is to say, there can be no solution if there is not a mutuality about the goals to be obtained. It is for this reason that group work, coupled with the study of group processes (which has as its aims the understanding of behaviour and the development of coping skills) is important. Such understanding should begin in the secondary school so that individuals possess the basic frame of reference on which operational skills can be developed at work. It is from thorough understanding of human behaviour that we will be able to foster efficiency, either among professionals or on the shopfloor.

The Shopfloor

Just as the professional associations have used education to restrict entry, so have the craft unions used apprenticeship for this purpose. Because of changing technology, the craft unions, with origins that can be traced back to the medieval guilds, have had to adapt painfully and slowly as they have seen the skill base of their work eroded. There has been considerable resistance to change, and very often there have been major inter-union disputes. There have also been philosophical disputes between central-union management and their members. Some of these are never resolved and operate side by side. For example, the union view that overtime should not be worked is in stark contrast with reality in Britain where there is much overtime. Some would argue that overtime is the means by which employers pay a decent wage!

The perceptions that union officials and workers have of an additional worker may differ considerably. As Hesseling wrote:

> To the central official, overtime appears to increase the supply of a particular type of labour, with which they are concerned, without bringing any compensating increase in their influence. On the other hand, an extra employee, while increasing the supply of labour, is a potential recruit for the union. The individual worker, however, sees the extra employee in his department as increasing the supply of his type of labour with few compensating benefits. For him, however, an increase in overtime supplies the extra labour, but raises his earnings and gives his workshop organization the possibility of using a cheap industrial weapon – the overtime ban.[22]

One familiar restrictive practice is the demarcation between one job and another that generally has the effect of under-utilizing labour. A major development in this field was the introduction of productivity bargaining. A study of productivity bargaining in the Esso refinery at Fawley showed that in return for substantial pay increases overtime could be reduced. The pay increases could be offset by greater productivity. In one department this was accompanied by a reduction in the labour force employed. However, the author of the study said that the objective of this productivity bargain was to reduce under-employment, and not simply to reduce labour costs or improve labour relations, for restrictive practices often prevent workers from developing their full potential.[23] They are the source of many unofficial stoppages. Because the closed shop is thought to foster restrictive practices, it was declared illegal in Britain in the 1980s. Yet when an examination of employer attitudes is made, it is found that, while they blame unions in public, they often support them in private. Restrictive-labour practices are not generally the subject of national agreements. While a national agreement will state a minimum wage, it has no control over, say, the overtime offered by management. Thus a minimum-wage agreement is no criterion of what will actually be paid in an individual organization. Restrictive practices are 'a result of an agreed decision by the working group' and therefore 'an integral – if disturbing part of the whole ethic of labour relations in a particular plant.'[24] Consequently when, as more than once has happened,

> employers have asked for a reduction of 'restrictive practices' in return for a wage rise . . . with the best will in the world the union leaders at those bargaining tables could not commit their members up and down the country to particular changes in working practices whose significance could be evaluated only on the spot.[25]

It is in this context that the link with the study of work groups needs to be made, for when we seek to evaluate the control that unions have over restrictive practices, we find so often that it is to the workplace or to the customs of society to which we have to return. An American observer of trade unionism quoted by Flanders wrote that trade unionism

> is rooted in the customary practices and social habits of wage earners at their work long before formal organizations appear among them. To protect their customary ways of living and working, cliques and other informal groups of workers habitually adjust employers' shop regulations to bring them into line with their own traditional codes of behaviour. Union rules and collective bargaining agreements, as we know them, are in effect legislative enactments bearing the same relation to unwritten customs and codes of work that statutes do to common law. In shops untouched by unionism, informal organizations of workers develop spontaneously and unconsciously to control and regulate group conduct.[26]

And, to quote another American,

> all workers live in the short run, they marry in the short run, they bring up their children in the short run, and they either starve or prosper in the short run between birth and the grave. Democratically conducted unions are the organs of expression of these short-run human beings and will respond to change.[27]

And this is apparently what is happening in Britain at the present time, in response to the decline in membership and new legislation. Indeed unions have found that they can use the new legislation to good effect within a national context.

One response is for the unions to join together into larger conglomerates. However, this may not solve their problems because some of the major industrial disputes in England have been between large unions or among their members, as in the 1985 miners strikes,[28] and most recently between the Amalgamated Engineering Union, the Electricians Union and the Trades Union Congress. In the case of the Amalgamated Engineering Union, it offered the Ford Motor Co. a single-union deal at a new plant to be built in Dundee. The TUC, at the instigation of the Transport and General Workers Union, blocked the deal and Ford cancelled their plan to build this plant.[29] The Electrical, Electronic, Telecommunication and Plumbing Union has been expelled from the TUC for entering into such deals. The problem is accentuated by the fact that many of their members aspire to middle-class values, and some large unions are responding to this by the provision of middle-class type benefits as, for example, private medical schemes.

Whenever there is change or change is proposed, it is bound to be resisted. A conglomerate threatens the identity of a union. Institutions that are seriously threatened often resist change to the extent that they destroy themselves, and this was nearly the case with the National Union of Seamen in 1988.[30] It could be argued that the legislation that prevented an all-out strike, that is after legal action, saved the union from demise. A similar battle is being fought by the technicians in the television industry.

There is no doubt that managers are much more prepared to confront the unions than they were a few years ago, although, as Felton and Harrison have pointed out, government has not always practised what it has preached in its relations with unions in the public sector.[31] A major factor in these developments was the limitations imposed on secondary picketing in the legislation (see below). It was this that defeated the National Union of Seamen because they were forced to restrict their strike to the company with whom they were in dispute. The fact that some unions are making very big changes in their attitudes has led some foreign observers to suppose that a new forward-looking unionism is being created.[32] It is also supposed that, in 1992, Europeanism will help force new attitudes to unionism. If it does not, then it is possible that if managements follow such successful companies as Marks and Spencer, IBM, Gillette and Hewlett-Packard, with high-level welfare policies and effective grievance-procedure schemes, that the need for unions will diminish. These enterprises are not unionized.[33]

The collapse of national bargaining in favour of workplace bargaining may strengthen this movement if management can provide the leadership. At the same time, there is no inherent reason why unions cannot adapt to these changes other than the weight of their own histories.

As with all extreme positions in Britain, there has been a reaction both in legislation and attitudes since 1978, and it is therefore important to assess the extent of change, as well as the depth of belief with which it is held. To what extent are these changes a function of persisting high unemployment, or legislation, or both? While it is too early to answer these fundamental questions, substantial changes would appear to be taking place.

Changes in the Pattern of Industrial Relations

Within the space of a decade there have been substantial changes in attitudes towards industrial relations in Britain. In 1973 a Conservative government was brought down by a miners strike, and their industrial relations legislation was immediately repealed by the incoming Labour government. Since 1979, a different Conservative government has brought in new but more limited legislation that has had an immediate effect on industrial relations. At the same time, the philosophy of the Conservative Party had moved away from support for Keynesian economics and the Welfare State, towards the position of, among others, Hayek, who believed that the monopoly effect of trade unions in wage bargaining held wages high and caused inflation.

A Royal Commission on Trade Unions had held that there was no need to legislate for trade unions, and this view was, and is, widely held by many academics.[34] Against their argument stood two principles. The first related to the simple idea that no organization can be above the law; the second related to the rights of individuals as opposed to groups. It was held that individuals were denied their rights in trade unions. One argument against the introduction of new legislation was that redress could be obtained within the law as it stood, and increasingly, resort to this part of the law has been made since it has been shown to be successful.

Since 1980, apart from the miners strike, industrial action has been at a relatively low level, so it is too early to evaluate the effects of the new legislation.

In the 1985 miners strike it was not used by the Coal Board. The actions that were brought against the union were by working miners. However, the combination of high employment and legislation does seem to be having a powerful effect on industrial relations. For example, in the north-east of England, which suffered severe unemployment in the Great Depression of the 1930s, union membership has declined dramatically, and there has been an increase in the number of companies refusing to recognize unions. This is a remarkable change in a region that has nurtured a strong union tradition.[35]

Unemployment – together with a drastic fall in trade union membership – coupled with the new legislation, have undoubtedly led to this state of affairs. Bright and his colleagues go so far as to argue that these changes reflect a fundamental process that is likely to be permanent. They suggest that greater statutory protection for individuals could lead to a situation where individuals no longer felt the need for union protection. This would be in accord with the desire of the Institute of Directors, and would represent a massive change of attitude. The employment legislation, they argue, will reduce the level of strikes, although other forms of industrial unrest will become commonplace. Early in 1987, the Conservative government began to consider legislation that would further secure individual rights.

During the 1980s, other changes took place in industrial relations, which included the collapse of industry-wide bargaining in favour of bargaining with a single employer.[36] It also seems that there has been a decline in piece-work payments, while more plant and group incentive-schemes have been introduced. These have been accompanied by rigorous work study and job evaluation. As might be expected in work-bargaining situations, the role of the shop steward has become enhanced.[37] Now they are able to seek equity and good relations with management who, in their turn, help to create an organization of shop stewards within the organization, so as to avoid, if possible, shopfloor bargaining.[38]

Among recent developments in employment practice have been the development of flexible work schedules. These are now common among clerical employees. Workers in five insurance companies were found to have improved their performance when flexitime was introduced. No relationship between flexibility and job satisfaction was found! Flexitime has also been found to reduce stress, which is related to child-rearing activities even though it did not change the pattern of chores undertaken in the family.[39]

An area of work practice that is receiving more attention is work-sharing as a means of reducing unemployment.

Work-Sharing

A few years ago it would not have been possible to discuss work-sharing as a possible solution to some types of unemployment. Workers who are put into unemployment by cyclical fluctuations in the demand for their products suffer considerable injustices, which may be overcome if everyone in the workforce takes a reduction in hours so that everyone can be employed on a continuous basis.

In Canada, where work-sharing is defined as temporary short-time working to reduce redundancies, it was found that while it was accepted at the local level, the unions at national level opposed this practice because, while it reduced the measured rate of unemployment, it also released politicians from the pressures to do something about unemployment. Management organizations in their turn suggested that work-sharing and the incentives associated with it postponed essential adjustments in the distribution and allocation of the workforce in the economy. The investigators who looked at these schemes concluded, in contrast, that the benefits in terms of better industrial relations and reductions in the costs of hiring and firing outweighed the disadvantages suggested by the central organizations.[40]

In Europe, there have been a number of work-sharing schemes and much has been written on the topic.[41] The troubled Westland Aircraft Company created a double day-shift for technicians in computer-aided design. The working week was reduced from 37 hours to 32.5 hours. It seems that in Britain, France and West Germany there is strong opposition from employers who believe that such schemes increase costs, reduce competitiveness and thus lower profit level.

In Europe, one response in West Germany has been to encourage early retirement, but this will only work if a nation has sufficient resources with which to pay the pensions. In France the number of jobs created by work-sharing was half that predicted. Small firms were found to behave in different ways from large firms. The smaller enterprises reduced production capacity and did not increase employment.

The reaction of the Confederation of British Industry suggests that work-sharing schemes have not been rejected out of hand. They would be more acceptable if, in return for more leisure, workers accepted less pay. The trouble is that leisure costs money, and in a low-wage economy this is likely to prove unacceptable. It has been suggested that unemployment could be alleviated by extra educational leisure, particularly for adults, sabbatical periods, and more flexible working weeks, all of which have been on the European agenda. Unfortunately, in Britain it seems that in the long run a reduction in hours tends to reduce employment, and that the drive for a shorter working week could cause workers to be less productive.[42]

Changes in the labour market during the last decade tend to support the negative view. The Manpower Services Commission has published data that shows the growth of a 'parallel' market for labour, which does not help the situation at all. Employers want part-time labour and they find it among housewives and others seeking 'second' jobs. They do not find it in the dole queue for full-time work. This explains the fact that between 1983 and 1986 while unemployment increased, the number of jobs increased faster than the number of people of working age.[43] At the same time, the number of school-leavers declined.

Individuals like work, and many of them seek part-time jobs because of their circumstances. Moral issues relating to unemployment are not considered and like many other issues of this kind, probably the only way to change the situation is through changes in the system of taxation and social security. Even then, women may want to work simply because of the distaste of permanent residence in the home.

Despite all these factors, the debate about work-sharing is likely to continue on both sides of the Atlantic,[44] particularly if high unemployment persists.

The Readiness for Change and Management

But change will not endure unless there are changing attitudes throughout society, and especially in management. There are many examples of sensible suggestions by workers that have been rejected by management.[45] If there is to be change, it is management that must take the initiative. Strikes may be caused by payment schemes presented in an unacceptable manner. A firm in financial difficulties may say that it will only offer a 2 per cent rise when most other firms are offering between 15 and 20 per cent. Such a rise may not be acceptable, if it is a large firm, and the workers believe that support for a strike would be forthcoming from the community. Their views are determined by the rise in retail prices. They are short-term in outlook. It might be better in such circumstances to offer nothing. In either case management needs to undertake a substantial preparatory exercise among the workers. It is, of course, possible that the workers are not 'ready' for such a change. Preparation is for 'readiness'. Judgements about the level of 'readiness' among a workforce are as important managerially as they are to teachers and parents in training children to read.

'Readiness' is the adequacy of a pupil, or a worker's existing capacity, to achieve an instructional or work objective. It is an 'entering behaviour' in solving a problem. Before a child can read, he or she has to have acquired other basic information before he or she can undertake the task. There is either specific training or preparation. In this sense there is no difference between formal training and discussion prior to negotiation. Both have the objective of enabling future learning. In the case of the worker, it will be learning from the point of view of understanding, which has been facilitated by prior discussion. Given this principle of learning, it is easy to assemble a case for worker representation in the management of organization.

It is a basic contention of this book that in many instances neither the workforce nor management are 'ready' for the interpersonal discussion necessary to handle the complexities with which society faces organizations and workers and, therefore, for participatory management. Moreover, this is due in part to the historical development of 'us' and 'them' attitudes and much associated injustice. It is also due in part to inappropriate schooling, and a failure of the education system to help students of all levels of achievement to develop interpersonal skills as well as skills in the areas of adaptation and control. One consequence is that the restrictive practices imposed by both workers and professionals become impediments to learning, and thus to adaptability.

. . . And Society

Change without a corresponding change in social attitudes may not be long lasting. The failure of the 1984 miners strike showed that, between 1973 and 1984, there had been a change in social attitudes toward the miners. During this period the more able persons in the mining communities left them for work elsewhere, leaving the lower achievers. Management had, therefore, to communicate with persons with very different and possibly limited frames of reference, who received very substantial support from their families to continue the strike. Musgrove, who discussed this issue, argued that this kind of circumstance must not be allowed to happen again, and that this is a problem for society.[46] If social beliefs and practices condition attitudes to work, how important are they? Does education re-inforce them or create them? How permanent are they? Is there such a thing as national character? To what extent are restrictive practices symptomatic of a more general social *malaise*?

The role of society in the determination of national achievement is considered in the next chapter.

Notes and References

1. Clarke, C. and Banks, P. (1982) How to tackle Japan, *Management Today*, February, pp. 50–3.
2. Reading, B. (1985) Cash markets waive the economists' rules, *The Sunday Times*, 22 September.
3. *Midland Bank Review* (1986) Capital markets boom in 1985 ahead of the 'Big Bang', Spring, pp. 14–23; and Peacock, A. (1984) Privatisation in perspective, *Three Banks Review*, no. 144, pp. 3–25.
4. Lord, R. (1988) Our farms should grow crops not subsidies, *The Times*, 9 May.
5. The reports were *Higher Technological Education* (1945); *Engineering Design* (1963); *Engineering Our Future* (1980) – all HMSO, London. An article taking the view that there was no shortage of qualified manpower is Heywood, J. (1974) Trends in the supply and demand for qualified manpower, *Vocational Aspect of Education*, Vol. 26, no. 64, pp. 65–72.
6. Lilley, S. (1970) *Technological Progress and the Industrial Revolution*, 'Fontana Economic History of Europe', Fontana, London.
7. In 1961, the Ministry of Education published a white paper, *Better Opportunities in Technical Education* HMSO, London. Later, business and technician education councils were created to control technician qualifications. Subsequently, they were merged.
8. Marshall, T.H. (1963) essay in *Sociology at the Crossroads*, Heinemann, London.
9. For a detailed description of Japanese high schools, see Rohlen, T.P. (1983) *Japan's High Schools*, University of California Press, Berkely, Calif.
10. *Ibid.*
11. The Engineering Council was established in 1984 and replaced the Council of Engineering Institutions. It regulates entry to the profession at all levels. The Chartered Engineer qualification is obtained by students who have taken an enhanced course at university. Such courses are equivalent to honours degree level. They are becoming of four, as opposed to three years' duration. An ordinary or unclassified degree will relate to the standard required for an engineering technician. The qualifications for this award will be the National Certificate awarded by the Business and Technician Education Council.
    The regulations provide that courses for the Technician Engineer level should be designed so that a student can 'proceed directly to Technician Engineer level'. The potential for transfer from Engineering Technician to Chartered Engineer seems to be more restricted as the council wants to see the courses take a new direction. Perhaps they will approximate to the American degrees in engineering technology.
12. Clements, I. and Roberts, I. (1981) Practitioner views of industrial needs and course unit content, in J. Heywood (ed.) *The New Technician Education*, Society for Research into Higher Education, Guildford.
13. Lawrence, P.A., Hutton, S.P. and Smith, J.H. (1977) *The Recruitment, Deployment and Status of the Mechanical Engineer in the German Federal Republic*, 3 parts, Department of Mechanical Engineering, The University of Southampton, Southampton.

14. *Ibid.*
15. Heywood, J. (1983) Professional studies and validation, in C.H. Church (ed.) *Practice and Perspective in Validation*, Society for Research into Higher Education, Guildford.
16. Thackray, J. (1988) Tightening the white collar, *Management Today*, July, pp. 80–4.
17. Golzen, G. (1988) Managers wary of charter, *The Sunday Times*, 3 July.
18. Mant, A. (1979) *The Rise and Fall of the British Manager,* Pan, London, regards this as one of the major factors that has led to Britain's continuing industrial decline.
19. Bradbeer, Sir D. (1988) Leaving regulations to the professionals, *The Times*, 5 July.
20. Fennell, E. (1988) Pop go the professions, *The Times*, 5 July. In 1989 the Conservative government introduced proposals to reduce restrictive practices in the legal profession.
21. McClelland, D.C. (1969) The role of achievement orientation in the transfer of technology, in W.H. Gruber and D.G. Marquis (eds.) *Factors in the Transfer of Technology,* MIT Press, Cambridge, Mass.
22. Hesseling, P. (1966) *A Strategy for Evaluation Research,* Van Gorcum, Assen.
23. Flanders, A. (1964) *The Fawley Productivity Agreements*, Faber & Faber, London – a highly regarded pioneering study in the field of industrial relations.
24. Cyrian, G. and Oakeshott, B. (1960) *The Bargainers*, Faber & Faber, London.
25. A statement by Professor Phelps Brown quoted by Flanders, *Fawley* (note 23).
26. Leiserson, W.M. (1959) *American Trade Union Democracy*, Columbia University Press, New York, NY, quoted by Flanders, *The Fawley* (note 23).
27. Gomberg, W. (1946) Union participation in high productivity, *The Annals of the American Academy of Political and Social Science*, Nov., p. 73, quoted by Flanders, *The Fawley* (note 23).
28. Lover, J. (1980) Why unions won't reform, *Management Today*, September, pp. 98–100.
29. Comments in the British newspapers for the first three weeks of March 1988.
30. Comments in the British newspapers for last three weeks of April, 1988.
31. Felton, D. and Harrison, M. (1988) Management on the offensive, *The Independent*, 12 May.
32. Bratt, C. (Director of the Swedish Employers Confederation) (1988) A Swedish view of UK labour, *The Sunday Times*, 24 April.
33. Newman, N. (1980) The joint industry solution, *Management Today*, April, pp. 60–5.
34. Pelling, H. (1976) *A History of British Trade Unionism,* Penguin Books, Harmondsworth.
35. Bright, D., Sawbridge, D. and Rees, B. (1983) Industrial relations of recession, *Industrial Relations Journal*, Vol. 14, no. 3, pp. 24–33. Unemployment in Britain has never stimulated much political action. For a commentary on this aspect, see Garraty, J.A. (1978) *Unemployment in History: Economic Thought and Public Policy*, Harper & Row, New York, NY.
36. Sisson, K. and Brown W. (1983) Industrial relations in the private sector, Donovan revisited, in G. Bain (ed.) *Industrial Relations in Great Britain*, Blackwell, Oxford.
37. Millward, N. (1983) Workplace industrial relations – result of a new survey of industrial relations practices, *Employment Gazette*, Vol. 91, no. 7, pp. 280–9.
38. Purcell, J. and Sisson, K. (1983) Strategies and practices in the management of industrial relations, in G. Bain (ed.) *Industrial Relations in Great Britain,* Blackwell, Oxford; and Pierce, J.L. and Newstrom, J.W. (1983) The design of flexible work schedules and employee responses, relationships and processes, *Journal of Occupational Behaviour*, Vol. 4, no. 4, pp. 247–62.
39. Lee, R.A. (1983) Flexitime and conjugal roles, *Journal of Occupational Behaviour*, Vol. 4, no.4, pp. 297–315.
40. Meltz, W. and Reid, F. (1983) Reducing the impact of unemployment through work sharing: some industrial relations considerations, *Journal of Industrial Relations*, Vol. 25. no. 2, pp. 153–61.
41. Jones, S.G. (1985) The worksharing debate in western Europe, *National Westminster Bank Quarterly Review*, February, pp. 30–41.
42. Symons, J.S.V. (1981) *The Demand for Labour in British Manufacturing*, Centre for Labour Economics, London School of Economics, Discussion Paper no. 91.
43. Hogg, S. (1985) Jobs: it's all a matter of timing, *The Times*, 10 July.
44. Olmsted, B. (1983) Changing times; the use of reduced work time options in the United States, *International Labour Review*, Vol. 122, no. 4, pp. 479–92.
45. Lee, M. (1982) Danger men at work. Why don't they ask?, *Management Today*, May, pp. 50–3.
46. Musgrove, F. (1984) Lost kingdoms of the mining men, *The Sunday Times*, 12 August.

9
NATIONAL ATTITUDES AND GROWTH

Introduction

What makes one country succeed and another fail in the economic sphere? This is the issue with which this chapter is concerned. It is argued that the system of values a society holds are crucial, or otherwise, for economic growth. It seems that in the long run, attitudes can and do change. Since 1950, West Germany has been the dominant economic force in Europe, and the USA was the world power. Now Japan has overtaken them, and there is a possibility that other countries in the Far East, such as China, Korea or Taiwan, will also make substantial inroads into the world economy.

Although Britain is a major power, it was for many years regarded as a dying economy. It was held that the British had a disease commonly called the 'British disease', or 'British *malaise*'. Within the last eight years, Britain has experienced a remarkable resurgence in its economy. This would seem to have been accompanied by a change in attitudes. It is too early to determine if this change in attitudes is permanent, or is a shift occasioned by severe unemployment. There is no evidence to suggest that there has been a change in attitudes towards industry. If this is the case, then Britain continues to have a problem. It seems that the USA has a similar problem. Britain is fortunate in having the *choc des opinions* of the single European market to look towards in 1992. It is also fortunate that among its major competitors in Europe, there is also a *malaise*. This seems to be particularly true of France.

That the economic fortunes of nations go up and down is well understood. Even West Germany is finding it relatively difficult going at present. Denmark and Sweden provide examples of this see-saw effect. This chapter opens with a short résumé of some developments in Europe, the USA and Japan.

Each culture has its own particular system of values, the orientation of which determines national growth. This view is introduced by McClelland's now-classical theory of the achieving society. Although Mant's study of the *Rise and Fall of the British Manager* was written at the height of the so-called British malaise in 1979, it contains a number of axioms that are as true today as they were then. These relate to the ability to fight within the European market, expertise and commitment in the top management of companies, and the general dislike of industry in Britain. A particular problem in Europe could well be a shortage of skilled labour.

It is important that societies should understand the values they hold, particularly in respect of the generation of wealth. The creation of wealth brings with it obligations as well as rights.

Recent developments in Europe, the USA and Japan

West Germany (the German Federal Republic) has been the most successful nation in Europe since 1950. Despite some ups and downs this success has been relatively consistent. As we saw in the last chapter, it has been put down to the positive attitudes the Germans have toward industry and technology. It was also suggested that German attitudes toward social status were significant. Some historians suggest that it was due to the industrial and economic bases that Germany established between the two wars.[1] Others relate it more generally to the characteristics of German nationalism as they have developed since the Industrial Revolution and the foundation of the modern State.[2] The Germans themselves consider that their dual system of education and training has had a major role to play in this development. Skilled work at the craft and technician levels is highly valued. In recent years, however, the German economy has been sluggish.

Apart from West Germany, Sweden has also been regarded as a highly successful country in the 1950s and 1960s. Its system of comprehensive education was held up as a model for other countries to copy: its system of industrial participation is still highly regarded.[3] Most recently, Denmark has also begun to make a remarkable recovery from a situation similar to that in which Ireland found itself in at the end of 1986, which was an economy in deep recession and considerable national debt.

It is widely held, and certainly the British take it to be the case, that from the mid-1950s, Britain's economic performance began to decline. A whole host of reasons were given. These included poor education and training, a lack of research, an inability to perceive the needs of the market and an equal inability to translate good ideas into marketable products. The British *malaise* or disease, as it was widely called in other countries, was widely associated with trade union power and the inability of managements to control that power. Much soul searching was done in Britain. A great deal of attention was paid to the performance of other countries and especially the American regeneration between 1980 and 1984, with its 'apparent' contradiction of economic theory and, more recently, its approach to taxation. There is a growing school of thought that now holds that these beliefs were a myth. If this is true, the beliefs that a country has about itself will be as important as the value system, if it is appropriate to make such a subtle distinction. This is a point to which we will return.

Some think that the American success is due to small business, but the statistics do not support this view. In any case, many American markets have become victims of Japanese competition. All the countries of the west have devoted much time to the study of Japan and the reasons for its economic success. Notwithstanding the American–Japanese economic relationship, the economic ties America has with the rest of the world are of profound significance. The means the USA uses to reduce its balance of payments deficit with the rest of the world influences the economic performance of the rest of the world.

Comparative studies of industrial practice in Japan now fill the pages of the journals and house magazines. Underlying all the findings is the importance of Japanese social structure and national attitudes. So it is that in the past few years there has been a willingness to entertain what may best be called 'economic psychology', in academic and political circles.[4] We are now prepared to ask the question, 'Are there national attitudes that influence performance?' Strangely enough, McClelland's classic study of this question – *The Achieving Society* – is more often than not ignored in this area of fascination.[5] It will be argued, however, in later paragraphs that it has considerable relevance to the understanding of national character.

Cairncross, in an address to the British Association, said

> that technological change has been the main spring of economic and social progress over the past two centuries, and that it remains the chief source of our increasing affluence. Whatever may be said to pooh-pooh or deride economic growth – economists are not behind hand in these flights – no one would want us to go back to the mode of living of 1770, still less to the lower standards to which the present population could be reduced if we abandoned every improvement in technology since then.[6,7]

How then, if at all, do national characteristics influence attitudes to growth and thus to economic and industrial efficiency? In this chapter we shall mainly consider the theories of McClelland and Mant,[8] although studies and polemics in this area are now a thriving endeavour.[9] It will be argued that there are national dispositions toward wealth and its creation through work, and that these influence entrepreneurship and, in consequence, economic growth. It will also be argued that the beliefs a nation holds about itself are as important as the other values that contribute to economic drive.

Achievement Motivation and Economic Success

The idea of achievement motivation is well understood and documented in education. It is sometimes called 'need for achievement' and was defined by McClelland, who gave it the letters 'Nach', for he believed it was as important as intelligence (to which psychologists had given the letter 'g').[10] He also thought it could be measured. The extension of the concept of achievement in this way was not received very well by psychologists, and a great many have ignored it altogether.[11] Other psychologists argue that there is no single scorable 'need for achievement', but several distinct functional sources, such as the self-assertive urge or self-sentiment, which may stand at quite different levels in the community.

Even so, the characteristics of an achieving person described by McClelland are readily acceptable. Thus de Cecco and Crawford, the authors of a textbook on eduational psychology, are able to refer to McClelland's work without referring to the concept of Nach.[12]

Need for achievement, or achievement motivation, is a learned motive to compete and to strive for success in situations where one's performance can be evaluated against some standard of performance. Because achievement motivation is learned, McClelland believed that it could be developed in adults. The characteristics such persons as a student or a manager with a high need for achievement possess are as follows:

1. A desire for positive feedback on their performance. (They need to know how well they are doing.)
2. A desire to be responsible for the task. (They need to feel satisfaction for a task well done.)
3. A desire to put their own work goals at a moderate level of difficulty. (Goals that cannot be attained because they are too difficult, and goals that are too easy will not yield satisfaction.)
4. A desire to take the initiative in the exploration of the environment.

A similar typology has been produced by Casson,[13] who distinguishes between enterprising and unenterprising workers thus:

> The enterprising worker may be defined as someone who is strongly committed to work as a means of generating income and improving his status, and who takes a broad view of his economic environment and a long view of his own employment prospects. The enterprising worker is therefore responsive to economic incentives such as higher wages, relatively unconcerned by the social disruption caused by migration, recognises the need for education and training, is hard-working in pursuit of promotion, and regularly scans vacancies in case there is a better job with another firm.

In contrast, the

> unenterprising worker may be defined as someone who is either committed to work only because he likes the kind of work involved, or he is not committed to work at all, but to leisure or social activities instead. He attaches little importance to economic advancement: income is demanded chiefly to support his leisure or social activities. His lack of interest in economic advancement means that he attaches little importance to education and training, he has a narrow view of his economic environment, and little awareness of what other opportunities are open to him. . . . The unenterprising worker who is interested in his work may well be skilled, but will be unadaptable and therefore occupationally immobile, the unenterprising worker who is uninterested in his work will be unskilled, unadaptable to semi-skilled work and geographically mobile.[14]

In a situation where structural unemployment is important, the possession of such attitudes in a community will have an important bearing on the nature and response to unemployment. It will also have a bearing on the approach governments take to unemployment.

A further psychological dimension in Casson's theory is the parallel he draws with old age. In the very long run, economies go senile, and it is possible that the

British economy has been going senile since the 1920s.[15] As we age, attitudes harden, so it is not surprising that workers who are in an enterprise of long-standing do not respond to change. In the open system in which we live, high prices and over capacity give newly developing countries the opportunity to enter the market because they offer the same goods or substitutes at a lower price.[16] Senility is characterized, it seems, by loss of markets. The political problem is, therefore, to provide an environment in which workers will want to be enterprising.

Thus, people with high levels of need for achievement set themselves realistic problems, which are just a little bit beyond their immediate grasp but which they perceive can be solved. McClelland argues that the making of a profit is by no means the most important incentive for such people. Drive is not inspired by the profit motive but because profitability provides the objective measure of competence the high-need achiever requires. Further, achievement satisfaction probably arises for individuals who have initiated an action and observe it becoming successful. For example, de Beneditti, the person who rebuilt the Italian company, Olivetti, in the early 1980s, is reported as saying

> A goal for instance is being able to become as we have done, the number one in Europe after IBM. This is a goal. This is a motivating theme for people. The profit is just a condition, but what does it mean to become the leader in Europe if you don't make profits? The human and professional objective is the company's growth, and the condition for having healthy growth is profit. And the way to see if you are going the right way is to see whether what you are accomplishing is with, or without profit.[17]

McClelland has designed training schemes to develop achievement motivation in business people. He does not claim 100 per cent achievement. Another American has attempted to apply these techniques to under-achievers in school. However, they were used during a summer school and not during time-tabled schooling. Recent developments in vocational preparation programmes and mini-companies will give teachers the opportunity to experiment with similar programmes to see if they have relevance in the school situation *per se*.

The student has to have reasons for developing a motive that is seen to be realistic and can be linked to everyday life, and it is the provision of realistic goals to motivate the low achiever that is both the major educational and industrial problem. The high-achieving student will record his or her progress in obtaining concrete goals, engage in self-study and want to belong to a successful group.

National Attitudes to Achievement

In his *The Achieving Society*,[18] McClelland argued that a person's need for achievement could be derived from the rate of frequency with which an individual spontaneously produces thoughts, as in telling stories to pictures. That can be coded objectively as dealing with doing something well or better than before or well or better than someone else. McClelland suggested that if children's literature influenced children's attitudes and subsequently the dispositions they take up in life, then books can be analysed for the values portrayed in their texts.

McClelland and his colleagues studied the popular literature of a number of countries at different periods in their history, and concluded that when this literature was achievement oriented, the rate of economic growth speeded up after a lapse of between 50 and 100 years.

As if to confirm McClelland's thesis Carey, a reviewer of a book that attempted to explain why there was a golden age in English literature, wrote if his argument is right then, a golden age in children's literature heralds a loss of national confidence. McClelland goes on to argue that popular concern with achievement motivation increases the number of business people with high levels of need for achievement (Nach), and it is this that leads to successful entrepreneurship and growth in a society.

Based on the analysis of children's textbooks, McClelland found that, whereas Britain was ranked 5 out of 25 countries in 1925, it ranked 26 out of 39 in 1930 by his parameters of achievement level. This led him to conclude that it was a lack of entrepreneurial leadership in Britain that was the cause of Britain's economic decline.[19]

In Victorian times, writes Bradley, 'business was seen as a romance and books by the score portrayed the lives of entrepreneurs both as gripping adventure stories and also as examples of high moral principle dedication to public service and concern for others'.[20] But in manufacturing industry, Britain was already on the decline, as historical tables of the parameters of the economy show.[21]

De Cecco and Crawford wrote that in education we sometimes call the need for achievement, the pursuit of excellence.[22] In history and sociology, we call it the protestant ethic. We can deduce from this that a nation that has the protestant ethic and loses it would go into decline. This would seem to be the view of such Conservatives in England as Mrs Thatcher, who call for a return to Victorian values. Within the context of McClelland's theory, it may be significant that many teachers in Britain do not believe in competition within schools and do not like the examination system, whereas in Japan, high-school students are subject to very severe competition, as we will see later.

The behaviour we adopt at work, or in the family, or towards our friends, or the demands we make of society, derive from the value systems acquired in our early years, and these are re-inforced or challenged as we grow up and interact with society.

Bureaucrats and Entrepreneurs

McClelland draws attention to the distinction between ambition and efficiency. Ambition is the goal of an achievement-oriented person. Once one problem has been solved, there is a loss of interest and a search for a new problem to be solved. The high-need achiever is always seeking new problems to solve. Routine tasks are accompanied by a loss of incentive. In contrast, effectiveness is the goal of the bureaucrat, which is not conducive to economic progress. Bureaucrats work hard and efficiently at everything, whereas there is a tendency for those with a high need for achievement to be selective.

Both types are required for the successful running of a nation, but it could be that at some time bureaucratic attitudes take preference over the entrepreneurial. These attitudes are learnt young in the family and society as children grow up. Entrepreneurially oriented parents will want the child to acquire independence and learn self-denial and self-control. The child learns that the world is a place in which things may be accomplished. It is a world view that encourages achievement. Contrast this child with one who is taught to value patience and conformity, who believes the environment can be trusted, who relaxes in an atmosphere relatively free of discipline, who sees the world as a benign place where one can get by through waiting to see what happens. It is a world view that helps people to be impartial – extreme types perhaps – but recognizable among our friends.

When it comes to making decisions about industry, the criteria with which entrepreneurs and bureaucrats view applications for government support will differ considerably. A bureaucrat is necessarily on the defensive. He or she will not be worried about performance but about whether or not he or she has acted correctly. Concern is for procedure rather than results. The same is true of both academics and lawyers. In contrast, the business person has to innovate to survive and in so doing he or she must take risks, and often against the advice of professionally oriented people. A bureaucrat is not allowed to take a risk with other people's money.

One effect of such attitudes is that it takes time for government departments to make decisions. Industry often requires quick decisions. For example, the chairman of the car manufacturer, British Leyland, thought three months was quite adequate for the government to vet a two-year corporate plan that required £1,200 million from that government. He argued that delay in approval would threaten the implementation of their next car range.[23] The distinguished scientist and war-time civil servant, R.V. Jones, in a letter to *The Times* (17 December, 1980), wrote:

> Much of the trouble arises from the isolation of civil servants from outside experience. Not for nothing are the heads known as mandarins, for the latter made the same mistake of isolating themselves from productive activity, wearing their finger nails long to show that they never did physical work. Although the American system, where senior civil servants change with the politics of the government, has obvious faults, this at least has the merit that men are perforce exchanged between the civil service and industry and other forms of administration, forming a corpus of men at each side who have experience of working on the other.

All this seems to lead to the idea that governments should not involve themselves in industry. At the same time, it is difficult to see how they can try to fund everything even in a limited way. Similarly, the view that governments should intervene is glamorized by the idea that expensive research will solve natural problems. Yet there is no need for such expenditure. There are many examples to show that the purchase of research from other countries can be equally as effective.[24] To do this requires a change. Concentration on research at the expense of the market can only lead to further decline. It is by no means certain that British business people are entrepreneurially oriented for, as Turner has pointed out,[25] many of them seem to have been more concerned to obtain such honours as knighthoods through contributions to government as advisers on national committees than with the activities of entrepreneurship. So it is that the Civil Service and the professions with reasonable-to-high salaries and index-linked pensions prove very attractive to the most able students. At all levels, the Welfare State would seem to have encouraged the security motive at the expense of achievement motive. If the working man from Merseyside, who is quoted below, is correct, welfarism can have serious consequences for the role of unskilled groups in society. Lee has written that

> A carefree class has arisen which knows that virtually everything can be obtained from the State. . . . If everything is provided, so long as the rules are complied with, the right number of children appear, and so on, then it must clearly seem rather immoral to do much and risk losing any of the benefits. Initiative is sapped, and ambition smothered, by the system that was supposed to foster them. Education is derided, but self-expression applauded, so that the services provided are rapidly degenerating, the cultural level becomes more crude, and activity gets direction more and more towards pleasing the self. It yields an extremely selfish and unhelpful attitude. In contrast there are those who 'are old fashioned enough to believe that one should only receive what one earns'. Thus, two contrasting cultures revolve around each of these two poles.[26]

The concept of the Welfare State is particularly suited to the intellectual who believes that the needs of individuals, and particularly those who are unable to fend for themselves, should be planned by the State. It becomes a substitute for the feudal lord and benevolent paternalism.

The views of the Conservative governments of the 1980s were that the bureaucracy was wasteful and gobbled up the nation's wealth. At the same time it created what is now commonly called a dependency state and took away responsibility from the individual. Therefore, the objectives of government were to reduce the role of the State in welfare and to foster a commitment to the idea and practice of individual responsibility. It was argued that these objectives could only be achieved if there was economic regeneration. It is clear that even if the politicians had not heard of McClelland's theory, they understood a theory that was remarkably similar. The trouble is that the practical application of a theory within a political framework often produces paradox to the extent that the theory is not supported. For example, there is no indication that the new educational curriculum in Britain will support the need for achievement.

Achievement Motivation and Japan

The Japanese system of education is the epitome of a meritocracy. It is totally oriented by examinations and thus by achievement. Selection takes place in the school system although up to about the ninth grade there is a tightly structured common curriculum. The development of élitist private schools to ensure entry to the most prestigious universities is a particular mark of this achievement-dominated society, which sees the utilization of human resources as fundamental. American investigators have concluded that the knowledge gained by a Japanese on leaving high school was equivalent to that of an American graduate leaving college.[27] The overall achievement of Japanese schooling is not in creating an élite but in establishing a higher general level of capability throughout the population. Underpinning the educational system is the dedication of the family to education and its commitment to the professional success of the household. The Japanese regard such competition as being in the interests of their country and they are motivated to work. This is in marked contrast to the findings of Deutsch[28] in America, who advocates co-operation rather than competition, and this is the belief of many teachers. The high schools stratify along class lines, and teachers in some vocational schools do experience a sense of *anomie* because their students have little prospect of taking university examinations. The widening of the intake has created problems for the slow learner because the pace of lessons has not changed. There is no attempt at mixed ability teaching, and it is among the slow learners – those who have a hard time in keeping up – where suicides are most likely, according to Rohlen.[29]

The schools are organized so that there is not a student counter-culture. Students remain in the same class throughout the day except for art, music and science. They travel to and from home, which is the other centre of their existence. Rohlen calculates that, excluding exercise and leisure, 5 hours per week are spent in social relations, 16 hours on television viewing and 15 hours at homework. This is in stark contrast to the USA, where adolescents do not stay at home in the evenings, and have plenty of pocket money. In Britain and Ireland, students in examination years would do up to 14 or 15 hours a week homework. Admittedly, the patterns of behaviour have moved away from such rigour. In Japan, patterns of behaviour learnt in the family and school are transferred to work in the larger companies, which provide permanent employment and status. There are considerable inequalities, as between the professional élite and those who work in the small sub-contracting organizations. The small-group loyalties of the latter tend to be within their own economic classes. Those who enter the large companies as permanent employees find their interpersonal relationships develop within the organization.

Overall, the rigid curriculum, the attention to detail that fact-finding examinations require, helps to create a workforce with a high level of skills and good work habits. Routine jobs are done well and, when necessary, longer hours are worked to solve problems. Japanese management techniques depend on values and attitudes that derive from the complex interaction of the organization with society, family and schooling. The organization complements them with company training. Compared with the USA, Japan spends much less on education for a much higher average level of ability. Part of this efficiency is obtained by a longer school day, and sixty more days in school in the year than in the USA.

Rohlen suggests that the Japanese system may be creating troubles for itself since, in order for Japan to assume a leadership role in the world, it will have to be more open and flexible. Both Duke[30] and Rohlen take the view that the education students receive is not open to the development of spontaneity and imagination. Listening is at the expense of writing and creativity. Taken together with the problem of the slow learner, it seems likely that the Japanese would, if they view these problems as crucial, follow their industrial practice and look for the best practices in the western world in order to incorporate them into the scheme of things.

Both Duke and Rohlen attempt to draw lessons for the USA from the Japanese experience. They say that America must recognize and try to match the accomplishments of the Japanese. To do this, argues Rohlen, those in America would have to

> reverse our retreat from the responsibilities of child rearing, to end our casual, laissez-faire approach to pedagogy, and to enshrine excellence in the academic fundamentals. These are basic challenges. We may also have to set national standards and acknowledge the tracking by ability in secondary education. All this may be seen to represent a retreat into traditionalism, but I prefer to see it as confirming two basic articles of faith: that life rests on social interdependence, and that the achievement of human potential is a fundamental social good. Individualism and freedom in any other context are sad illusions, and progress toward social equality that cannot be integrated with the pursuit of general excellence has no long-term viability.[31]

Several American educationalists are saying the same.

One reason suggested for the Japanese success is that, whereas in Japan most children were in primary schools at the beginning of the twentieth century, this was not the case in Britain. This made available to Japanese industrialists an educated workforce, and they were prepared to provide additional training. In contrast, the industrialization of Britain took place without an educated workforce and many employers still do not think that substantial training is necessary.[32]

The evidence is surely that there is something in the national-character argument, for Japan, like Germany, has picked itself up twice. It seems likely, therefore, that British attitudes to industrial and commercial life are an influence on performance.

The British 'Miracle'

An OECD report published in 1986 shows that, for the period 1982 to 1986, Britain was at the top of the growth table.[33] The percentage change in gross national product averaged 14 per cent, whereas between 1977 and 1981 it was 3.2 per cent and between 1972 and 1976 it was 12.5 per cent. Smallwood, commenting on this report, suggests that it shows that, contrary to the view that Britain was in a state of decline, that the level of affluence is comparable to the greater part of Europe and Japan. The argument is based on the view that in the past, the comparisons with other countries have been misleading, for they have been given in terms of income per head. The only possible way to arrive at a measure of affluence is to compare the purchasing power of those average incomes. When relative prices, including rents, were calculated by the OECD, it showed that the Japanese are only slightly more prosperous, although the Americans appear to be 50 per cent better off.[34]

Congdon, in another article, argues from a different set of statistics that there has been a fundamental change in the British economy since it stayed at the top of the growth league from 1982 to 1986[35] (14.2 per cent change in the ratio of GDP/GNP). In the previous five-year cycles, the change was 3.2 per cent (1977–81), and 12.5 per cent (1972–6). He suggests that the economic policies pursued by the government in this period provided a more congenial environment for enterprise, saving and growth. They created more business opportunities. He bases his argument on those put in the previous chapter relating to the removal of restrictive practices and financial liberalization, which has brought a new prosperity to the City of London. But he hesitates to draw the conclusion that this change of direction is permanent, for he argues that monetary restraint has broken down since the middle of 1985. There has been a substantial increase in credit and inflation has begun to increase. At the time of writing, interest rates were substantially increased: 'Sceptics may reasonably doubt the success of the rejuvenation therapy if the sick man shows signs of slipping back to his bad old habits so soon after his supposed return to health.[36]

In contrast, although to be fair his objectives and statistics are different, Smallwood takes a different view. He finds to his surprise that the picture communicated to him, year in and year out, that Britain was in decline was simply not true. Worse, it

> provided a depressing backcloth throughout most people's working lives. The psychology of failure has damaged industrial confidence and enterprise, weakened faith in our national institutions, caused people to resign themselves with a sense of fatalism to shoddy and declining standards in the public services, and reduced the country's political influence abroad.[37]

Translated into the classroom, we see in Smallwood's picture the low achiever – the student who continually fails his or her examinations, who fails because he or she anticipates failure. Such students lack confidence, and confidence is gained from success. So much research on achievement shows that success breeds success. Thus, if the British turnaround is to be successful, it is important that Britons should gain a confidence in what they do. A measure of this success will be the extent to which manufacturers can once again persuade Britons that British goods are best.

Is there anything in the past that would indicate the permanence or otherwise of this revival?

Attitudes Towards Industry

Have attitudes towards industry changed? The idea that the British believe industry 'to be not quite nice' has been around for a long time. One should not get one's hands dirty, either through practical work or shady financial deals. The southerners who regard themselves as the English never come into contact with 'real' (heavy and dirty) industry that is, or used to be, conveniently stowed away somewhere in the north. Mant argues that the English attitude to industry is an example of 'binary' thought, which can be traced back to Sir Francis Drake.[38] To achieve wealth he did things that were not quite nice, but by doing these things in the name of the Queen, he gained patronage and kept some of his wealth. The 'binary think', as Mant calls it, is that the English believe a great deal of money cannot be made without a 'fiddle'. A little dishonesty is acceptable if it receives patronage. The 'small matter' of the fiddle is forgotten or swept under the carpet. If it does not receive patronage, and is found out, it is unforgivable (for example, the Guiness affair).

Industry is associated with making wealth, and this makes it dirty in two senses. The first is that it openly seeks wealth. Second, it is dirty in the physical sense. It is very convenient that industry was located away from London. It can be mentally swept away to the middle and north of the country. It is not without significance that the high-technology light industries have grown in the south of England, or that the London commuter belt serves the City of London. This raises the question as to whether the English were ever very serious about industry, and it also questions, as we have seen, the motives of those who own industry, and this despite the importance of the Industrial Revolution. But in a real sense the Industrial Revolution was not in the mainstream of the British tradition, which stemmed from country life.

As we saw in Chapter 7, the person who put money into the business did so not because he or she was interested in the product, but because he or she was interested in the return on their investment. Money was lent to entrepreneurs for capital. The entrepreneurs often, in their turn, employed managers or were at one and the same time managers. The shareholders did not have a commitment to industry. Their commitment was to their land and property. There is no evidence that this commitment has changed. There is no evidence of a real understanding of industry, either in Parliament or the financial centre – the City of London – although the City can claim to create wealth through the 'export' of invisibles and its loans to industry: 'Factories and cotton may have been two symbols of the first half of the nineteenth century but so were the public schools, the canals, and the new importance of Manchester primarily as a centre for commerce rather than manufacturing'.[39]

If it is correct that those in power were motivated by other reasons to invest in technology, and were not truly part of the technological revolution itself, then the failure of British industry to receive support in the latter half of the twentieth century can be understood, for the motivation in the financial markets is the return on investment in the short run.

Nevertheless, because of our concern for material objects, industry is still thought to be important. So it is, writes Mant, that 'School teachers are exhorted to direct their best charges into industry, not for its intrinsic attractions, but because otherwise the country might go broke'.[40] But students respond to the market and they will go where the money is likely to be. There is no evidence of a substantial interest in manufacturing. If anything, the situation is rather like that Iacocca believes to exist in the USA:

> If quick paper profits replace long-term competitiveness as the prime reason to invest in American industry, I don't want to think about where we're going as a nation.

I'm particularly troubled by the deeper issue that has brought on this recklessness: the deteriorating values of businessmen today, especially the freshly-minted ones. It's time somebody started to question the system that breeds these people.

Why is it that talented young men and women aren't interested in going into industry but flock to Wall Street? They're all hoping that by the time they're 30 they'll be making $5m or $6m a year.[41]

Which is to return us to the problem of mergers and the relationship between the worlds of finance and industry.

As we saw in the last chapter, there is still much fighting going on in industry. Mant has contrasted the industrial structure of West Germany with Britain. He points out that after the Second World War, the industrial structure that developed from its pre-war base enabled it to be aggressive and competitive. National character enabled Germany to fight. The upper board on whom the workers depend in a German company is able to fight for the company. These boards are composed of experts and have a commitment to the product. In contrast, the boards of British companies operate like a monarchy. The board of directors becomes the court. These courts have many directors who are non-executive and who, while having little commitment to the company, give it respectability in society. They can and do act, as was seen in the 1987 Guinness affair, and this may lead to changes in the attitudes of non-executive directors to their role. Nevertheless, Lord Wilfred Brown[42] believed that a third of British companies were in the hands of chief executives who were inadequate.

Mant, who seems to have been the first to describe Britain as a culture of dependence, argued that British company boards created a culture of dependence within their workforce – an extension, we might add, of the paternalism of the landowner into industrial organization. Within this culture, be it a family or a work group, there is a dependency on a particular person who can be relied on to sort out the problems in the group.[43] In the case of the company it is the board. The workers are the family and it is within the family that the fight breaks out. Thus fighting in British companies takes place within them when there are discontinuities in organizational structure. In the past, much of this fighting has been with trade unions.

For example, within companies there has been a failure to sack the poor executive, and when individuals 'depend' on their jobs, they will not readily seek to remedy the faults easily seen in the system in which the job is done. It is easy to blame someone else. In one organization I investigated, the maintenance of key plant, involving electrical, mechanical and chemical components, became impossible because the electrical technicians would say a fault was mechanical, and the mechanical technicians would say it was electrical. Such was the effect of their training on their adaptability.

As we have seen, there is still much fighting going on between unions, and between unions and companies. At the same time, there is evidence of change, as we saw in the last chapter. It is possible that those who advocate different work patterns (work-sharing, part time) underestimate the need for individuals to earn substantial sums of money. This could provide unions with a new *raison d'être*.

Similarly, if non-unionized low-wage labour is seen and comes to feel that it is exploited, unions may also find a *cause célèbre*. All extremes in British society eventually come to grief, for it is part of national character to avoid the nasty, and this is done by consensus that is sometimes achieved by the morally wrong. But as moral wrong increases, so there is a pressure to return to the moral right, and no amount of exhortation not to legislate 'against' trade unions, such as that by the Royal Commission on Trade Unions, would have prevented the enactment of very limited legislation in the 1980s. And this swing continues with proposals to enable trade union members to have a statutory right to sue their unions. Even so, there are those on the right of the Labour Party who would counsel caution.

However, the major fight/flight issue relates not so much to the union issue but to the thrust British industry gives to its entry into the single European market. There is much concern about this in Britain, and British management is criticized for not utilizing the most advanced management techniques. A report by International Survey Research shows that among British top managers, 42 per cent are seen to be bureaucratic, and only 28 per cent entrepreneurial by their own managers.[44] This is to suggest that an entrepreneurial culture is not being created, and to underline the continuing importance of the studies by Mant and McClelland.[45]

It is clear that considerable changes in the attitudes of top management, management and workers will be required if Britain is to succeed in the European market. Among the important changes that will be required will be those that influence the relationships between workforce and management, particularly if there is to be effective participation.

Participation, Obligations, Rights and Education

If participation is to be successful, it has to be as a felt experience[46] and this can only come about through greater understanding and the acquisition of higher skills, which is the theme of this book. Chapter 2 demonstrated the importance of perception in this respect, and subsequent chapters by inference have shown the significance of organizational structure. In Britain, perceptions of the performance of organizations and the behaviour of managers and workers have been found to vary with size. Workers and managers in larger organizations may, without good reason, be hostile to each other if, as a starting-point, for example, managers in large organizations believe workers are more militant. It also seems that both workers and management in small organizations greatly exaggerate the tolerance and understanding found in their organizations. The investigators who drew attention to these findings also reported that job satisfaction was less in the larger organization.[47] It seems, therefore, that small and medium-sized organizations would seem to be better able to provide the structures for effective participation.

In this respect, the West German approach is of considerable interest. Each workshop is encouraged to share responsibility; everyone is involved in co-determination (*Mitbestimmung*), and it is this that has helped Germany return to prosperity. This brings us back to concepts of national character, national will and national neurosis.

It seems evident from all that has been said that companies in Britain require a much higher degree of commitment from their managing boards and shareholders than they currently receive. Just as workers and managers have rights and obligations, so too, do senior managers and shareholders. Because shareholders have no obligations to the company, they can hardly be expected to have a high level of commitment to its future. How to obtain this commitment is a matter of considerable concern.

The Demand in Europe for Skills

Various writers have suggested that a major problem all the European countries will probably have to face is a shortage of skilled labour. The birth rate in West Germany has fallen below the replacement level. In the mid-1990s, the population in the 16–25 year age range will drop by over one and a half million. The consequences of this could be a severe shortage of skilled labour. The need for a flexible and skilled workforce will increase as high technology continues to change the techniques of work.

Values: Their Significance and Evaluation

McClelland's and Mant's theories have several aspects in common. In the absence of any other suitable explanation of economic behaviour, the ideas of underlying emotional patterns and drives that communicate themselves to large aggregates of people seem rational. It also seems that changes in attitudes take place over very long periods of time, and this would be consistent with a very long trade cycle. It seems that the self-fulfilling hypothesis goes to work so that a nation will continue to believe it is a failure long after it has begun to succeed. Similarly, it may become so obsessed with success that failure is not recognized. Clearly, patriotism of some kind is important for the drive to achieve in the economy. At the same time patriotism, such as that generated by the Falkland Islands war, can be self-defeating. At the time of writing, the government was opposed to Britain joining the European Monetary System. It is argued that if it does not, London could lose its place as the first centre for finance in Europe. This would have serious implications for the future development of the City of London. But of more significance, it is argued, there can be no single European market without monetary union (see note 30, page 173).

In McClelland's model the key difference is between achieving and non-achieving people. These have many of the characteristics of the enterprising and unenterprising workers, discussed in the next chapter. In Mant's model the difference is between being and doing. In McClelland's theory it is achievement motivation, and in Mant's it is dependence and fight/flight. Both draw on the historical development of cultures for support, and both are led back to the individual as the basis of the aggregate. When compared with Japanese culture, there are strong grounds for supposing that the family and religious commitment are major influences in performance, more so than perhaps we would like to believe. It is in this respect that the role of parents needs to be considered. The family has been little considered in political debate, but slowly it is being brought into the discussion of educational programmes in Europe.[48]

It is important that societies should understand the values they hold, particularly in respect to the generation of wealth. Not only is the use of profits at issue, but also its use by each individual in society. One potential impediment to the British dream is the attitude of individuals to money, when money is readily available. If it is put into consumption, then it is not available for other, more productive investment. Past experience suggests that this is a particularly strong impediment to economic progress. Educators have a major role to play in the development of such understanding as do politicians, for all change depends on the advancement of ideas that will find acceptability in that aggregate of persons called the community. It is learning that will lead to economic responsibility, and it is towards this end that the leadership of nations should be directed.

Bailey has said

> The process of redefining transcending (traditional) values must usually be a lengthy one, the outcome not just of many experiences but also of many alterations. People compete to impose on one another their definition of what an innovatory item is and what its likely consequences will be. An innovation, consequently, always has the potentiality of being a threat to some part of an established order: if its adoption results eventually in a change of values (as when peasants give up the goal of maintaining their family intact) this change is likely to come only after debate, argument and sometimes conflict.[49]

I would not wish to imply that there are no transcending values. The creation of wealth also brings with it obligations, as the scandals in the New York, London and Paris stock exchanges showed in 1987 and 1988. Like Carter, I do not believe that 'wealth will be put in its right place without a major rediscovery of man as a spiritual being'.[50] There is no doubt that the non-conformism of the great British entrepreneurs of the nineteenth century was to combine social progress with commercial progress. Perhaps it is the failure of the modern entrepreneur to do this that necessitates organizational theory. It is this, along with conflict between the individual and authority, that presents religion with its major problems at the end of the twentieth century.

Education provides a forum for debate and argument at all levels about the role of man and woman in society. Within that context it has to ensure that everyone is provided with the widest range of frames of reference possible, and these must include a consideration of the potential of governments to change attitudes and condition learning. It is with this aspect of the management of the economy that the next chapter is concerned.

Notes and References

1. Abelshauser, W. (1982) West German economic recovery 1945–1951. A reassessment, *The Three Banks Review*, no. 135, pp. 34–53.
2. Lilley, S. (1970) *Technological Progress and the Industrial Revolution*, 'Fontana Economic History of Europe', Fontana, London.
3. Jones, H.G. (1982) The Swedish regenerates, *Management Today*, May, pp. 74–7; and Rubenowitz, S., Norrgren, F. and Tannenbaum, A.S. (1983) Some psychological effects of direct and indirect participation in ten Swedish companies, *Organization Studies*, Vol. 4, no. 2, pp. 243–59.
4. Reynaud, P.L. (1981) *Economic Psychology*, Praeger, New York, NY; and Sen, A. (1983) The profit mofit, *Lloyds Bank Review*, January, pp. 1–20.
5. McClelland, D.C. (1961) *The Achieving Society*, The Free Press, NY.
6. Sir Alec Cairncross, presidential address to the economics section of the British Association, Swansea, The advancement of science annual meeting, 1971; more recently, (1988) Britain's industrial decline, *The Royal Bank of Scotland Review*, no. 159, pp. 3–18, in which he questions the statistics that purport to show a British recovery, and where he argues that the end of Britain's industrial decline has not yet been reached.
7. See for example an economist who takes an opposite view, Mishan, E.J. (1967) *The Cost of Economic Growth*, Penguin Books, Harmondsworth.
8. Mant, A. (1979) *The Rise and Fall of the British Managers*, Pan, London.
9. Among the authors who have recently published in this field are Barnett, C. (1986) The truth of the British decline, *Management Today*, April, pp. 84–8; and Weiner, M. J. (1981) *English Culture and the Decline of the Industrial Spirit, 1850–1980*, Cambridge University Press.
10. McClelland, D.C., Atkinson, J.W., Clark, R.A. and Lowell, E. (1953) *The Achievement Motive*, Century-Crofts, Appleton, NY.
11. Kunkel, J. in R.L. Burgess and D. Bushell (eds.) (1969) *Behavioural Sociology – The Experimental Analysis of Social Process*, Columbia University Press, New York, NY; and Butcher, H.J. and Cattell, R. (1968) *The Prediction of Creativity and Achievement*, Bobs Merrill, Indianapolis, Ind.
12. de Cecco, J.P. and Crawford, W.R. (1974) *The Psychology of Learning and Instruction*, Prentice-Hall, Englewood Cliffs, NJ.
13. Casson, M. (1983) *Economics of Unemployment: An Historical Perspective*, Robertson, Oxford.
14. *Ibid.*
15. The tabulations of performance of the British economy since the eighteenth century, and the history of technological innovation, would certainly seem to support this view. See, for example, Barratt-Brown, M. (1970) *What Economics is About*, Weidenfeld & Nicolson, London.
16. It is trade with developing countries and the Middle East that has prospered manufacturing in Britain. It is for this reason that it is not only necessary to increase overseas aid but also to ensure that it is effective. Such aid is an act of benevolence, as many would seem to think, for mutual support is brought about by trading. It is also for this reason that there is increasing interest in the Chinese market. Lomax, D.F. (1986) The investment implications of China's offshore oil development, *National Westminster Bank Quarterly Review*, February, pp. 50–69, writes: 'The excess capacity in the world economy for most industrial products, including oil refining capacity, shipping, steel, investment goods, and commodities, means that China is extremely well placed to make up for any gaps in its investment planning by the selective and flexible use of the world market place'.
    Dearden, E. (1986) EEC membership and the United Kingdom's trade in manufactured goods, *National Westminster Bank Quarterly Review*, February, pp. 15–25. Gives figures that show a substantial manufacturing imbalance between Britain and Europe.
17. Nichol, P. (1985) Italian in the fast lane to success, *The Times*, 3 May.
18. McClelland, *Achieving Society* (note 5).
19. McClelland, D.G. (1969) The role of achievement orientation in the transfer of technology in W.H. Gruber and D.G. Marquis *Factors in the Transfer of Technology* MIT. Press, Cambridge, Mass.
20. Bradley, I. (1987) *Enlightened Entrepreneurs*, Weidenfeld & Nicolson, London. This includes studies of Cadbury, Colman, Lever, Morley and Rowntree. But see also Lilley, *Technological Progress* (note 2), for a broader perspective.
21. See, for example, Barrett-Brown, *What Economics is About* (note 15).
22. de Cecco and Crawford, *Psychology* (note 12).

23. Sir Michael Edwardes quoted in *The Times*, 10 December 1980.

24. Federation of British Industry (1961) *Industrial Research in Manufacturing Industry 1959–1960*, London; and letter from D.B. Welbourn in *The Times*, 27 February, 1987:

> May I suggest that this country is doing very much too much research and not nearly enough development. If British industry will not do the development of our research, doing research merely helps the competition. May I give you one example? In 1965 I was responsible for initiating research into Cadam (Computer-aided design and computer-aided manufacture) in the Cambridge University Engineering Department. Later, as the University's Director in Industrial Cooperation, I tried to get British industry and Government departments to use and to develop the most promising of the various potential money-spinners which we had produced as a result of the research effort.
>
> Of British firms, only the Delta Group plc, under Lord Caldecote, got interested. British Leyland tested Duct (a Cadcam programme which specifically programmed the skills of the patternmaker) in a half-hearted manner; Sulzer, in Switzerland, tested thoroughly, but finally decided to back a somewhat similar Swiss package; while Volkswagen and Daimler-Benz tested it thoroughly, took licences and put a lot of money into cooperating in the development: this despite the fact that they both already had Computervision, an American product which Austin Rover has been trying to foist on to its subcontractors.
>
> In October, 1985, Daimler-Benz published a paper showing the financial savings which they are making by 'buying British'.
>
> If you study balance-of-payment figures you will discover that both Germany and Japan spend very large sums in buying other people's research; into this they put large development efforts, in particular into designing and redesigning products for manufacture.

25. Turner, G. (1971) *Business in Britain* (Revised edition), Penguin Books, Harmondsworth.

26. Lee, M. (1980) The working class divide, *Management Today*, May, pp. 50–3.

27. Rohlen, T.P. (1983) *Japan's High Schools*, University of California Press, Berkely, Calif.; and Duke, B.J. (1986) *The Japanese School*, Praeger, New York, NY.

28. Deutsch, M. (1985) *Distributive Justice: A Social Psychological Perspective*, Yale University Press, New Haven, Conn.

29. Rohlen, *Japan's High Schools* (note 27).

30. Duke, *The Japanese School* (note 27).

31. Rohlen, *Japan's High Schools* (note 27).

32. Dore, R. (1973) *British Factory, Japanese Factory*, Allan and Unwin, London.

33. Organization for Economic Co-operation and Development (1986) *Economic Outlook*, December.

34. Smallwood, C. (1987) Britain explodes the pauper nation myth, *The Sunday Times*, 10 May.

35. Congdon, T. (1987) Thatcher's rejuvenation cure, *The Times*, 6 March, who gives a précis of the OECD report cited in note 23.

36. *Ibid.*

37. Smallwood, Britain explodes (note 34).

38. Mant, *The Rise and Fall* (note 8).

39. Forres, M. and Lawrence, P. (1978) What is industry? *New Society*, October, quoted in full by Mant, *The Rise and Fall* (note 8).

40. Mant, *The Rise and Fall* (note 8).

41. Iacocca, L. (1988) *Talking Straight*, Sidgwick & Jackson, London.

42. Brown, Lord W. quoted by Mant, in *The Rise and Fall* (note 8).

43. Mant takes his theory of dependence from the work of Bion, W. (1961) *Experiences in Groups*, Tavistock, London. Bion suggested that below the level of task performance, groups of human beings function according to certain basic assumptions. He called them dependence, fight/flight and pairing. Large aggregations of people often act on these assumptions. Thus a group may depend (dependence) on a charismatic leader. Or it might attack or flee from a more or less real bogey. They may be viewed as group ego-defence mechanisms.

44. International Survey Research, reported by Rudd, R. *The Times*, 5 July 1988.

45. The Institute of Marketing. The popular journals and newspapers frequently recount the life-stories of Britain's self-made people, for example, Chittenden, M. (1988) Self-made men: graduates of the university of life, *The Sunday Times*, 10 May; and, in the same newspaper for 17 May, The money spinners, by P. Beresford.

46. Rubenowitz, Norrgren and Tannenbaum, Some psychological effects (note 3).

47. Stephenson, G., Brotherton, C., de la Afield, B. and Skinner, M. (1983) Size of organisation, attitudes to work and job satisfaction, *Industrial Relations Journal*, Vol. 14, no. 2, pp. 28–40.

48. The Education Reform Act 1988 in England makes specific provision for parents in the management of schools.

49. Bailey, F.G. (ed.) (1973) *Debate and Compromise: The Politics of Innovation*, Blackwell, Oxford.
50. Carter, C.F. (1968) *Wealth*, Penguin Books, Harmondsworth.

10

COMPLEXITY AND SIMPLICITY: MANAGING THE ECONOMY

Introduction

Governments, and through them ideologies, have a major role to play in the development of new attitudes or in the persistence of prevailing value dispositions in society. Legislation can be used to encourage or impede change. Governments are necessarily involved in economic activity. How they involve themselves in that activity determines the value dispositions we take. Governments can reserve to themselves a range of statutory instruments that do not require legislation for their implementation.

Among the decisions they can make are ones relating to the allocation of funds for research in the public sector, and industrial support in the manufacturing and construction industries. Other decisions relate to the control and financing of education, health and social security. Overriding all of these considerations are decisions that affect the economic climate in which industry has to function. These in their turn influence taxation, and rates of interest and exchange. Underlying these decisions are the ideologies of the governing party.[1]

The nations of the western world are open systems in exchange with each other. To create wealth, a country needs both to sell and to buy from other nations. It needs to have a 'healthy' balance of payments between income generated from exports and money expended on imports. This in its turn requires an exchange rate that at one and the same time attracts investments from overseas, and is favourable to its own exporters. Overseas investors (not speculators) are attracted to economies that are said to be 'sound'. Soundness might be described as a reasonable rate of growth without inflation; what is 'reasonable' changes with changing economic circumstances, and not even West Germany or Switzerland are free from small rates of inflation.

Since the early 1970s, when excessive increases in oil prices caused substantial inflation in the western world, governments have been particularly concerned to

157

keep inflation at a low level. In the latter half of the 1970s, the number of unemployed began to rise in European countries. It has been the subject of much concern, but recently the number of unemployed has begun to fall. Nevertheless, while there is still much concern about the high level of unemployment, paradoxically it does not seem to worry the electorates in Europe at the moment.

What appears to be simple is found to be complex and today, governments employ economic advisers to assist them to develop their policies. When, in Britain, in the late 1970s the political consensus broke down, a sharp divide was seen between economists who followed the approach of Keynes, and those who were influenced by monetarism. The Conservative governments since then have followed an approach that leans heavily towards monetarism. The political ideology that has shaped thinking is that the Wefare State leads to dependence, that State and semi-State organizations are inefficient, and that competition is the essence of efficiency.

Governments undoubtedly influence attitudes by the policies they foster as, for example, the desire to own a home. Political expediency often dictates decisions that may have the opposite effect on their policies. The major problem for the British economy is to consume less and save more, when the desire to consume is felt deeply.

Since the individual influences policies through voting behaviour, it is important that individuals should be able to make judgements about the different approaches to the economy proposed by the political parties. Given the importance of industry as the main creator of wealth, it is important that individuals judge policies in the light of their potential to assist companies create that wealth. Because it is a characteristic of economic behaviour that countries and, therefore, companies, experience regular booms and recessions, the discussion of the different approaches to economic theory that follows is based on the different analyses that have been made of the trade cycle.

Governments, like individuals and institutions, are learners. Unfortunately they are committed to particular value judgements. Faced with complex decisions, they are more likely to revert to the simple drives of their philosophy than adapt to the complexities of the problem to be solved. In this respect they are no different from individuals and learners. In the future, as life becomes increasingly complex, society will expect governments to become more adaptable, and this may require substantial changes in political outlook and approaches to politics.

Individuals, when faced with complex data that challenge their value dispositions, are likely to fall back on their own beliefs, and such dissonance may make attitude change difficult. It should, therefore, be a requirement of all education programmes that they provide for a practical understanding of the economic system.

The Trade Cycle

Various economists have held that the process of economic activity is unceasing, and that a slump is not a deviation from normality but part of a normal process.

Schumpeter, who held this view, suggested that the cycle was caused by the fact that in a boom people not only become more prosperous but also tend to go into debt because it is easier to borrow money.[2] This seems to be the case today. However, because it is necessary to cancel debts, there will be a time when the money available for spending will be reduced. This will cause deflation and the conditions necessary for expansion will be reduced. Rees-Mogg has likened the cycle of economic activity to the piston in a petrol engine. The downward stroke necessarily comes back. It prepares for the rise just as the upward stroke prepares for the downward. Thus the swings in the business cycle are inevitable and therefore normal: 'It is therefore deflation rather than debt building which points towards the restoration of future prosperity. Both processes are self correcting but unfortunately have a tendency to overshoot'.[3] The problem of timing exists as it does in a petrol engine. Von Mises, an Austrian, suggested that at the beginning of the recovery period, because banks have a lot of funds, they lend at low rates of interest that industry uses to purchase plant and equipment in order to get value for their money. But this reduces the supply of money from the banks and interest rates rise, and in consequence it no longer becomes profitable for industry to invest and so borrow more money. Deflation (or recession) begins the restoration process. In this process the effect of an increase in government borrowing is to increase rates of interest. If the expenditure is excessive, it can help to bring about the downward movement and recession.[4]

Perhaps the most influential interpretation of the trade cycle apart from those of Marx and Beveridge[5] came from Keynes, for his theory had a major impact on the post-war economic activities of the nations in the western world. His work was greatly influenced by his experience of the Great Depression in Britain.

Keynesianism

Keynes, believed that involuntary unemployment was the cause of mass unemployment in the 1930s, and that this was due to inadequate aggregate demand and a lack of co-ordination between savings, on the one hand, and investment on the other. In order to smooth out a depression, investment had to be encouraged in order to create demand. Investments could be increased if interest rates were reduced, or by an increase in government spending, or both. Thus in a recession a government would increase its spending, and this spending would decrease unemployment.

Governments have a number of mechanisms at their disposal to control consumption and investment in the economy – such as rates of interest, direct and indirect taxation – that should be used to smooth out the depression. The levels of drive to consume, invest or save are called the propensities to consume, invest or save. When we receive *extra* income the use to which it is put holds the key to change. The size of income is determined by investment. But savings and investment are not necessarily made by the same people or if they are, decisions to save and decisions to invest are not necessarily made at the same time. Beliefs about the state of the economy will influence these decisions. When individuals decide to spend money on consumer goods, they cause the production of consumer goods. If they decide to invest, they provide money for capital goods. A decision to save rather than to consume will not guarantee a decision to invest, and this is the heart of the problem for if these savings do not lead to investment then there will be a reduction in business activity. When the rate of return on an investment approximates to the rate of interest on the borrowing necessary for capital investment, the entrepreneur will not be encouraged to invest. Thus the return on an additional unit of investment (the marginal efficiency of capital) will decrease as the volume of capital is increased. Ultimately, stagnation occurs. Either interest rates have to fall, or the marginal efficiency of capital has to increase if unemployment is to be reduced. Thus to reduce the effects of the depression there needs to be investment.

As with other theories, it is assumed that individuals do not spend their money fully on consumption. Some will be taken up in taxes. Since the level of employment is determined by the level of investment, there must be sufficient investment to take up the excess of total output. Thus, when there is deflation the inducement to invest falls. In order to restore investment governments can intervene by creating public-works programmes, lowering the rate of interest and increasing its own consumption as, for example, increasing Unemployment Benefit. Such manipulation is called demand management, and in support of this technique it has been pointed out that the Depression of the 1930s only ended when demand expanded, and full employment only returned with re-armament and the war.[6]

However, demand management or fine tuning, as it came to be called, seemed to work satisfactorily from the end of the Second World War until there was a very rapid advance in inflation in the early 1970s. This inflation was due, in the first place, to heavy expenditure by the Americans on the war in Vietnam. Wage rates increased, and commodity prices doubled within an 18-months period. The most devastating pressure on prices came in 1974 when the oil-producing nations quadrupled the price of crude petroleum in anticipation of real shortages.

During the Conservative government of 1970–4, there was a massive expansion in credit. The banks' liquidity ratio was changed, cash reserves fell and individuals and companies were able to borrow much more money. Some £5,000 million came into the economy in this way, and so substantially increased the money supply. While unemployment went down, which would be expected from the Keynesian approach, the newly created demand increased prices, inflation accelerated and the balance of payments went down.[7]

By 1977, Keynesian methods were in disrepute in Britain since the injection of funds into the public sector, with the related increase in the amount of money borrowed to finance these activities (Public Sector Borrowing Requirement), was thought to increase inflation substantially. Because of increasing prices, there were demands for increases in wages, and the positive response to these demands led to further increases in prices. And in this way companies priced themselves out of the market and the unemployment figures began to spiral.

In these circumstances it was possible for an incoming Conservative government to take measures that, it believed, would stop the inflation. They thought that the money supply should be rigorously controlled and at the same time State agencies should be privatized so that they would become more efficient because they had to compete in the market. They also believed in tax reform (supply-side economics)[8] and the limitation of trade union power.

The Conservative Years

The blend of approaches the Conservative government used toward the economy was called 'monetarism'.[9] Early on, the party strategists had undoubtedly been influenced by Milton Friedman's criticism of Keynesianism. Friedman, an American economist,[10] recognized that the weakness of the Keynes approach was that if a government was committed to full employment, it removes the threat of unemployment due to high-wage claims. He argued that there is a natural rate of unemployment and that if unemployment was kept below its natural rate, the rate of inflation would continually accelerate. Therefore, governments should commit themselves to the reduction of inflation and not full employment. In order to do this the growth of money incomes has to be stabilized. It follows that the public-sector borrowing requirement has to be reduced. In the years that followed, the Public Sector Borrowing Requirement was reduced so much that, in 1988, income tax was substantially reduced in the UK. In this respect, policy followed that in the USA. Jenkins, a well-known commentator on British affairs, considered the budget of 1988 to be a symbol of change in political philosophy for in it the Chancellor abandoned the concept of taxation as a tool of equality.[11]

Conservative policies had the effect of reducing expenditure in every government department as well as in the local authorities responsible for municipal activities (for example, police, fire, education, roads, housing). In keeping with the view that Britain should become a nation of house owners, local authorities have been forced to sell the houses they rented to persons mainly from the skilled, semi-skilled and unskilled socio-economic groups. Also in keeping with their philosophy that competition breeds effectiveness, they set about privatizing many State-run institutions (for example, telephones, gas, aerospace), and in support of their free-market philosophy, abandoned exchange-rate controls. At the same time, as we have seen, the Public Sector Borrowing Requirement was reduced.

Although these severe monetary strategies reduced inflation, they did not have the immediate effect on unemployment that they were supposed to have. By 1988 it had been reduced to 2.5 million, and by January 1989 it was at 2.0 million, which some observers regarded as excessively high. Whatever else may be said about high unemployment, it is a considerable cost to the community, even when a government is in the black to the tune of £15 billion.

Nevertheless in Britain it is not, it seems, an issue of moment and Keynesian economists in both Britain and the USA, who regard high levels of unemployment as scandalous[12] believe that this lack of interest in the subject will lead many individuals to consider that high rates are also the natural rates of unemployment. The problem is that when there is a high rate of unemployment, myths of the kind generated in the 1980s come to be believed. Such myths are that most of the unemployed are either unemployable or prefer unemployment to taking a paid job. This seems to be somewhat harsh, given the very large expenditures in education aimed at giving low achievers employable skills.

There are others of a more conservative frame of mind, who believe that there is a certain amount of truth in these views: 'What they cannot see is that voluntary unemployment covers a thousand kinds of cases, from real misconduct through immaturity and naivety to the condition of being a bullied victim running away'.[13] If Casson, Stone and Walden are correct, then there are fundamental issues of great moment to be faced, for a nation cannot tolerate for long the creation of an underclass of individuals who are alienated from the social system in which they live.[14] The complexity of unemployment, so they would argue, is simply not understood.[15]

The British Government has adopted an economic strategy many economists on both right and left question. The only instrument of control they used in the 1980s was the interest rate. High interest rates have the effect of reducing credit at home. The contradiction such economists as Blackaby and Reading perceive in these policies is that governments expect restrictions on credit simultaneously to restrain imports and stimulate exports.[16]

For example, in the middle of 1988 it became clear that in Britain inflation was rising. At the same time, a huge balance of payments deficit accrued to the order of £12 billion. It was argued that the rise of inflation was due to excessive wage demands, and that the balance of payments deficit was due to high consumption expenditure. The two are, of course, inter-related. Therefore, so the logic goes, if interest rates are increased, consumer expenditure will be reduced, sterling will increase in value, funds will be attracted to Britain, and because of the need to remain competitive in the overseas market, companies will restrain their wage awards. The net effect is supposed to be that inflation is brought down without an increase in unemployment. But Reading has pointed out that employers can, in these circumstances, choose to lower their output. This reduces their labour costs.

At the same time, many consumers are house owners with mortgages. They are forced to redirect their expenditure into increased mortgage payments on which the government has to pay higher tax relief. Thus the increases in mortgage-interest payments contribute to inflation, and about half the 6.8 per cent inflation in 1988 could be accounted for by these payments. As we have seen, such payments do not contribute to industrial growth and for this reason it is agreed that tax relief on mortgages should be stopped.

Expectations

More generally, a major paradox relating to policy is that having encouraged increased productivity, successful employees are now to be penalized by restraints on their earnings. This illustrates the fact that too often economists and politicians misunderstand the economic behaviour of individuals. They forget that their policies create expectations and that these in turn cause economic behaviour. So it is conceivable that, if those who have been successful in the past have their rewards reduced, that in the future they will not be so willing to increase their productivity.

For example, the Keynes approach to management of the economy gives rise to false or different expectations from those that would have occurred if the economy had been left to its own devices.[17] Full employment is expected as a right, therefore those who seek to protect jobs impose an obligation on society to support them in that task. If at the same time they seek high wages, society is expected to support them, even if it means increasing the price of the goods they produce. High wages, therefore, contribute to inflation. Thus in Britain, there have been policies to control incomes and prices in order to influence wage settlements.

Incomes Policies

It would be contrary to present Conservative philosophy to impose income controls. Nevertheless, they have been concerned about the level of wage settlements and have exhorted industry to make low wage settlements. In this respect their record as an employer has not been good. In 1986, for example, the public settlements were higher than those in industry.[18] It seems that increasing unemployment does not stop those in work seeking wage rises above the rate of inflation, and it is for this reason that there is a great deal of sympathy among economists for an incomes policy.[19]

Carter makes this point:

> The danger with any prices and incomes policy is that it will prevent desirable changes in relative prices and relative incomes, and thus make the economy less efficient. Nevertheless they cannot be regarded as expedients to be used for a few months of emergency, and then abandoned. Its purpose will not be fulfilled until deep-seated ideas of what is 'reasonable' and 'just' have been changed, and that cannot be achieved in a short time.[20]

There is strong opposition from the Institute of Directors in Britain to government interference in wage bargaining because it is a complex activity involving many variables. A pay offer is a complex weighing up of many factors, for example, business demand, the competitive costs of being short of capacity, the cash and profit penalty of having excess capacity, availability of special skills, other competitive threats, targets for market share, the state of labour relations in the company, and possible hopes of renegotiating or buying out bad working practices. Politicians, argues Hoskyns, the Director General of the Institute, do industry a disservice when they treat pay as a unique variable.[21] Labour costs do not fall as a result of political exhortation but because of variety and competition in the market-place.

Because of these complexities, a general reflation in the circumstances prevailing in Britain will not, it is thought, greatly increase employment. Therefore when a government that is opposed to incomes policies is in power, it must orient its policies towards the problems of the long-term unemployed. These are of two kinds and they must go hand in hand. The first kind relates to interest rates, stable money and taxation (fiscal). The opposite to reflation is to create a situation where low interest rates and stable money prevails. This will help the small and medium-sized companies to increase jobs. Administrative and taxation changes can also be introduced to help the small company.

Profit-sharing also requires considerable changes in attitudes. Thus, the second kind of policy has to relate to attitudes. These include the revision of education programmes to prepare young people for work, and the counselling of the long-term unemployed (called RESTART in 1986 in the UK). Such counselling includes a discussion of the type of work a person is looking for, training needs, interests and other possibilities. There are other schemes that help the unemployed set up their own businesses, and allowances to employers for helping young people.

Unfortunately, governments may take the wrong action in order to achieve a short-term gain. Some commentators have argued that what is offered are palliatives rather than solutions.[22] For example, in Britain, training schemes will only work if there are enough jobs to go round. Long-term benefits will only accrue if there is universal vocational education based on the workplace. This is the view of several commentators on the British scheme.[23] There are commentators who believe that not enough is being done in these areas and that, given the new wealth, there is room for greater public sector expenditure.

Incomes policies do not deal with the fundamental change in attitudes that is required, and that relates to the propensity to save in a country where money is spent rather than saved.

Policy and Attitudes

Governments in the western world have, during the last ten years, become more sharply divided between right and left over the relative freedom that should exist from government intervention and planning. In Britain, as we have seen, a Conservative government began to unravel the Welfare State in 1979 in the belief that freedom from interference would foster competition, which in turn would create wealth. To do this it had to reduce inflation and stop the high wage rises that were pricing British goods out of the market. Rather than introduce an incomes policy that was not part of its philosophy, it chose to make drastic reductions in the Public Sector Borrowing Requirement. This meant that there would be fewer jobs available as a result of government expenditure. Unemployment rose and remained at a high level for sometime before falling below the three million mark. Many observers consider the lower rate still to be too high.

On the left and towards the centre, as we also saw, it was argued that more public expenditure would lead to a substantial reduction in unemployment. Part of the policy was to privatize State-owned concerns. Naturally there was much opposition on the grounds that it was selling off valuable national assets. These arguments continue.

One of the major criticisms of the policies of that era was that they did not assist industry. It was argued by Lever, a former Labour minister, a millionaire, that all governments ignored the national economic problem because they were not selective in their approach to consumption and investment. This problem continues, for Britain saves a smaller proportion of output than the world average for industrial countries or even for the leading European countries.

Lever and Edwards[24] argued that monetarists act as if the central question is the quantity of money, and their opponents as if it is the quantity of demand. The focus of their argument was that governments from either side of the political divide favoured the individual and his or her consumption needs at the expense of industry's needs for capital. It was much easier for an individual to obtain credit from banks, building societies and insurance companies, than for industrialists to obtain money for capital investment, particularly in the medium and the long term. The banks in successful countries provided much more of the capital for investment to industry, and on very much better terms. As a percentage of Gross National Product, bank lending to industry was 20 per cent in the UK, 25 per cent in France, and 38 per cent in West Germany and 96 per cent in Japan. They argued that in circumstances where the average life of plant and machinery was 35 years, the need for such investment was self-evident. They also argued for a financial structure that would enable the banks, like the building societies, to borrow short and lend long. This would inevitably mean a substantial change in the balance of investment to consumption expenditure, and necessarily require curbs on the latter. As we have seen, one way to do this would be to abolish the tax relief on the interest paid by home owners on their mortgages (mortgage relief), and it is interesting to note that this is being done gradually in Ireland.

As national wealth grew in Britain, so more people came to own houses and the mortgage relief increased (see Table 10.1). This meant that people became more credit worthy and more money could be borrowed. The consumers began to borrow more and to save less to the extent that debts in the personal sector were 80 per cent of disposable income. Although a great deal of saving is done, it is illiquid because it is in pension funds and mortgage repayments. The tax allowances draw savings into the housing sector rather than to other sectors where it could be used for investment in industry and, at the same time, reduce

Table 10.1   Some of the subsidies paid by the British government in 1985

£billion	Subsidy
2.7	Mortgage relief
0.7	Housing subsidies
2.4	Rent rebates and allowances
4.3	Industry
1.3	Youth Training Scheme
1.1	Farmers
2.0	Cost of troops in Germany

the rates of interest, which are held high because of excessive consumption.

Since 1985 there has been a considerable boom in housing, and this was associated with substantial consumer spending in 1988 that led to increases in interest rates in order to dampen down this spending. Newspapers and economists sympathetic to the government once again drew attention to the fact that such spending reduced the money available for investment and, moreover, that it was inflationary.[25]

To make the changes necessary would require a substantial change in the expectations and attitudes of the public. Table 10.1 illustrates this point: the largest sum is for mortgage relief, and much of this goes to the middle classes. In that same year, suggestions that mortgage relief through income tax should be abolished, and that middle-class parents should pay university fees, were dropped. The first decision was entirely consistent with the political philosophy that Britain should become a property-owning democracy. Any change would operate against that philosophy.

Looking back over the past thirty years, it seems clear that as soon as money becomes available, private borrowing increases, and consumer spending relates directly to the amount that can be borrowed. If this is the case, it might be argued that government policies re-inforce a disposition to spend rather than to save or invest. Indeed, this might be a key component in the British disease, which has yet to be unravelled.

Unfortunately, one of the difficulties is that governments exist in the short term and as such are held captive by the electorate, or by a dominant but minority pressure group system.[26] For this reason it has been argued on the basis of experience in California that there should be constitutional restraints on fiscal and monetary powers so that governments are protected from minorities.

Mitchell argues that 'no one in politics knows the value of anything'. Politicians do not have reliable information, or the time for study, and if they did they probably would not allow it to influence their beliefs.[27] In any event, many governments find it very difficult to take bold actions in spite of the fact that bold and quick action may probably be better than a series of small actions spread over a long period of time.[28] Taxation can influence social attitudes in many ways. It can be used, for example, to reinforce the family as a social institution, or reduce its value. Thus, until recently in Britain there were considerable tax advantages to be accrued from mortgage relief by couples who did not marry but lived with each other. Similarly, if child benefits are stopped in an economy where they are paid, this is likely to impede rather than enhance the desire to procreate. In western economies, the low birth rates are already posing problems for the payment of old-age pensions in the first twenty years of the next century.

But governments not only exist for their homeland but live in the real world, and it is the open economy that so often dictates action in the absence of any programme of fundamental change.[30]

The Open Economy

No nation is free from the economic activities of other nations. Thus, exchange rates and home interest rates are interlocked. Industrialists require exchange rates that will enable their goods to sell, and interest rates to be low so that they can invest. The problem is that these rates fluctuate in the relatively short term and this makes it difficult to plan. Above all, industrialists want a situation that is relatively stable if they are to plan and compete in international markets. High exchange rates price them out of the market. So it is not surprising that one or two commentators have called for a return to the gold standard in order to get exchange-rate stability.[29]

Because of the international money market, money flows from where it is cheap and plentiful to where it is scarce and expensive, that is, to where speculators perceive the returns will be highest. The country that offers the best returns will have the strongest currency, and this may cause its goods to be priced out of the market. But a currency that is not a major currency like sterling, may have one price against a major currency, such as the dollar, and another against European currencies, especially the mark. A country whose currency is highly priced may import goods because they are relatively cheap and so go into a trade deficit. Thus, instead of the trade deficit causing a fall in currency, it is the strong currency that causes the trade deficit.

The major economic problem is the financing of the imbalances that occur between countries. Because West Germany and Japan save too much, they have a balance-of-payments surplus. Similarly, because Britain and the USA spend too much, they have a balance-of-payments deficit. It is these imbalances that destabilize foreign-exchange markets. One effect of the American trade deficit is that if action is taken to restore the balance by increasing the rates of interest, money will be drawn from other countries that might otherwise be invested in those countries. In either case they are financing the American debt.

An interesting feature of the world economy in 1988 was the fact that Germany, which had a substantial trade surplus raised its interest rates to stem inflation, which was running at 1.6 per cent. This had the effect of increasing the value of the mark. If both debtor and creditor nations raise their interest rates, then a severe worldwide recession is the likely outcome.

In Britain, policy aims both to reduce inflation and to maintain a stable pound. Those who put inflation as the first priority would make interest rates rise so that money is squeezed. This should reduce house-price inflation since mortgages become dearer as the lending societies compete with banks to offer better terms to savers.

If, on the other hand, policy puts the stability of the pound before inflation, then a steady rate of exchange is required. It is argued that the best way to achieve stability is to link sterling to a non-inflationary currency. This would mean that Britain would have to join the European Monetary System (EMS) in order to link the pound to the mark, and this in turn would mean, in the long run, sponsoring together with the other countries in the EEC a Euro-currency.

Just as industrialists require stability, so the foreign-exchange markets should be enabled to operate within a psychological framework of certainty, as it is uncertainty about a government's intentions that leads to speculation. As Smallwood who has written several articles on this aspect says, if there is total uncertainty in the market, the operators in the market 'will simply follow the crowd, and react to each piece of news as it comes up without taking notice of "fundamentals" '.[31] He argues that the collapse of a fifth of British manufacturing industry between 1979 and 1982 was due to the loss of markets caused by a rapidly rising pound. Moreover, Cairncross argues that in the long run as well as in the short, the pace of industrial recovery in Britain will be largely dictated by other countries.[32]

It is, therefore, important for governments to try to forecast what is happening in the world as it is for them to understand what is happening at home.

The Complex Nature of Social and Economic Decisions

The trouble is that economic phenomena are complex, and decisions involving many variables have to be made all the time. As yet, complex social phenomena are not always open to the methods of laboratory investigation used in the physical sciences. Unfortunately, factors that are measurable gain importance in the social sciences precisely because they are accessible to measurement. But 'such a demand quite arbitrarily limits the facts that are to be admitted as possible causes of events in the real world'.[33] And this brings us back to the factors that impede learning.

By and large, educational programmes do not develop the skill of synthesis. Individuals are not trained to think in system terms. Their training is in analysis. When they are faced with complex phenomena, they sometimes return to the simplicities of the ideological system they hold, so that black can appear to be black and white appear to be white. This may be particularly acute in the political sphere when beliefs have to be confined to a party line.

When a person or a learner is faced with a complex problem that cannot be related to or challenges his or her value system, dissonance may occur. Although a voter or a student may like a politician or a teacher, the messages they send may be untenable to that individual, and this may cause the voter, or student, to change their regard for the politician or teacher. Another reponse to the apparent receipt of unpalatable information is for the recipient to change its meaning, and to say, for example, 'I don't think X meant that – but this'. The problem of cognitive dissonance, as this response to complexity and/or conflicting values is called,[34] is particularly severe when the problem or issue runs counter to the recipient's strongly held predispositions. There is, in human behaviour, a persistent tendency to believe in the advantages of one's own arrangements. Social science phenomena, which challenge previously held positions, are prone to dissonance, especially when they are complex.[35] In these circumstances, the problem may be ignored by the recipient or a simplified problem introduced in its place. Because of dissonance, especially that caused by complexity, the specialist acquires significance as an adviser.

One effect of dissonance is that it makes it unlikely that politicians will change the values held deeply or otherwise with which they are associated. They will want to simplify the complex. Unfortunately, economic problems are complex. Sometimes they receive re-inforcement from society, at other times they don't. It may be supposed that in Britain lack of enthusiasm for the European Common Market is a factor in the repeated refusal to join the European Monetary System. Equally, given the view that high interest rates reduce inflation, it would be very difficult for politicians to accept the view that interest rates should be drastically cut, yet that is what one independent economist has proposed. Reading argues that they should be brought down to 5 per cent because *making money cheap also makes it scarce.*[36] Lenders are not so ready to lend when the rates of return are small, except when the purpose of the loan is investment in industry. And, as others have argued, the way to solve the jobs' problem is to help industry sell more in the export market. Such a position is probably outside the plausibility structure. It would require a very substantial change in beliefs, and we have to recognize that the operation of the economy is as much a function of psychological belief as it is about the reality of the system. To make the change required here, politicians and society would have to be persuaded that Britain is very successful and that the consequences of success lie in this direction.

Cognitive dissonance illustrates the need for the curriculum to provide the widest possible range of frames of reference with which to handle the information of everyday life. We no longer accept that journalists, either in newspapers or on radio and television, present entirely dispassionate accounts of the economy or political dispositions. There is plenty of hidden bias. Second-level education cannot escape from this problem. A fundamental component of the curriculum must surely be the provision of learning experiences that will enable students to begin to develop skills in economic and political literacy. That it will not be possible to escape from bias in this area is no reason for not attempting the task, although it will increase the professional responsibility of teachers. Such a programme will be very different from that traditionally provided in the subject of economics, and might even follow the pattern of this book. In any case, if the programme is confined to economics, it will have to be far more professionally and vocationally oriented than it is at present. But just as changes in the curriculum are necessary, so are changes in the structure required if individuals are to be better prepared for life.

Notes and References

1. While we may not go along with all the views in *Where There's a Will* (1987, Hutchinson, London) by a former Conservative minister, M. Heseltine, it illustrates the power of government and shows how the organizational structure of the Civil Service can impede policies because of the relationship the different departments of State have to Parliament.
2. Schumpeter, J.A. (1938, 1964) *Business Cycles*, McGraw Hill, New York, NY.
3. Rees-Mogg, W. (1981) The cause of depression in prosperity, *The Times*, 13 January.
4. Mises, Ludwig Von, (1949) *Human Action*, Hodge, Edinburgh.

5. In *Das Capital* (1946), Vol. 1, Allan and Unwin, London, Marx explained unemployment in terms of an 'industrial reserve army' that was created when the cycle of economic activity bottomed. When expansion occurred it was given work. He supposed that society comprises only of industrial capitalists and wage workers and in consequence that production depended on the power of the non-producing classes to consume. However, the power of the consuming class was limited by the laws of wages and by the fact that it can be exerted only so long as the labourers can be employed at a profit by the capitalist classes. It is the poverty and therefore restricted consumption of the masses which is the last cause of real crises.

    Beveridge thought that unemployment was caused by rigidities in the transfer of training and wages. Workers who possessed out-dated skills would resist movements in wages designed to encourage innovation and competitiveness. The trade cycle began with the introduction of new techniques. Greater output led to a boom. These techniques caused labour to become disorganized so that spending power is reduced and in consequence the boom is ended. Therefore, governments should seek to maintain the spending power of workers. To achieve this goal, the unemployed should receive benefits during their unemployment. The idea that the British labour force is not sufficiently trained for change continues to this day.

    Beveridge defined three types of unemployment: seasonal, structural and frictional. Some industries as, for example, tourism, substantially increase their demand for staff in certain periods of the year. Outside of these periods there is a reserve pool of labour. A.C. Pigou, one of the classical economists, gave as examples of frictional unemployment segmentation and boundaries in the use of skills as between trade unions. He thought that governments might help the unemployed by extra expenditure on public works. Structural unemployment arises when there is substantial change due to the introduction of new technologies. In many nations, the changes in the coal-mining and steel industries, including the USA, are examples of structural change.

    Beveridge thought that labour exchanges should concentrate on placing people in available jobs so that the inefficient are squeezed out. Those in 'frictional' unemployment could be retrained for work in newly established industries. But the Great Depression, with unemployment at three million in Britain, could not be accounted for by Beveridge's theory of frictional unemployment.

6. Tomlinson, J. (1982) Unemployment policy in the 1930s and 1980s, *Three Banks Review*, no. 135, pp. 17–33.

7. For a simple description, see an economics text written after the period. For example, Heertje, A. and Robinson, B.R.G. (1979) *Basic Economics*, Holt, Rinehart & Winston, London.

8. Supply-side economics is the study of the influence of taxation on relative prices, savings and work. See Bartlett, B. (1985) Supply side economics: theory and evidence, *National Westminster Bank Quarterly Review*, February, pp. 18–29.

9. Burton, J. (1982) The varieties of monetarism and their policy implications, *The Three Banks Review*, no. 143, pp. 14–31. See also note 15.

10. Friedman, M. (1975) *Unemployment Versus Inflation*, Institute of Economic Affairs, London.

11. Jenkins, P. (1988) A ground-breaking, rich man's budget, *The Independent*, 16 March.

12. Blackaby, F. (1988) Monetarism's forgotten people, *The Sunday Times*, 29 May.

13. Eric Heffer, in the House of Commons, quoted by Pearce, E. (1988) A heartless way to live now, *The Sunday Times*, 6 March.

14. Studies of Britain in the late nineteenth century show that two economies grew alongside each other. While on the one hand foreign competition was beginning to make itself felt, causing loss of jobs and falling profits, there was, on the other, a boom caused by falling food prices. Individuals were now able to buy other things and so expand the economy. Thus in parts of the big cities decent housing began to be erected for skilled workers, while in other parts of the cities an economy of the dependant prevailed, who undertook work that was rewarded by falling wages. Norman Stone, in *Sunday Times* (1988) Drink-Sadden History of the Docklands Underclass, 3 July review of a book that describes these circumstances says that there are three things that stand out, which are, to quote, 'skills unfortunately of great importance to us'. They are as follows:

    1. That an underclass is living in hopeless, hereditary despair.
    2. The influx of Jews into the East End of London did not cause a violent reaction even though there was some anti-semitism.
    3. The attempt by the middle classes to introduce the working classes to the world of the mind

did not work. The university created for them in the East End was soon taken over by middle-class students.

The first point follows from what has been said previously. It raises questions about how the under-privileged will be dealt with in society. The problem in Britain is that the system of benefits and its relation to the system of taxation cause a poverty trap to be established, from which it is difficult to escape.

In respect of the third point, Brian Walden, a British commentator, also written in *The Sunday Times* (1987) Hope for Workers Caught in a Trap, 20 Dec. has drawn attention to the fact that technology has replaced many of the jobs that were done in the past by the 'labouring classes'. The work these people did has disappeared, and more significantly, the culture of the factory, with which it is associated, has declined. Walden believes that society underestimates their sense of rejection. He takes the view that retraining, as opposed to education, will not solve the problem, for what is required is education. The purpose of that education is to shatter 'the nexus of self pity, lack of vision, and innate pride in ignorance that keeps people resentfully chained to life without prospects'. 'We ought', he says, 'to want to help people to change their lives for the better from purely altruistic motives.' This altruism is missing.

M. Casson argues in *Economics of Unemployment: An historical perspective* (1983) that it is the failure to be mobile that leads to unemployment, on the one hand, and vacancies, on the other. Thus in part, unemployment is better understood in terms of the factors that affect the mobility of workers. He argues that the most probable reason for lack of immobility is an unwillingness to take on new working methods or to learn new skills, and that is in no small way a function of attitude. Just as managers should be more entrepreneurial in their outlook, so should workers be entrepreneurial in respect of the acquisition and utilization of their skills. Thus it is that formal education has to be concerned with the provision of this skill base, even though the determination of the characteristics of that basis is complex.

However, it is clear that the new technologies have displaced persons in all socio-economic groups. No group has escaped entirely. Thus education for adaptability has to be a general function of general education for all.

15. Complexity invades any discussion of unemployment as soon as attempts are made to define the phenomenon. J.A. Garraty, *Unemployment in History* (1978) the author of a substantial history of unemployment, goes so far as to state that he has avoided the issue. If he had attempted this task he would probably have shown that the definition has changed many times in history. Ideas about idleness and unemployment have certainly changed with time. Nowadays there is little talk about idleness as a cause of unemployment. Today it is generally accepted, for the most part, that unemployment arises from a shortage of jobs in specific industries and regions, and that jobs can only be created or maintained in sufficient numbers if a nation can continually increase its wealth. Nevertheless, there is still a niggle that some individuals may prefer unemployment, and the benefits associated with unemployment to work.

Our views about unemployment and our behaviour are determined in no small way by the attitude society takes to the unemployed. As Garraty puts it, 'Prostitution may not actually be the oldest profession, but whether a prostitute is a legitimate worker or a parasite depends on the attitudes of society and indeed of the individual prostitute' (*ibid.*).

He goes on to say

> Unemployed persons have been treated as criminals who must be isolated from society or driven to hard labour, and as sinners to be regenerated by exhortation and prayer (their own as well as those of their betters). They have been viewed as wayward children who must be taught how to work, as lazy incompetents best left to suffer the consequences of their sloth, and as innocent victims of forces beyond their control. Nearly every scheme for both improving their lot and sustaining them in their misery that is currently in vogue, along with many no longer considered workable, was known and debated at least as far back as the sixteenth century. What actually has been done for the unemployed and about unemployment has depended upon the interaction of moral and religious attitudes, the sense of what is economically possible, the focus of political power in society, and the exdtent which those who possess the power are aware of how unemployment affects both its victims and their own interests (*ibid.*).

Fundamental to the notion of unemployment is the notion of the right to work. Trade unions claim this to be a fundamental right – but is it? In any event, who has this right? Is it all males and females over school-leaving age? Is it a right that both partners in a marriage should be allowed to work? Is it a serious matter, when both husband and wife are working, that one of them should become redundant? In times of unemployment, should married women teachers allow themselves to be replaced by new, unmarried, female teachers? During this century there has been a remarkable change in attitudes towards women working, and this has been accompanied by a considerable increase in the number of jobs available. Thus one question in a debate about unemployment is, 'how many jobs ought there to be available?' Answers to this question are complicated by the fact that the number of jobs created does not necessarily mean that unemployment is reduced. Similarly, the number of jobs lost in a week does not necessarily mean that unemployment is increased. Raw statistics suggest that in Britain, four million new jobs are created each year. It is also necessary to distinguish between the long-term unemployed and the short term, if the rate of change within the labour market is to be understood.

In many countries, moonlighting is not taken into account in the statistics. Many individuals who have jobs that are counted in the statistics also do other jobs for other people, for example, house repairs, which are not reported to the tax authorities or anyone else. These jobs create an informal or 'black economy', as it is known, and it is growing in Europe. An unemployed person may be involved in the 'black economy'. Although that person might have the equivalent of a job, they are not recorded as having a job. Unearthing the real facts about unemployment is extremely difficult.

But just as there is a concept of unemployment so there is a concept of *under-employment*. Workers who are unable to perform tasks well within their ken – because of restrictive practices – are under-employed. But such practices can also lead to over-employment in the sense that more people are employed than are actually required to perform the task satisfactorily. Under-employment is also thought to occur among the highly able, such as managers, technocrats and technologists.

In under-developed countries, it may be preferable to have large numbers of people who are under-employed than to have a correspondingly large number of people unemployed.

16.   Blackaby, Monetarism's forgotten people (note 12); and Reading, B. (1988) Battle of the money bulge, *The Sunday Times*, 22 May.

17.   Phelps, E.S. (1968) Money wages dynamics and labour market equilibrium, *Journal of Political Economy*, Vol. 76, pp. 687–71 and in Phillip Curves (1967) 'Expectations of inflation and optimal unemployment overtime', *Economics*, Aug.

18.   Smith, A. (1981) The informal economy, *Lloyds Bank Review*, no. 141, pp. 45–60.

19.   See Vines, D. (1986) Macroeconomic policy after monetarism, *Royal Bank of Scotland Review*, no. 152, pp. 3–19, which also summarizes the major differences between Keynesian and monetarist approaches. The Employment Institute was founded by R. Layard, whose book, *How to Beat Unemployment*, was published by Oxford University Press in 1985.

20.   Carter, C.F. (1973) *The Science of Wealth*, Arnold, London.

21.   Hoskyns, Sir John (1985) Pay's let the bosses decide, *The Times*, 5 Dec.

22.   Rowley, K. and Wiseman, J. (1983) Inflation versus unemployment. Is the government important?, *National Westminster Bank Quarterly Review*, February, pp. 2–12.

23.   Ryan, P. (1984) The new training initiative after two years, *Lloyds Bank Review*, no. 152, pp. 31–45.

24.   Lever, Lord and Edwards, G. (1984) in *The Sunday Times*. The situation was no different in 1987, and commentators were making the same points, for example, Searjeant, G. (1987) Spendthrift consumers crowd industry out, *The Sunday Times*, 2 March.

25.   *The Sunday Times* (1988) The problems of success (editorial), 3 July.

26.   Kindleberger, C.P. (1980) Responsibility in economic life, *Lloyds Bank Review*, no. 138, pp. 1–11.

        Peter Jay has argued that policies in Britain were monetarist between 1974 and 1979. In contrast to the prevailing view of government policy, they were expansionary after 1974 *but* had the same effects as a monetary policy in that inflation decreased in 1981 to single figures; this deflation was accompanied by a considerable increase in unemployment, which continues to remain high.

27.   Mitchell, C.W. (1988) *Government as it is*, Institute of Economic Affairs, London.

28.   Hayek, F.A. (1975) *Full Employment At Any Price*, Institute of Economic Affairs, London.

29.   Among those who have argued strongly for a return to the gold standard is a former editor of *The Times*, William Rees-Mogg. For a recent discussion of reforms to the monetary system, see Rybczynski, T.M. (1987) The approaches towards the reform of the International Monetary System, *National Westminster Bank Quarterly Review*, February, pp. 2–11, who takes an opposite view.

30.   In June 1989 Britain committed herself to become a member of the EMS at an appropriate time and when other countries removed their exchange controls. In any currency alignment success depends on the relative valuations of the currencies being aligned. The alignment of sterling to

the Gold Standard in 1925 is cited. It is argued that because the pound was overvalued that Britain suffered slow growth and rising unemployment 'For' and 'against' arguments were set out by Smith and Reading in *The Sunday Times* July 2, 1989. T Congdon (*The Times*, June 26, 1989) argued that the deep-seated financial incompatibility between members of the EMS made it impossible for Britain to join. The most interesting comment came from P Brimelow (*The Times* July 8 1989) who pointed out that the decision was political not economic. After all the largest bilateral trade flow in the world took place between Canada and the USA, and they had found neither a common currency or a fixed exchange rate to be necessary.

    See also Charles, R. (1989) Canada – United States Free Trade Agreement: A Canadian's Personal Perspective. *National Westminster Bank Review*, May, pp. 17–26.

31.   Smallwood, C. Economic Editor of *The Sunday Times*, in numerous articles between 1986 and 1988, for example: 13 Dec. 1987, 3 Mar. 1988, 27 Mar. 1988 and 3 July 1988.

32.   Cairncross, A. (1988) Britain's industrial decline, *The Royal Bank of Scotland Review*, no. 159, pp. 1–18.

33.   Phillips Curves, P. Expectations of inflation (note 17).

34.   Festinger, L. (1959) *A Theory of Cognitive Dissonance*, Tavistock, London.

35.   Marshall, S. (1980) Cognitive-affective dissonance in the classroom, *Teaching Political Science*, Vol. 8, pp. 111–17.

36.   Reading, Battle of the money bulge (note 16).

11

LEADERSHIP

Leading and Following

Ultimately, effective management depends on people, and we have expectations of those persons. More often than not, we become disappointed with the performance of people in top posts and their charisma fades. Most of the people regarded as leaders who have been asked to discuss the qualities of leadership can be shown to have made many mistakes when their total careers are taken into account. The popular management journals and the business columns of the newspapers are full of success stories of companies that, a year or so later, are found to be wanting. It would seem almost as if leadership is a short-lived quality directed to a particular problem at a particular time. The most important art in leadership may well be to know when to give up and hand on to someone else. This may not be important if there is sustained growth, but come the time of stagnation or renewal, different qualities may be required. It is not surprising, therefore, to find that writers and researchers on leadership often classify leaders into 'types'. So what is a leader, what is leading, what is leadership?

Leading implies following. To the extent that we set ourselves goals, and to the extent we set about obtaining those goals, we both lead and follow. Just as every individual is a manager so, too, is every individual a leader. Because this is the case, each individual has with him or herself the attributes of leadership. What distinguishes one person from another as a leader is the use to which they put their attributes of leadership in the varying situations in which they find themselves. Leadership is, therefore, partly a function of personal disposition, personality if you like, and partly a function of the situation that embraces the individual at a particular time. This is as true of the individual who seeks a goal that is largely independent of others, as it is of the individual who has to direct and control a group of persons in pursuit of a common goal. Thus it is that leadership may involve the leader in management. But that is not all there is to leadership, because some people, like the prophets, cause people to follow whatever it is that they are called upon to follow, without actively involving themselves in the organization. Others do the management for the leader. Evidently, the study of leadership is complex. So what is it we want from the person whom we call 'leader'?

Leadership, Styles and Traits

Many attempts have been made to understand the factors contributing to leadership in organizations.[1] There have also been many studies of leaders in the military and political fields that have contributed to our understanding of the many facets of leadership, and to the development of leadership training programmes.[2] The approaches to the study of leadership that have been taken relate to trait theory, style theory, situational theory and path-goal theory.

Adair calls qualities, such as 'initiative', 'perseverance', 'integrity', 'humour', 'tact', 'compassion', etc., traits. There are many more. These particular examples are taken from Adair because he uses them in pairs to show that they relate to three areas that embrace an organization and its goals. These are the task, the team and the individual. For example, initiative and perseverance have functional value in respect of the task; integrity and humour in respect of the team; and tact and compassion in regard to the individual. In the early trait research, no account was taken of the needs and personalities of employees – neither was their relative importance specified. It will be seen that Adair's use of qualities takes care of these objections. His scheme of leadership training is designed to help individuals to understand the characteristics of leadership, if they possess them, and if they don't, to perceive whether they could develop themselves through such training. Adair's readers are invited to rate, for their importance in leadership, 25 items, such as enterprise (13), astuteness (15), capacity to speak lucidly (14), willingness to take risks (12), ability to meet unpleasant situations (10) and analytical ability (7). The numbers in brackets show how they were ranked by a cross-section of managers. The first 5 from the 25 in order of significance were the ability to take decisions, leadership, integrity, enthusiasm and imagination. I would suggest that this is what any group (students, family, sports people, industrialists, members of the church, politicians) expect of their leaders. The other qualities are important but not as important, so it seems. Leaders do require self-confidence, justice, moral courage and consistency. Examination of the programmes for social and life-skill development in schools among the older pupils shows that some of them are mini-programmes in leadership. It is not, therefore, without significance that, apart from intelligence, differences in achievement are often accounted for by teachers in terms of traits. For example, the low-achieving student is often said to lack confidence and motivation.

Trait theory will always have some importance if only because it uses the terms commonly employed to describe leaders. We like leaders to demonstrate initiative, self-assurance and decisiveness. These qualities are components of the style people bring to jobs, and leadership style has been much studied. Early studies contrasted production-centred with employee-centred styles. They are similar to teacher-centred and child-centred teaching. Perhaps the best-known typology is the contrast between the authoritarian style and the democratic style of management.[3] These styles are similar to teacher-centred and child-centred teaching. One of the most-used typologies is the Blake-Mouton Grid, which relates the degree of concern for people in a 9-position matrix. The 1.1 style describes a person who makes minimum effort to get the work done required to sustain membership of the organization. The 9.9 style obtains work from committed people, and creates interdependence throughout the organization through a common purpose. A 9.9-style leader creates relationships of trust and respect.[4] The same kind of studies of effectiveness in learning as a function of teaching and learning styles have been made with similar results.[5] The teacher's task is made difficult by the fact that there will be several different learning styles among the pupils. The same must apply to managers. Given that a company is a learning system, then managers will benefit if they understand the learning styles of their workers. Management has to obtain a balance between the differing styles of its workers in all parts of the organization; if not, the whole organization will become ineffective. The attainment of balance is the function of control and integration, since an organization 'is the co-ordination of the different activities of individual contributors to carry out planned transactions with the environment'.[6] It implies the building of teams. As such, managers have to understand the interaction between the style, the subordinates' expectations, task complexity and the factors that contribute to the environment.[7]

Leadership, Control, Integration and Change

The effectiveness of control is a function of the levels of commitment within the organization, for, as Barnard has said, individuals may be thought of as contributing activities to an organization rather than being totally in it.[8] As we saw, any individual exists in a plurality of social systems and the level of commitment changes as the goals of some of these systems become relatively more important, and vice versa. One managerial or leadership function is to integrate the role of people in the organization and, in some organizations, this may be a specific task.

Managers who have integrative roles do not supervise actual work. Their job is to assist those who do, and it is a common-place function in industry. Its purpose in large organizations is the co-ordination of decisions. In the company described in Chapter 6, project engineers played an important role in integration. Projects necessarily utilize the resources of more than one department, and this is one reason for the interest in matrix forms of management in which the company's departments are integrated to provide resources for a number of development and project teams. As we saw, within a matrix a manager may play a role both in the department and in a project, and so he or she obtains dual responsibility. This kind of organization is almost necessary in such companies as those in the aircraft industry, where large projects are undertaken.[9] Integrators, whether in school, college or industry, have often to exercise a chairperson's role. Their problem is how to influence without authority. Such integrators have to develop a high level of mutual trust, and so their personal disposition is of considerable importance.

They will very often have to repress their own ideas or see them substantially changed. In much of their work they will seem to be almost passive agents, as Lawrence and Lorsch say:

> For a leader, such functions as rejecting or promoting ideas, according to his personal needs, are out of bounds. He must be receptive to information contributed, accept contributions without evaluating them, posting contributions on a chalk board to keep them alive, summarize information to facilitate integration, stimulate exploratory behavior, create awareness of problems of one member by others, and detect when the group is ready to resolve differences and agree to a unified solution.[10]

Like the dean of the faculty in a university, the integrator gains his or her power through his or her ability to communicate in different 'languages' between departments with different psychological (language) orientations. This power is based on knowledge and information to which he or she has access over and above the groups he or she is integrating.

There are examples to show that departments can isolate individuals who have been put into integrating roles. For this reason, the integrating function should be coupled with the management system so that the integrator has a formal role in the decision-making process. Galbraith has called it a managerial linking role. An integrator has the job of 'standing between two groups without being absorbed into one of them or accepted by neither of them'.[11]

It is evident that the direction an organization takes may be changed by the intervention of either individuals or groups. How the mechanisms of control are perceived by individuals is an important factor, for there cannot be control without integration, and vice versa. Interest in the USA, in particular, has centred on the planning of strategies to change the direction of an organization. Leadership in industry might be regarded as the ability to change an organization, so that it continually achieves those goals essential to the maintenance of its effectiveness as an organization.

Disposition and Personality among Individuals and Groups

It is self-evident that style is a complex function of personality and the situation – both task and people – with which the individual interacts. Surprisingly enough, there has been little discussion of the relationship between the style, the situation and the leader. Style data, argues Hunt, is readily available, but the collection of situational data, especially about superiors, subordinates and peers, has been neglected. Similarly, little time is spent in collecting data about the task, and the people who have to perform the task.[12]

Just as individuals have personality dimensions, so do small groups. As we have seen, departments in an organization can develop their own language system. Moreover, the emotional commitment of their members will be to the common task or values they share. A newcomer will have to adapt to the needs of the group and share their emotions. We have seen that when different departments prefer different solutions to the same problem, as may occur between a design and production department, conflict occurs. Such conflict relates to the level of certainty contained in the task as well as to the emotional orientation of the work, and both may be re-inforced by, or in conflict with, the task. Predictable tasks cause well-defined procedures and mechanisms of control. These are in contrast with many technical tasks where the outcomes are uncertain and the mechanisms of control a response to that situation. Therefore, in fitting an individual to a task it is important to evaluate the emotional orientation of the persons to that work.[13] For example, a research worker will not like being put to work on a job that is essentially care and maintenance, although his or her disposition may change with age, and at some later time he or she may be better deployed in such a task.

Individuals also vary in their orientation towards time:

> The technologist spends hours analysing ambiguous problems and uncertain relationships in order to complete a design due in three months. He will not know if it is successful until a moon shot is completed two years from now. Contrast him with the operations foreman, who quickly loads three jobs on his machines, shifts manpower assignments, ships two completed lots, and knows at the end of the day how well he has performed. These different time perspectives are necessary for their respective tasks.[14]

The level of responsibility a person feels in a job relates to the time it takes for the longest task to be completed, so argues Jaques.[15] The structure of organizations is not a matter of chance, but a reflection of the way individuals differ in their capability to exercise discretion over increasing periods of time. Support for this time-span of discretion theory has come from Stamp, who suggested that different kinds of capability are required to cope with the five time-span levels identified by Jaques when the theory is applied to leadership.[16] For example good policy formulators who may not be good at implementing them may require a time span of up to ten years for the kind of internal analysis and reflection which they do. Some academics come into this category except many have to deal with particularities and details with which other policy formulators are impatient.

This is in contrast with the short time span (no more than 3 months) which practitioners, who are not good at articulating new policies and plans, and who may be impatient with them because the reality of the situations with which they like to cope is perceived by them to demand immediate and pragmatic responses.

Those who are likely to be good in line management will often work by trial and error. Their maximum time span is not likely to be more than a year.

Thus the possibility of selecting persons for tasks by reference to their behavioural time spans emerges. A mismatch may well be accompanied by stress.

Because personalities differ, both at the level of the individual and the group, it is inevitable that large organizations will require a combination of leadership styles and research seems to support this view.[17] The problem for some leaders is that they may not be able to change their style to meet the needs of the groups to whom they have been transferred. This brings us full circle to the beginning of this book, for leadership is a form of role-playing, and we have seen the significance of perception to both role performance and adaptability. Hunt puts it this way:

> The relevance of the style adopted is a function of the degree of perceptiveness or sensitivity of the individual to the demands, tasks, expectations etc. of the situation. If the preferred behaviour needs modifying to produce a new balance of power or to

disrupt one (or whatever), then the perceptive leader will modify his behaviour. Conversely, the insensitive leader will not modify his behaviour to meet the situational demands.[18]

Thus training for leadership begins with learning, and learning with perception. A major problem is that there is very little opportunity to learn systematically from experience in the workplace. This must be the task of leadership development, but it is also the task of compulsory education. Such a programme will be largely experiential, in which evaluation is a key factor. However, the success of groups, families and role-sets in organizations depends as much on the led as it does on the leader, for it is their combination that gives the organization its culture. We turn therefore from research to the potential that each one of us has for leadership.

Every Individual a Leader

So much for the theory. In Chapter 6 the view is put that learning and decision-making are the same and that in all our everyday activities we show skills in management. The same applies to leadership. We all take on leadership roles in one way or another – mostly, I suspect, to get our own way but sometimes to help a group or a family cohere. We may even intervene in the role-set at work. In some work situations, such as the school and college where there is a high level of democracy, we might even want to wield power through the group or committee.

Participation is the 'in' thing. This is as it should be, for are we not now better educated and better equipped to participate? Is it not a fact that participation will be forced on us? Apart from this fact, and because there is no best leadership pattern, the frame of reference for the future understanding of the behaviour of a leader will be focused on the reality of the situation. Collinson calls this 'reality-centred' leadership,[19] in which we all have a leadership role to play.

One of the reasons conflict emerges and leadership is made difficult is that we don't really want anyone to lead. Leadership implies change and many of us do not want to change. Peters and Waterman quote Ernest Becker, who in *Denial of Death*, wrote of the paradox in individuals that

> Man thus has the absolute tension of dualism. Individuation means that the human creature has to oppose itself to the rest of nature (stick out). Yet it creates precisely the isolation that one can't stand – and yet needs, in order to develop distinctively. It creates the difference that becomes such a burden: it accents the smallness of oneself and the stickoutness at the same time.[20]

Our play in groups is in no small measure a reaction to our perceptions of ourselves.

We make judgements about our own capabilities and decide whether or not we can or would wish to lead. If we are deprived of leadership or do not enter the stakes, the tendency is to 'let the other chap get on with it . . .'. We are no longer responsible.

It follows from the view that every person is a manager that everyone is a leader.

Each role requires leadership, for each role requires the exercise of responsibility: each role requires that the individual understands the contribution he or she can make to the group leader's task. It is this philosophy (principle) that is missing from so many institutions. Thus it is that the first task of many leaders of large and small groups is to build a value system acceptable to all, the pursuit of which engulfs the energy of the group.

If organizations have personality, so they also have culture and values. Systems or organizations may be viewed as sets of ideas, 'the meaning of which has to be managed'.[21] Leaders give the culture shape through the creation of language, ideology, myth and ritual.[22] Peters and Waterman contend that the successful organizations they studied were rich in legend and parable, whereas unsuccessful companies were not. They go on to argue that where the culture was very dominant, the highest levels of true autonomy were to be found. It is within the culture that meaning is found and needs thereby satisfied.

It also brings us full circle to role theory, and the understanding we have of our roles (Chapter 2). Just as we will develop better skills of critical thinking if we work to a model of critical thinking, so we will perform better in groups the more we understand our roles. Belbin brings the idea of the role presented in Chapter 2 into sharp relief in terms of leadership in and the management of groups. He argues that each member in a team (group) has a functional role and a team role. Thus, while presenting the functional aspect, the individual will do this within the framework of a predetermined disposition. He also argues that the team roles individuals adopt are limited to eight, which he calls chairman, shaper, plant, monitor-evaluator, company worker, resource investigator, team worker and finisher.[23]

In brief, the chairman is concerned with the attainment of objectives. Characterwise, while dominant, he or she will not be assertive. The shaper is the person who, in a group, always wants to bring everything together so that a project can be initiated and completed. Shapers are bundles of nervous energy able to challenge and to respond to challenge. The plant is the person with imagination who, when the team is bogged down, looks for new ideas. Together with the monitor-evaluator, he or she is highly intelligent. The monitor-evaluator brings dispassionate critical analysis to the problem. Tse calls him or her a 'cold fish'.[24] The company worker is the individual concerned with practical implementation. His or hers is a disciplined approach that requires plenty of character. The resource investigator looks outside for ideas and brings them back to the group while the team worker is the one who understands the emotional needs of the group. The team worker tries to promote unity and harmony. The finisher is the anxious one: the individual who worries about detail; who wants to get things done properly.

Similar types to those listed by Belbin will be found in any group, and teachers in a departmental or staff meeting are no exception. They will be found in gangs of children. Each type has its strengths and weaknesses, which Belbin has documented. While it would appear that individuals have a natural predisposition to some roles and always behave in the way associated with the role, it is possible in training exercises to develop them in these roles. They can also be located within the organization in such a way that its structure demands that they play a role.

The Servant Leader

The idea of the servant as leader is to be found in a small pamphlet by Greenleaf. He said that in the early 1960s there was a crisis of leadership, and that this was in part due to the fact that individuals allowed the problems of our times to be dealt with wholly in terms of systems, ideologies and movements.[25] Put in this way, we can see at once how pressure groups have arisen, and how the tendency of many people in all social classes to let others get on with the job is self-imposed alienation. In Greenleaf's dictum, individuals often deny themselves wholeness and creative fulfilment by failing to lead when they could. However, I have argued that most individuals do not perceive leadership to be a possibility. Nevertheless, with appropriately chosen learning strategies throughout their formal education, they can be brought to a greater understanding of leadership and the dependency factor in leadership. Like Greenleaf, the thesis of this book is founded on the view that the total process of education is indifferent 'to the individual as servant and leader, as a person and in society'.

Greenleaf holds to the prophetic view that there are prophetic voices of wisdom and clarity speaking all the time. There are times when they are not heard, and these occur, as now, when the level of seeking and the responsiveness of the hearers is low: 'The prophet grows in stature as the people respond to his message'.[26] Thus it is the seekers who make the prophet and the led who make the leaders. Both, by the action of choice, have obligations to each other: 'We listen to as wide a range of contemporary thought as we can attend to. Then we *choose* those we elect as prophets – both *with old and new* – and mould their advice with our own leadings. This we test in real life experiences to establish our own position'.[27]

We do the same with the small things of life, the family, the local community and the job or the new job. Greenleaf puts his argument thus:

> A fresh critical look is being taken at the issues of power and authority, and people are beginning to learn, however haltingly, to relate to one another in less coercive and more creatively supporting ways. A new moral principle is emerging which holds that the only authority deserving one's allegiance is that which is freely and knowingly granted by the led to the leader in response to, and in proportion to, the clearly evident servant stature of the leader. Those who choose to follow this principle will not casually accept the authority of existing institutions. *Rather, they will freely respond only to individuals who are chosen as leaders because they are proven and trusted as servants.* To the extent that this principle prevails in the future, the only truly viable institutions will be those which are servant led.[28]

One of the problems Greenleaf sees, and it has been one of the several themes in this book, is that education is far too occupied with criticism and analysis. This is at the expense of those skills essential to creative leadership, which is to help everyone to grow as a person. It is leadership of community, of listening and understanding, of language and imagination, of acceptance and empathy, of awareness and perception, of healing and serving, of conceptualization, and of action. But such leadership, as Collinson points out, has to be tempered by realism.[29] Effective planning, for example, can cause human problems. Friendship does not mean that everyone should like each other. It does contain the ability to express honest hostilities while maintaining co-operation. The incongruity of present developments in education in the European Economic Community is that it is the programmes for low achievers that contain all the ingredients of leadership training!

The concept of leadership put forward by Greenleaf will be understood by Christians, who may see it as modelled by Christ. But the notion of servant in the Gospel is somewhat different, and Christ is careful to point this out:

> A man can have no greater love than to lay down his life for his friends. You are my friends, if you do what I command you. I shall not call you servants any more, because a servant does not know his master's business: I call you friends because I have made known to you everything I have learnt from my Father.[30]

Modern education and the media, especially the media, have made us know and want to know our master's business but they have not made us friends. Therein lies the challenge to education in the last part of the twentieth century.

Notes and References

1. See, for example, Dessler, G. (1976) *Organization and Management*, Prentice-Hall, Englewood Cliffs, NJ; and Hunt, J.W. (1979) *Managing People at Work*, McGraw-Hill, Maidenhead.
2. Adair, J. (1983) *Effective Leadership: A Self-Development Manual*, Gower, Aldershot.
3. Lippitt, R. (1940) An experimental study of the effects of democratic and autocratic atmospheres, *University of Iowa Studies in Child Welfare*, no. 16, p. 45.
4. Unfortunately, when the Blake-Mouton grid and other instruments are used to collect this kind of data, they often give different results when tested on the same people. Thus Hunt, *Managing People* (note 1), says that it is arguable that the controversy about styles is probably about the methodology of the instruments used rather than the theory.
5. See, for example, Grasha, A.F. (1984) Learning styles. The journey from Greenwich Observatory (1796) to college classroom (1984), *Improving College and University Teaching,* Vol. 32, pp. 46–53; and Hymann, R. and Rosoff, B. (1983) Matching learning and teaching styles: the job and what's in it, *Theory into Practice*, Vol. 23, no. 1.
6. See Hunt, *Managing People* (note 1). This definition is from Lawrence, P.R. and Lorsch, J. (1967) *Organization and Environment*, Harvard Graduate School of Business Administration, Boston, Mass.
7. The study of such interactions is called goal-path theory.
8. Barnard, C. (1950) *The Functions of the Executive,* Harvard University Press, Cambridge, Mass.
9. Youngman, M., Oxtoby, R., Monk, J.D. and Heywood, J. (1977) *Analysing Jobs*, Gower, Aldershot.
10. Lawrence and Lorsch, *Organization and Environment* (note 6).
11. Galbraith, J. (1973) *Organization Design*, Addison-Wesley, Reading, Mass.
12. See Hunt, *Managing People* (note 1).
13. See Lawrence and Lorsch, *Organization and Environment* (note 6).
14. Galbraith, J. *Organizational Design* (note 11).
15. Jaques, E. (1976) *A General Theory of Bureaucracy,* Heinemann, London.
16. Stamp, G. (1980) Personal capacity: an expansion of capacity, *Leadership and Organization Development Journal,* Vol. 1, no. 3, p. 17.
17. Storm, P. and Shou, A.J. (1980) Leadership style and leadership flexibility: some transnational observations, *Leadership and Organization Development Journal*, Vol. 1, no. 2, p. 26.
18. Hunt, *Managing People* (note 1).

19. Collinson, L. (1985) How to plan for people, *Management Today*, June, pp. 94–8.
20. Quoted by Peters, J. and Waterman, R.H. (1982) *In Search of Excellence: Lessons from America's Best Run Companies,* Harper & Row, New York, NY. See also notes 21 and 22.
21. Martin, J. (1980) Stories, scripts and organization sellings, Research Report no. 543, Graduate School of Business Study, Stanford University, Calif.
22. Pettigrew, A.M. (1976) The creation of organisational culture, Joint EIASM/DANSK Management Research Centre Seminar, Copenhagen, p. 11.
23. Belbin, R.M. (1981) *Management Teams: Why They Succeed or Fail*, Heinemann, London.
24. Tse, K.K. (1985) *Marks and Spencer. Anatomy of Britain's Most Efficiently Managed Company*, Pergamon, Oxford.
25. Greenleaf, R.K. (1973) *The Servant as Leader*, Windy Row Press, Peterborough, NH.
26. *Ibid.*
27. *Ibid.*
28. *Ibid.*
29. Collinson, How to plan (note 19).
30. John, 15: 13–15.

12

EDUCATION, INDUSTRY AND SOCIETY

Introduction

Advanced technological societies require individuals to adapt continually. Such adaptation, to paraphrase Heiko Steffens, should be creative.[1] In the preceding chapters, the factors that enhance or impede individual and societal adaptation have been shown to be the same as those that enhance or impede learning. It is concluded that a prime concern of any education system is with the development of skills in learning and that this necessarily implies an understanding of how both individuals and institutions learn. One trend in western Europe has been to develop work preparation and life-skills programmes for those of average and below-average attainment. However, there is a general need for individuals across the range of ability to be technologically literate if they are to be involved in policy formation at either the institutional or self levels. In so far as people, organizations and society are concerned, individuals require philosophical, economic and socio-psychological perspectives with which to examine their own as well as society's performance. This book has considered a limited number of key concepts in the areas of learning, interpersonal relations, organizational behaviour, economics and societal development, which together provide a framework for the understanding of individual and societal adaptation.

Since there is much interest in the so-called 'British *malaise*', one theme of this book has focused on this issue and to compare that dilemma with the experience of other countries, Danzin[2] would argue that, by comparison with Japan, the *malaise* extends to Europe as well. This chapter continues with these comparisons, more especially as they relate to education and industry, and it begins with a warning that such comparisons, particularly at the statistical level, are extremely difficult to make.

In Britain, there has been a thirty-years dogfight between education and industry. Educationalists have argued that industry makes insufficient use of its products while, in return, industrialists have said that they are not the products they want. Government policies have and continue to respond to this debate. In this chapter it will be argued that such social engineering through the curriculum is unlikely to solve the British *malaise* towards industry and manufacturing. Comparative studies of the educational systems of France, Japan, West Germany and Britain do not show that there is a particular curriculum that will solve the problem. Even when account is taken of the limitations of comparative studies, McClelland's thesis seems true that it is national attitudes that are the principal determinants of economic behaviour. Since the curriculum and its teaching follows rather than leads social attitudes, it is questionable if changes in its contents can lead to substantial changes in attitude that are not a response to perceived societal needs.

Nevertheless, education does have a role to play in the development of creative adaptability, for education is concerned with the development of intelligence. Given that intelligence is the purposive adaptation to and selection and shaping of real-world environments relevant to one's life, then any educational programme must be concerned with the development of skills in learning how to learn. Such skills must be acquired through frames of reference that will help to generate an understanding of the socio-economic system and the potential of technology to effect change.

Misleading Numbers

Many commentators, including historians, are apt to be confused by national statistics when they are used for comparative purposes. For example, the statement that 'only 13% of young people in Britain receive a higher education, which compares poorly enough with the U.S. figure of 43% and Italy's 30%' is totally misleading.[3] This is because the definition of higher education differs between these countries. When such comparisons are made, they should attempt to measure the efficiency with which a system produces graduates. In these circumstances, it is possible to argue that the British system is more efficient than the American. When the drop-out rates for higher education in the USA and the universities in Britain are compared, the apparent wastage rates are found to be much higher in the USA than in Britain, that is, of the order 40 per cent as compared with 11 per cent. Thus it might be concluded that the British universities are more efficient than their counterparts in America. However, any measurement of efficiency has to take into account the input level, or what are loosely called entry standards, of the students. When this is done, it is found that the input standard of a university course in Britain is much higher than that in the USA, since the A-level of the GCE is at least the equivalent of first-year university courses in such countries as Ireland and the USA.

It might be argued that a lower standard of admission will enable more students to participate in higher education, but this is to ignore the fact that in Britain there is a larger further education sector concerned with a wide range of vocational courses. It does seem, however, that the numbers of skilled craftworkers and their equivalent is much higher in West Germany than it is in Britain, so it is possible that the economic success of West Germany is linked to the dual system of education and training.[4] Whatever else it does, it certainly reflects a much more positive attitude towards training for industry in Germany.

West Germany

A surprising feature of the West German school system is that it continues to resemble the British system of the 1960s. That is to say, that it is essentially tripartite in nature, although there is an increasing number of comprehensive schools. Although the success of the West German education system has been put down to the dual system of educational training that follows on from school, the Germans have been interested in the relationships between education and work within the school curriculum for many years. During this period they have developed *Arbeitslehre* (education for work), which integrates craft, mechanics, electronics, information technology, home economics incorporating family studies and consumerism, and career studies into a single integrated programme. The programme, which also embraces work experience, is designed to develop skills that will be of value in work and life. The method of achieving this is through projects that develop skills in problem-solving (understanding problems and planning for their solution, realization and evaluation).[5]

While such courses in the comprehensive and technical schools cannot be said to account for the so-called West German miracle, they have reflected the view now prevalent in Britain that students should be introduced to vocational studies of a general kind during their schooling. Like Britain, these studies have had little impact on the Gymnasium (Grammar School), although it seems there is more concern for the general educational issue such studies raise for the bright, academically oriented students than perhaps there is in Britain. It is at the level of higher education that the difference between British and West German attitudes is most clearly seen.

Barnett has recorded that 'on the eve of the war, Germany was turning out 1,900 graduate engineers a year, plus 2,000 fully qualified practical engineers from her engineer schools to Britain's 700 graduate engineers'.[6] But this figure is also misleading for it should include the number of graduate scientists produced in Britain, since many of them also became engineers. It should also include the number of persons who qualified by part-time education.[7] Nevertheless, the different ratios of engineers to scientists produced in Britain and West Germany may be indicative of different attitudes towards engineering as between the two countries. In the 1950s, the total number of graduates in these two subjects produced by each of the two countries was about the same. However, West Germany produced twice as many engineers as scientists, whereas Britain produced twice as many scientists as engineers. By the 1970s these ratios were 1:1 and 1:2. In fact, Britain had, in 1979, a higher proportion of science and engineering graduates than West Germany, Japan or the USA.[8] These ratios tempt the deduction that Britain was/is oriented toward the 'pure', whereas West Germany was/is oriented to the practical. Inspection of the curricula and their relative status in these countries seems to support this view.

A major difference between the curricula offered in these two countries has been that a West German education in engineering was much longer. It also embraced engineering design. These facts have contributed to the view that engineering courses in Britain should be of four year's duration. Within recent years, public and professional policy has encouraged the lengthening of courses in engineering to four years. An equally substantial difference between the two curricula was the fact that in the British approach the emphasis was on the application of science and not on any rounded preparation for manufacturing technology in industry.[9] Design and manufacturing were not a concern of this education. It is only within the 1980s that a serious attempt has been made to rectify this position.

The debate about 'pure' versus 'applied', which has dogged British education for the last thirty years, arises from the culture in which it was bred. Pure science was the activity of the 'gentleman', and it was and is pure science that holds the status among the subjects of the curriculum. Pure science holds that in its application it is the engineering method. In contrast, in West Germany status is associated with income and power and not with personal refinement, education and breeding. There is no divorce between theory and practice, and because of this the technical universities (Technische Hockschulen) have had parity of esteem with the universities ever since they were created in the nineteenth century. This was not the case with the colleges of advanced technology in Britain. Specifically created to emulate the Technische Hockschulen in the 1950s, they sought university status and, even when it was granted, became relatively low-status universities subject to enormous financial cuts even though they were apparently doing what was needed. As in West Germany, so too in France: the Grandes Ecoles, which embrace the study of administration and technology, have the highest status within the system of third-level education.

In West Germany, the distinction found in Britain between the arts and science and the pure and applied does not exist. In West Germany, the distinction is between *Kunst, Wissenschaft,* and *Technik. Wissenschaft* denotes all formal-knowledge subjects, arts, science, and social science in our terms. *Kunst* denotes art, where the *raison d'être* is aesthetic; and *Technik* denotes craft and engineering where the criteria are skill and utility. Engineering has a stronger cultural validation in West Germany under the independent heading of *Technik* than it has in Britain under the misnomer of *applied science*, which gives engineering a subordinate status. Hutton, Lawrence and Smith point out that West German education is specialist, not generalist.[10] Although they do not come down in favour of either approach, they argue first that specialism enhances the status of the engineer because the engineer's specialism has practical application and, second, that in Germany it gives an engineer *a priori* claim to enter industrial management. In contrast to Britain, the majority of industrial managers in West Germany are engineers and they are paid more in absolute terms than British engineers. Relative to their position, West German engineers are paid more than university professors and senior civil servants. This is not to argue that engineers in Britain have been successful when in senior management positions. It could be argued that the opposite is true, and this may be a composite function of disposition and the narrowness of an education that was rigid in the applications of science.

Nevertheless, the pay (status) of engineers reflects value dispositions in society to which education can only respond. Education can provide curricula but it cannot ensure that the most able students will take the courses offered. They know 'what is what', even if only vaguely.[11] If able students are to pursue careers as entrepreneurs and industrialists, they have to be persuaded that they are worthwhile. As it is, in Britain, careers in industry have not carried high rewards for graduate engineers. Security is found in the realtively high remuneration of the Civil Service, and entrepreneurship and risk in the financial markets of the City of London. Access to either sphere is relatively difficult for the engineering graduate. But these are cultural not educational problems. They relate to national character, attitudes and values.

For example, it would seem that in Germany during the nineteenth century the desire to create a unified State (the drive of nationalism) was worked out through industrial success.[12] The same components of national character came to the front in 1945 when the German people had to embark on a massive reconstruction of their State. The significant goal, which could be legitimately pursued, was economic success.[13]

The lesson of West German success since the end of the Second World War is not, it seems, about the relative merits of two different educational systems, but in the value dispositions to be found in society. It is to be found in a society that, unlike British society, has not been shackled by an 'us' and 'them' class structure,[14] reinforced by the educational system it produced. While changes in the school curriculum are being encouraged in Britain, in craft, design and technology, it is questionable whether they will achieve the goal of a more entrepreneurially and technologically-oriented society, as reflection on recent developments in the curriculum in France suggest.

Recent Developments in England, France and Ireland

Apart from the developments in craft, design and technology in England, increasing unemployment has caused the government to provide schemes that prepare young persons, who leave school at the compulsory age of 16, for work. These may be undertaken in schools and colleges or at centres developed for these purposes. These Youth Training Schemes led to the view that courses within school should have more relevance to the needs of the students and, in consequence, should have a vocational component. The Department of Employment intervened in the world of second-level education, and its Manpower Services Commission has intervened in the school curriculum in order to provide a vocationally-oriented curriculum as an experiment in schools for the 14–18 age group (the technical vocational education initiative: TVEI). Since the programme runs in parallel with the school curriculum, which prepares young people for higher education (universities and polytechnics), it can hardly be expected to attract the more able. In reality, it is a response to the changing pattern of industrial and commercial needs. It is hoped that this particular group of students will be occupied in endeavours they perceive to be constructive. The general aims relating to industry and society, as set out in the TVEI curriculum objectives, could apply to any set of courses at any level of the education system. At the moment, they are only taken by a section of average and below-average pupils.

There is a long-established tradition of teaching woodwork and metalwork in schools. However, these subjects have low status. The fact that the universities do not, by and large, accept them for entry contributes to the low esteem in which they are held. There is no guarantee that the inclusion of technology in the core curriculum will increase the status of the subject in school, or generally change attitudes towards industry, even if the universities take notice of them for admission purposes.

Although its inclusion in the core curriculum may be thought to have brought the English curriculum into line with France, where technology is a compulsory subject in the *collège*'s curriculum (12–16 years of age),[15] it does not have the thrust being given to its implementation in France. This difference arises from the educational and philosophical traditions in the two countries.

Whereas in England there has been a long tradition of teaching craft subjects in schools, no such tradition existed in France. In England, teachers were specifically trained in colleges of education and served what was the equivalent of an apprenticeship in a particular material, for example, wood or metal. In France, individuals without this background were retrained first in the craft area (there is no woodwork in the French technology scheme), and then retrained again for technology. The courses of retraining lasted one year. Thus, whereas the craft teachers in England had to change their skills to encompass multi-media work, the French teachers began their work without a long tradition of craftwork from which they had to be changed.

In the search for status for their subjects, the English teachers not only had to embrace multi-media studies, but they also embraced design through which they came to the idea that the chief aim of their subject was to develop problem-solving skills through student participation in the design-realization process.[16] Then the goals changed from the development of perfectionist skills in wood and metal to the appreciation of materials and processes through design-and-make activities. Information technology and science in their applications were embraced through the applications of electronics, pneumatics, etc., to the devices being made.

At present, the proposals for assessment of technology show a broadening of the concept of what technological activities are in school. The fact that they include aspects of home economics suggest similarities with *Arbeitslehre* programmes, which operate in comprehensive and technical schools in West Germany. The question that has to be answered is whether these changes will produce the shifts in attitudes among the pupils, which would appear to be essential if there is to be a more general and positive response in society towards industrial regeneration.

My impression from discussions with teachers, the programmes of conferences

Table 12.1　The aims of the transition year in Ireland expressed in terms of skills and competencies (1986) *Planning, Introducing and Developing Transition Year Programmes: Guidelines for Schools*, Interim Board for Curriculum and Examinations, Dublin

The experience of transition: skill and competencies
Each student should, at the end of The Transition Year (TYO):

- have been exposed to a broad, varied and integrated curriculum and have developed an informed sense of his/her own talents and preferences in general educational and vocational matters (*transition skills*)
- have developed significantly the basic skills of literacy, numeracy and oracy (It is assumed that most students will have developed these skills before the end of junior cycle, but specific reinforcement may be needed for some through TYO) (*literacy/ numeracy skills*)
- have developed confidence in the unrehearsed application of these skills in a variety of common social situations (*adaptability*)
- have experienced, as an individual or as part of a group, a range of activities which involve formal and informal contacts with adults outside the school context (*social skills*)
- have developed confidence in the process of decision-making, including the ability to seek out sources of support and aid in specific areas (*decision-making*)
- have developed a range of transferable thinking skills, study skills and other vocational skills (*learning skills*)
- have experienced a range of activities for which the student was primarily responsible in terms of planning, implementation, accountability and evaluation, either as an individual or as part of a group (*problem-solving*)
- have developed appropriate physical and manipulative skills in work and leisure contexts (*physical*)
- have been helped to foster sensitivity and tolerance to the needs of others and to develop personal relationships (*interpersonal/caring*)
- have been enabled to develop an appropriate set of spiritual, social and moral values (*faith; morals*)
- have had opportunities to develop creativity and appreciation of creativity in others (*aesthetic*)
- have developed responsibility for maintaining a healthy lifestyle, both physical and mental (*health*)
- have developed an appreciation of the physical and technological environments and their relationship to human needs in general (*environment*)
- have been given an understanding of the nature and discipline of science and its application to technology through the processes of design and production (*science/ technology*)
- have been introduced to the implications and applications of information technology to society (*information technology*)

This list of skills and competences is not exhaustive and new ones may emerge through the experience of schools.

and research,[17] lead me to believe that the teachers and trainers have not given major consideration to the relationship of their subject to the world of work. While many design-and-make activities have been, and indeed are, encouraged by industrial and community needs, teachers' attitudes were not oriented to the market or industry.

This is in marked contrast to the French approach, which has as its fundamental philosophy that France will not survive in the twenty-first century unless its pupils are conversant with technology as a major force in the market. Thus from the age of 12, students learn technology through the project method. Each project begins with a market survey and the pupils have to produce for the market. To achieve this goal, the class is divided into teams that have at their centre a management group. Other teams work on fabrication, construction, electronics and information technology. The pupils are given time to study theoretical concepts as, for example, how a capacitator works, as the course progresses. Important features of the programme, therefore, are the inclusion of information technology and basic business economics and management.

In Ireland, there is a similar tradition to that in England in the vocational schools, where both woodwork and metalwork are taught, and a syllabus very similar to that in England is being developed around a task-oriented methodology. However, in the secondary schools, where there is little or no tradition in this area, the curriculum research unit of the Christian Brothers and the University of Dublin have developed an alternative approach to technology, which is of interest.

In a limited number of schools students are able to spend a year from the time

Introduction	*General programme*	
	Applications of science	*Mini-company(*)*
Manufacturing (*)	Imformation technology/electronics (*)/ systems engineering/control technology	Market research
Technology	Management 1/organization & individual (*) technology of organization people and machines	Product innovation
		Implementation
Materials & processes		
Project based problem solving techniques	Management 2 marketing/product innovation/quality control	Technique & organization
	Technology and society	Marketing
	Continuation of manufacturing technology	

Stage A 3 to 4 weeks → *Stage B 10 to 22 weeks* → *Stage C 3 to 4 weeks*

Figure 12.1 Experimental research programme on the transition year for cost-effective integrated technology (from Owen, S. and Heywood, J. (1988) Transition Technology in Ireland, paper presented at the First National Conference on Design and Technology: Educational Research and Curriculum Development in Design Technology, University of Loughborough)

they take their Intermediate Certificate (15 years) in vocational, community and general education studies, which are free from the stress of examinations. The goals of this year are set out in Table 12.1. They resume their studies for the Leaving Certificate examinations when they have finished this year.

The Christian Brothers' research unit perceived that a programme in technology could satisfy the objectives of the year as set out in Table 12.1. Their model of the curriculum is shown in Figure 12.1. It begins with an intensive course in manufacturing technology that introduces students to materials and processes through the task-oriented method. This course has been run successfully with both boys and girls. Indeed, the girls adapted more successfully than the boys.[18] Formal studies in the various components of technology, which include management and economics, culminate in a mini-company exercise. A management

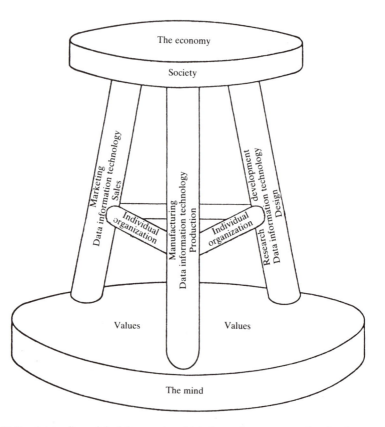

Figure 12.2   A 'stool' model of the way in which the various aspects of technology support the economy and society (from Heywood, J. (1989) Towards technological literacy in Ireland: an opportunity for an inclusive approach, in Heywood, J. and Matthews, P. (eds.) Technology, Society and the School Curriculum. Practice and Theory in Europe, Roundthorn, Manchester

course for schools has been designed, implemented and evaluated by teachers working with 200 pupils.[19]

It will be seen that how technology emerges in the curriculum is very much a function of the cultural tradition in which the subject is developed. In England there was not a very strong craft tradition and what has emerged is a response to the changes technology has caused in material uses and product design. The same is true of the developing curriculum in the junior cycle in Ireland. However, where these traditions are not strong, new approaches are possible. Thus in France, technology is seen to be crucial to survival. The model of technology developed by the Christian Brothers also begins from this point and attempts to reconcile values in society with economic well-being. Their model is pictured as a stool (Figure 12.2).[20] It only shows the essential links.

The base represents the power of human beings as represented by their minds. It is the mind that is the source of ideas and decisions. Information is passed from and to the mind along the legs and for convenience this flow is shown at the centre of each leg. The legs contain the technologies of action that support the economy and embrace society. The horizontal support, which is attached to the technologies of action, represents the binding forces brought about by the interaction between individuals and their organizations.

They considered that the purposes of their curriculum were to make up for

- lack of understanding of the role of industry and commerce in creating wealth;
- lack of achievement motivation with its consequences of the level of risk-taking and entrepreneurship;
- lack of good management and its consequences for the effective utilization of personnel; and
- lack of response to the market and its consequences for competitiveness arising from poor product quality and design, poor styling, poor delivery and poor aftersales service.

And from this they deduced that a curriculum in technology should provide an appreciation of the following:

(1) The potential and limitations of materials and processes.
(2) The potential and limitations of machines for the manufacturing process.
(3) The determinants of cost and quality in the manufacturing process.
(4) The significance of product design in engineering and design in styling.
(5) The potential of electronic devices in information technology, the solution of scientific and design problems and control technology.
(6) The assistance that the application of scientific principles can give to design and development.
(7) The significance of industry in wealth creation and the role of the entrepreneur.
(8) The significance of the market to product design and manufacture.
(9) The role of government in the creation of wealth.

(10) The voting contribution of the individual as a determinant of prevailing and future socio-economic models.
(11) The understanding of human behaviour and the factors that contribute to personal and interpersonal competence.

The contents of this book have been used on the basis for in-service training programmes for teachers in Ireland who were developing programmes for the Transition Year as indicated above. They, in their form modelled courses on this outline, and implemented them, together with mini-company activities.

Finally, it will be appreciated that tolerance towards the ideas of others which is a characteristic of both the British and the Irish is a cultural disposition that is accompanied by a great deal of ambivalence. For example, in Britain ambivalent attitudes exist towards large enterprises. There is a fear of monopoly, multi-nationals and the USA! There is also a fear of interventionist policies, such as mergers, which will put all the eggs in one basket. Thus, like sport, talent becomes spread thinly across all the sectors of industrial activity and more especially research. The play with too many kinds of industrial activity in a relatively closed and secure system does seem to have been, and continues to be, a major cause in the decline in British manufacturing industry. There has been no consensus that would allow government to operate a department of State that would function in the way that the Japanese Ministry for International Trade and Industry does. It is the British and Irish way to let people do their own thing, if at all possible. Individualism is encouraged at the expense of the group, and perhaps this is the lesson both the British and Irish have to learn from Japan.

In Contrast with Japan: Industrial Parameters

We saw in Chapter 8 that there seems to be an inherent trait in Japanese workers that leads them to be able to do dull jobs well even when they have had a university education. Since there cannot be satisfaction in every task, this is a great advantage to society. We have also seen that the education system tends to re-inforce such attitudes, at least among the more able. While it is clear that there is dissatisfaction among the less able in Japan, it is the large organizations that have the pull on the workforce and thus, like Marks and Spencer, maintain the drive for quality. Lord Nelson, in an address to the Institution of Electrical Engineers, said that British products, which were formerly renowned for their quality, no longer have this reputation. There is, he said, 'no reason why this position, which largely reflects an attitude of mind, cannot be quickly reversed.'[21] One of the reasons that the Japanese have increased the quality of their products is that management and workers have a commitment, not merely to quality as a nation, but to its solution through effective management–worker relationships and appropriate organiza-tional technology exemplified by the use of quality circles. It is a paradox that, whereas family firms in Britain have not been particularly successful innovators, it is family methods of management the Japanese have brought to their corporately owned enterprises. Management arrive at work at the same time as the workers and they participate in shopfloor work. However, their paternalism, unlike that of their British counterparts, extends to the encouragement of personal involvement in the enterprise. The Japanese use a variety of managerial methods in the companies they run in England.

There are no status divisions in the Japanese approach to management. As we have seen, the class structure of British society is thought by many observers to be the most significant cause of the British failure. Most recently, Harvey Jones, a former Chairman of ICI, Britain's largest enterprise, has said

> In too many firms there are too many distinctions between the shop floor, office and management. People are not treated – in some cases, not allowed to be treated – as individuals who are part of the same firm. Industry is above everything a team job – our team versus the competitor team.[22]

We have seen how successful British firms were when they dropped their status divisions.

At one time, employees in British firms remained with them for a lifetime as they do in the larger firms in Japan. This is no longer the case. The mergers of the 1960s caused many people to lose their jobs in manufacturing industry, and there was a corresponding loss of loyalty to the organization. Poor rewards undoubtedly contributed to their loss of loyalty. Just as in football, frequent changes between teams undoubtedly reduce a player's commitment to the team, so it is with the enterprises when job changes are part of career-planning based on commitment to the individual. In such cases, companies are used by the employee as steps in the promotion ladder. This is one of the legacies of paternalism that gave poor rewards. We shall return to this problem again in the section on schooling.

The large Japanese companies support their employees by very substantial programmes of training for graduates from universities, colleges and high schools alike. This training continues throughout their careers. Quality circles are a means of simultaneous problem-solving, staff development and training. As we have seen, they are firmly based on principles of learning. Used across the range of industrial and commercial activity, they influence marketing, design, research, product development, plant, manufacturing and workforce. More significantly, each activity is informed by good intelligence. Lord Nelson said that in only one of these areas had England performed well and that was research. He argued that companies in Britain have two weaknesses: the first is the failure to collaborate: each company wants to do its own thing and in consequence there is much duplication of effort. The second is the conversion of research into competitive products. There continues to be, as Burns and Stalker found in the 1950s,[23] a communication gulf between research, marketing and production. The British have not been able to exploit the new markets that have been opened up to them. More significantly, a large trade deficit in manufacturing has developed with the EEC.[24]

The 1979–87 Conservative government did perceive these issues: they understood that a change of attitude was necessary if wealth was to grow, and set about dismantling the influence of government in many sectors of the economy. They believed in the value of competition and that labour-market rigidities were a major contributory cause of the British *malaise*. However, some of the actions of that government, such as high exchange rates, had the opposite effect on manufacturing, for it became more difficult to sell goods abroad. Cognitive dissonance, it was argued, is inevitable since the value dispositions carried by politicians are considerably in-built in their mental structure. Thus the arguments become black and white and those industrialists who, like Nelson, would wish for government support are seen to be wanting their hand to be held. Given the history of British industry and its relations with government, this is not an unreasonable judgement in the absence of any clear plan about the role of industry. Unfortunately, black-and-white debates prevent evaluations of such institutions as the Japanese Ministry for International Trade and Industry, and the role it plays in industrial development. As Aitken has pointed out,[25] the Japanese miracle was not an example of 'the success of free competitive capitalism'. They did and do impose restrictive tariffs on imports; they have had a substantial deficit; they do protect their industries; and so, as Aitken puts it, Japan provides a conundrum for western observers. Market pressures in the short term could operate against the long-term national interest.

In Contrast with Japan: Schooling

Reference has already been made to the Japanese high-school system. Attention has been paid to the examination system, the high level of competition and the problems of the slow learner. Little attention was paid, however, to the system of classroom organization, apart from the fact that the very high levels of achievement, which are obtained relative to other systems, seem to be derived from mechanical methods of teaching and learning.

There are four other aspects of the system that western observers highlight and that support the contention that it is the relationship of the education system to the prevailing value system that is the key to understanding how education informs economic success.[26]

The first is the expectations society has for its education system. In Japan, parents, and thus society, have high expectations of their children and thus of their schools. Children are expected to persevere and schools are expected to help them persevere. The outcome of such attitudes is that a very large proportion (which embraces the average and below average) have what are regarded as very high levels of literacy and numeracy by comparison with the USA. And this is achieved in spartan conditions with class sizes of between 40 and 50.

The second feature is the relationship of the teacher to the community. There is no shortage of teachers as there has been in the UK and the USA. The teacher is still respected in society. This is no longer true of the UK or the USA. And this position is re-inforced by the fact that starting salaries are similar to those for graduates entering industry.

The third feature is the importance attached to the teaching of economics in high school where it is a compulsory subject.

The fourth and perhaps most important feature of the system is the way it reinforces group loyalty. On entry to the primary school, the child learns the importance of loyalty to the group. Duke argues that this has not made them a nation of lemmings. The very success of the Japanese points in the opposite direction. Thus Duke is led to argue that

> We in the United States must work toward this goal – the voluntary commitment of oneself, the loyalty that implies sacrifice to the welfare of the group – in order to promote the well-being of our industries and well-being of our society. This commitment does not mean blindly following the leader or the department manager. It does not involve meek acceptance of orders from the foreman.[27]

However if Kinsman is correct, the trend in western societies is away from the group toward individualism. If it is the case that group loyalty is a key feature of the Japanese economic success, then the implication of Kinsman's theories need to be considered in some detail.

Individuals and Institutions as Learners

Another fascinating typology to try to explain national behaviour has been suggested by Kinsman.[28] Although it is not largely different from McClelland's, it does throw additional light on the issue.

These typologies are representative of three philosophies for living. They are called sustenance, outer-directed and inner-directed. The sustainers cling to their existing standards of living. Kinsman suggests that they are the residuals of an agricultural society where a 'grim determination to survive' was necessary.[29] With the Industrial Revolution came a new group, the outer-directed, motivated by success and conspicuous achievement. Some of those with a grim determination to survive remained together with these outer-directeds or, as McClelland would say, achievement-motivated individuals and groups. This group still is in the majority in Japan, West Germany and the USA. There is now, however, a third group – the inner-directed – that is eroding the position of the second. Their interest is in 'self-development and a balanced complete existence'.[30] The picture presented by Kinsman is very similar to that of the British outlined above. He says, 'They do not feel particularly involved in the competitive rat race, they are co-operative by nature, concerned with a sense of meaning and purpose, involved in individualistic, caring and quality of life issues'.[31] This seems to be an extension of McClelland's bureaucratic type. So long as they feel comfortable, they are not distinguished by class, or so it seems to this writer. Kinsman illustrates the attitudes of the three groups by their answers to the question, 'Why are you eating less?' The inner-directed reply would be, 'Because it is healthier', whereas the outer-directed would reply, 'Because I can't get into my trousers', and the sustainers would say, 'Because I can't afford it'. The difficulty with this model is that it is probably both age and socioeconomically related. Individuals may, of hidden necessity, find themselves answering in all three ways at different times because of changes in their circumstances. The point is that one or other disposition remains uppermost and in Kinsman's thesis the more tenacious inner-directeds are on the increase. Newspaper comment seems to support this view. This could well be a problem for all the industrialized nations in the future if the rise of the Green parties is anything to go by.

This picture of the inner-directed merges with the view of the British presented above, for ultimately, as Kinsman says, 'individualism rules, fragmentation is the fashion'.[32] It feeds on democracy at all levels of society and thrives on pressure groups. Ultimately it produces a democracy that is self-defeating. It is not possible to improve standards of living without increasing wealth in the economic structures we have. Individualism has the effect of reducing national commitment and it is this that is one of the major differences between Britain and Japan.

Kinsman uses his thesis to argue that, in Britain, this individualism will promote strains on management. A much deeper understanding of people's behaviour will be required of managers. The military style of management will go and co-creation will begin. It differs from worker participation in management since each cell (working group) takes responsibility for its own work and has to stand on its own feet. If individuals are necessarily managers (see Chapter 6), then the organizational structure that will emerge must be one of co-creation, in which the leader is servant (see Chapter 10). For this to be achieved, everyone will have to understand the principles of management, and the sooner students begin such learning, the better.[33]

Even so, there remains the problem of adaptability. If wealth is to be increased, people at all levels have to become increasingly adaptable. They will also have to understand how wealth is created. Education does have a role to play in this, for it is concerned with the development of intelligence.

Following recent work by Sternberg described in Chapter 1, intelligence was defined as the purposive adaptation to, and the selection and the shaping of, real-world environments relevant to one's life. To achieve this goal, it is clear that an educational system should be concerned with the development of skills in learning how to learn and the acquisition of frames of reference, which will help to generate an understanding of the socio-economic system and the potential of technology to effect change. This might be called 'technological literacy'. If Britain is to take any notice of developments abroad, then it is to France, Ireland and Japan that it ought to look for changes in curriculum and method. As we have seen in the Japanese high schools, all students participate in the study of economics, which is clearly oriented to show how national aspirations can be met. More than that, the students are task-oriented. Motivation is an important component of intelligence in our recent understanding of that concept. In France, all students in the State schools (*collège* curriculum) take technology that embraces modern technology literacy (electronics and mechanical), technical skill development, information technology and economics.

In Britain, this type of education is being given for the wrong reasons to the wrong group. Unemployment has led the government to give this type of education to below-average students of the 14–18 age group. Not only does this serve to reflect and preserve the class groups, but it fails to tackle the problem with those who could in future years be in financial institutions or government, and who could influence the expenditure of money. National character fails to recognize and to accept the need for competition. Unless the whole status of industry is raised and salaries paid commensurate with that status, industry will remain uncompetitive and in a separate world, which is not part of mainstream thinking. The significance of manufacturing to the British economy is not understood.

Cairncross has recently argued that, contrary to the popular view, industrial productivity in Britain has been increasing at no greater rate than in the 1960s. If that is the case then, if countries like West Germany and France, which are now slack, began to produce at higher rates, Britain would have difficulty in competing with them successfully. We have, he says, not to explain either the rise or the fall in productivity but why Britain lags behind Europe. In his explanation he cites some of the obstacles to innovation mentioned in previous chapters. Perhaps his severest criticism is for the education system:

> What has mattered more are cultural influences expressing themselves in weaknesses in the education system. On the one hand has been the English preference for learning on the job rather than first engaging in study and training; on the other, the effort to contain public expenditure, including expenditure on education, and a reluctance to entrust the state with responsibility for higher education.[34]

The two points are not, in my view, necessarily related, as the success of the more or less private system of higher education in the USA shows. However, they do illustrate both sides of the *malaise*, to which reference was made in Chapter 9. It is no accident that a Conservative government should introduce a licensed-teacher programme based on a master/apprentice relationship that by-passes formal training in college. A government that apparently has the right aim is unable, it seems, to extract itself from the straitjacket of culture. If there is to be change, then everyone has to understand the principles of change. History has to show how culture conditions and how those empires that became complacent failed. Such history teaching involves the learner in understanding how we learn, and what bends our prejudices, on the one hand, and what releases them on the other.

Charles Handy has argued 'the British have hither to relied on a Darwinian belief that the best will come through in the end, that belief is a wasteful and cruel philosophy in a world where good jobs are precious and talent rare. The intelligent organization has to be a learning organization'.[35]

But firms cannot be learning organizations unless the people in them know how to learn. It has been the contention of this book that for most of us learning is haphazard and often ineffective because we have never formally learnt what enhances and impedes learning. Such learning has to begin in school and be reinforced and developed in higher and further education. Moreover, it has to be for all and not the select few. It demands a radical change in our understanding of what the curriculum should be, not only in regard to knowledge, but in respect of the methods to be deployed.

For example if it is true that we are becoming more individualistic, then we need to understand early the moral obligations we have towards and within the activities of management and leadership.

Handy's contention that because computers necessarily jump barriers organizational structures will become flat as opposed to hierarchical is surely correct.[36]

The ability to work in such organizations will not only require considerable adaptation on the part of workers and managers alike but in the cultural forces which shape attitudes and social structure. Greenleaf's[37] concept of the leader as servant is not an ideal, for as Handy[38] points out, a leader's authority will depend on a person's ability to help others to do the job better. In such organizations no one will be able to escape a leadership role for to allow another to lead is an act of leadership, just as to allow someone else to manage is an act of management.

Just as demands will be made on individuals so too will demands be made on nations.

As the world becomes a more open system, so the nations of the world, in particular the UK and the USA, France, West Germany, Ireland and Japan learn from each other. Britain, Ireland and the USA for example, have much to offer in their approaches to the creative dimension of life in their education systems.

Technological literacy embraces both the human and creative dimensions, and without their inclusion our understanding of ourselves, the persons with whom we work and the impact of technology, will be seriously limited to the detriment of economic progress within a developing framework of social justice. It is for this reason that education's prime concern is with effective learning for adaptability. It has therefore to help students acquire skills in learning how to learn within a curriculum concerned with human understanding and values, on the one hand, and technological change on the other.

Notes and References

1. Steffens, H. quoted by L. Bonnerjea (1985) *Thinkers and Makers Education for Tomorrows World*, Policy Studies Institute, London.
2. Danzin, A. (1985) Adaptability to new technologies of the USSR and East European countries examined. A NATO Colloquium: NATO Information Service, 1110, Brussels, Belgium.
3. Barnett, C. (1986) The truth of the British decline, *Management Today*, no. 139, pp. 84–8. Some of Barnett's statistical interpretations were challenged by Sir Bernard Lovell in *The Times*, 13 March 1987 (in response to a letter by Barnett on the same theme).
4. Cairncross, Sir A. (1988) Britain's industrial decline, Royal Bank of Scotland Review, no. 159, pp. 3–18.
5. Murray, M. and Heywood, J. (1986) Education for work in the Federal Republic of Germany, in J. Heywood and P. Matthews (eds.) *Technology, Society and the School Curriculum: Practice and Theory in Europe*, Roundthorn, Manchester.
6. Barnett, Truth (note 3).
7. Payne, G.L. (1960) *Britain's Scientific and Technological Manpower*, Oxford University Press, Oxford. Gives complete details of the output of scientists and technologists from the different educational routes.
8. Marris, R. (1986) Higher education and the economy and the concept of completion, *Studies in Higher Education*, Vol. 11, no. 2, pp. 131–54.
9. Bosworth, G.S. (1963) Toward creative activity in engineering, *Universities Quarterly*, no. 17, pp. 286–300.
10. Hutton, S.P., Lawrence, P. and Smith, J.H. (1977) *The Recruitment, Deployment and Status of the Mechanical Engineer in the German Federal Republic* (3 parts), Department of Trade and

Industry, University of Southampton, Southampton. These reports are based on substantial comparative studies made *in situ* in West Germany and England.

11. Heywood, J., Mash, V. and Pollit, J. (1966) The schools and technology, *Lancaster Studies in Higher Education*, no. 1, Apr. pp. 154–300.

12. Lilley, S. (1970) *Technological Progress and the Industrial Revolution*, 'Fontana Economic History of Europe', Fontana, London.

13. Tse, K. K. (1985) *Marks and Spencer, Anatomy of Britain's Most Efficiently Managed Company*, Pergamon, Oxford.

14. See Lilley, *Technological Progress* (note 13); and Mant, A. (1979) *The Rise and Fall of the British Management*, Pan, London.

15. The syllabuses for the *collège's* curriculum are published in a paperback under that title. It is an official book of the French Ministry of Education.

16. Department of Education and Science, 1987 *Craft, Design and Technology 5–16*, HMI series, Curriculum Matters No. 9. HMSO, London.

17. Toft, P. (1989) doctoral thesis, University of Salford.

18. Owen, S. and Heywood, J. (1988) *Transition Technology in Ireland*, First National Conference on Educational Research and Curriculum Development in Design and Technology, University of Loughborough.

19. Murray, M. (1989) thesis, School of Education, University of Dublin.

20. Heywood, J. (1986) Toward technological literacy in Ireland: an opportunity for an inclusive approach, in J. Heywood and P. Matthews (eds.) *Technology, Society and the School Curriculum: Practice and Theory in Europe*, Roundthorn, Manchester.

21. Nelson, Lord (1984) Export competitiveness; a factor of management and/or design, *Institution of Electrical Engineers Proceedings*, Vol. 131, A, no. 8, pp. 626–34.

22. Quoted by Eglin, R. (1986) *The Sunday Times*, 6 April (Sir John's formula for industrial recovery).

23. Burns, T. and Stalker, G.M. (1961) *The Management of Innovation*, Tavistock, London.

24. Dearden, S. (1986) EEC membership and the United Kingdom's trade in manufactured goods, *National Westminster Bank Quarterly Review*, February, pp. 15–25.

25. Aitken, I. (1986) Tokyo commentary *Guardian*, 3 March.

26. Duke, B. (1986) *The Japanese School. Lessons for Industrial America*, Praeger, New York, NY.

27. *Ibid.*

28. Kinsman, F. (1986) Managing the future, *Management Today*, April, pp. 77, 126 and 128.

29. *Ibid.*

30. *Ibid.*

31. *Ibid.*

32. *Ibid.*

33. Heywood, J. (1988) Leadership, management and education. Lessons for and from Schooling, Association of Teacher Educators of Europe Conference, Barcelona, Sept.

34. *Ibid.*

35. Handy, C. (1989) *The Age of Unreason*, Hutchinson, London, quoted by him in an article in *The Sunday Times* 23 Apr. 1989.

36. *Ibid.*

37. Greenleaf, R.K. (1973) *The Servant as Leader*, Windy Row Press, Peterborough, NH.

38. Handy, *The Age of Unreason* (note 35).

INDEX